Law and Property in Algeria

Studies in the History and Society of the Maghrib

Edited by

VOLUME 10

The titles published in this series are listed at *brill.com/shsm*

Law and Property in Algeria

Anthropological Perspectives

Edited by

Yazid Ben Hounet

BRILL

LEIDEN | BOSTON

This volume was published with the support of the French National Agency for Research (ANR), as an outcome of the research project "Property in Moslem Transitional Environments" (PROMETEE) that was conducted within the frame of the German-French program FRAL and associated teams affiliated to the Centre Jacques-Berque (CJB) of Rabat and the Erlanger Zentrum für Islam und Recht in Europa (EZIRE).

Centre Jacques-Berque
مركز جاك بارك
études en sciences humaines et sociales
للابحاث في العلوم الانسانية و الاجتماعية

Cover illustration: Shepherd in the daira of Ain Sefra (wilaya of Naama). PHOTO BY SANDRA GUINAND, MAY 2005.

The Library of Congress Cataloging-in-Publication Data is available online at http://catalog.loc.gov
LC record available at http://lccn.loc.gov/2017058812

Typeface for the Latin, Greek, and Cyrillic scripts: "Brill". See and download: brill.com/brill-typeface.

ISSN 1877-9808
ISBN 978-90-04-35762-4 (hardback)
ISBN 978-90-04-36211-6 (e-book)

This book is printed on acid-free paper and produced in a sustainable manner.

Contents

Acknowledgments

The editor wishes to thank the Department of Law at the University of Algiers 2, and specifically Professors Fillali and Belhimer, who hosted our intermediary workshop there. He also wishes to thank the Centre Jacques-Berque and all the people who contributed under its auspices to the success of the project, as well as Saskia Brown and Carol Rowe for their translation and editing work.

Note on Arabic Transliteration

Authors have exercised some flexibility in the way they transliterate Arabic and Berber words, some preferring to use a formal method, while others choose to reproduce the sound of words as they are spoken.

Where a formal approach is adopted, the following transliteration system for Arabic is used:

ا	*ā*	ط	*ṭ*
ب	*b*	ظ	*ẓ*
ت	*t*	ع	ʿ
ث	*th*	غ	*gh*
ج	*j*	ف	*f*
ح	*ḥ*	ق	*q*
خ	*kh*	ك	*k*
د	*d*	ل	*l*
ذ	*dh*	م	*m*
ر	*r*	ن	*n*
ز	*z*	ه	*h*
س	*s*	و	*w* or *ū*
ش	*sh*	ي	*y* or *ī*
ص	*ṣ*	ة	*a* (or *at* in *iḍāfa* constructions)
ض	*ḍ*	ء	ʾ (omitted at the beginning of words)

Introduction: Anthropological Perspectives on Law and Property in Algeria

Yazid Ben Hounet and Baudouin Dupret

With a surface area of 2.5 million km^2, Algeria is the largest country in Africa – the tenth largest in the world – and one of the continent's leading economic powers. Its economy is still highly dependent on oil and gas exports. It has the highest GDP per capita in North Africa (US$ 7,534 in comparative purchasing power figures from 1 January 2014), and the fourth-highest GDP on the African continent (US$ 206.1 billion in 2013). With close to 40 million inhabitants (38.7 million on 1 January 2014), of which 98% are Muslims, Algeria is the ninth-largest country of the Muslim world in terms of population.

However, in spite of this privileged place on the African continent, in the Muslim world and in the MENA region (Middle East and North Africa), Algeria remains little known, and works relating to contemporary Algerian society published outside of Algeria are rare. The colonisation of Algeria by the French, and the Algerian War of Independence, are the subject of many publications in the French- and English-speaking worlds,[1] but social science publications on Algeria today are still few in number, compared, for example with those on Morocco and Egypt. This is particularly true of social and cultural anthropology, a discipline which, up to the early 1990s, was somewhat despised by the authorities. They considered it a colonial science,[2] and suspected it of promoting the theses of, and giving a university base to, Berber movements (Moussaoui, 2005). It was only in the 1990s, as the country began to embrace a multiparty system, that departments specialising in anthropology started to develop in Algeria.[3] However, the violence and insecurity of the "black decade" (*décennie*

1 For the French-speaking world, we might mention the works of Charles-Robert Ageron, Mohamed Harbi, Benjamin Stora, Daho Djerbal, Gilbert Meynier, Sylvie Thénault and Malika Rahal, and for the English-speaking world, the works of James McDougall and Todd Shepard.

2 Ahmed Ben Naoum (1993: 29) speaks of this frustration, linked with "the guilty conscience of belonging to an 'ethnographied' society".

3 Anthropology (social and cultural), the daughter (offspring) of colonialism, in Claude Lévi-Strauss's words, had a singular fate in Algerian academia. Criticised and rejected in the first decades following Independence, the discipline is today advocated by numerous scholars. Courses (masters, doctoral, etc.) in anthropology are also being developed in Algerian universities and research centres. Some works exist on criticism of anthropology as colonial knowledge (notably Lucas and Vatin, 1975); and a few on the analysis of the institutional development

 | DOI 10.1163/9789004362116_002

noire)[4] of violence (from the early 1990s to the early 2000s) made thorough field research almost impossible. Consequently, ethnographically documented anthropological works based on data collected directly in the field have been limited in number.[5]

This volume, which focuses on law and property in Algeria from an anthropological perspective, thus seeks to contribute, however modestly, to our understanding of Algerian society today, through its relationships to property and to law. Beyond this, the book's objective is to propose, using a comparative approach proper to anthropology, new theoretical and methodological perspectives by which to apprehend the anthropology of law in a Muslim context. Algeria, as a post-colonial and post-socialist state, whose population is overwhelmingly Muslim, proves to be a particularly interesting case to study. Focusing on property law in practice, on the conflicts inherent in it, and on the strategies deployed to circumvent the law, is a particularly fruitful perspective from which to view the effects of a rapidly changing society.

In this Introduction, we shall first explain the book's theoretical framework – property law from an anthropological perspective – and our aim – to substitute the anthropology of Muslim law for a legal anthropology in a Muslim context. We shall then discuss certain specificities of property law in the post-colonial and post-socialist state that is Algeria. We shall, lastly, present the individual chapters.

Law, Anthropology and Property

In their introduction to *Changing Properties of Property*, Franz von Benda-Beckmann, Keebet von Benda-Beckmann and Melanie G. Wiber (2006: 2) emphasise that:

---

of anthropology in Algeria since Independence (notably Moussaoui, 2005; and publications by the *Centre de Recherche en Anthropologie Sociale Culturelle* (CRASC) on the social sciences in Algeria). These academic publications address a number of debates on the modes and types of knowledge produced on Algeria, as do scholars in anthropology and the related university courses.

4 On this issue, see, for example, Luis Martinez (1998) and Abderrahmane Moussaoui (2006). Moussaoui (2006: 13) rejects the term "civil war" used by Luis Martinez as it "is not quite appropriate when this violence remains 'localised' in certain regions and limited to certain categories". We shall use the local term – "black decade" (*décennie noire*) – to define this decade of violence.

5 Among the rare anthropologists to carry out field research during the 1990s and the early 2000s, we note Abderrahmane Moussaoui, Susan Slyomovics, Judith Scheele and Tassadit Yacine.

> Property is always multifunctional (…). It is a major factor in constituting the identity of individuals and groups. Through inheritance, it also structures the continuity of such groups. It can have important religious connotations. And it is a vital element in the political organisation of society, the legitimate command over wealth being an important source of political power over people and their labour, no matter whether we think of domestic or kinship modes of production, capitalism or communism. Property regimes, in short, cannot easily be captured in a one-dimensional political, economic or legal model.

In addition to the multifunctional aspect of property, these authors remind us that the property models in force, which claim universality, are in fact largely based on Western legal categories. The most important of these is the notion of private and individual ownership, "often regarded as the apex of legal and economic evolution as well as a precondition for efficient market economies" (von Benda-Beckmann, von Benda-Beckmann and Wiber, 2006: 3).

The issue of property and its transmission is at the very heart of any socio-anthropological investigation. It is the foundation of the economic and political relations in a society, and these relations constitute the central object of legal regulation. Social changes are also reflected in the evolution of property relations, as has been emphasised in anthropology, as well as in other disciplines in the human and social sciences.

Durkheim (1950: 152), for example, considers the protection of a "human person's property" as the second rule of human morality. He regards contract law as an extension of this situation, in the form of the acquisition and transfer of property, of which inheritance is one particular mode. Contrary to classical conceptions, for which property is linked to work and is a kind of natural law – John Stuart Mill asserts that property does not imply anything other than the right to one's personal talents, and hence to what can be produced by applying these – Durkheim remarks that property, and consequently its transfer as well as the kinship links justifying it, is a social fact. But a social fact may, by its very existence, eventually assert itself as the "nature of things", when "a certain arrangement of facts and circumstances appears unavoidable once its existence has been acknowledged" (Foriers, 1982: 809).

Kant (2003) considers property an intellectual link, since it associates a person and a thing without any need for a physical connection. This relation implies reciprocity, since for other people to admit that one has a right to something they do not possess, one must admit the equivalent right of other people to certain goods. And for this reciprocity to be established, the things must initially be possessed by a collectivity. Durkheim, starting from the

Kantian conception, seeks a definition of the right to property that is abstracted from the particular modalities it may have assumed in different times and places. The first element he identifies is the existence of an appropriable thing, whose definition obviously varies from one population to another, as does the definition of who is entitled to possess. The second element is the relation between the owning subject and the owned thing, which Durkheim specifies as the exclusive enjoyment of the good, even if the effective enjoyment is postponed, as in the case of usufruct. This prevents other people from taking advantage of it. The question of this relation is also at the heart of the definition of property suggested by Levi-Strauss (2002). It is no longer an objective relation between the subject and the object, but a relation between people, a relation with other people and the social structure (2002: 100), which can be described as "mediatised" by the good owned. We should also mention the materialist approach, represented by Godelier (1982), for example, who considers that forms of property express relations of production. Law is considered here as a superstructure concealing the actual content of these relations of production, and sometimes even out of step with them (law as only a fiction).

The study of property obviously cannot be reduced to Kant, Durkheim, Lévi-Strauss and Godelier. The aim here is to emphasise that all these authors engaged in a quest for an ontology of property, that is, a search for the essential properties that provide the "essence" of property. In certain respects, however, this ontology is reduced to a metaphysical approach, inasmuch as the essential nature of this "essence" worries these thinkers more than the conditions of its deployment. We shall suggest, from the Algerian context, that one should hold on to this issue of the essence of proprietary right in order to explore its praxeology, in other words, to describe the related practices ethnographically. This involves identifying the modes of appropriation of a good, the ways of certifying a right to property and exercising this right, the reasoning employed to establish causes, effects or relations, the role played by the spoken or written word, and the way important notions such as the person–good, movable–immovable, property–ownership, property–possession distinctions, etc., play out in real life.

From an Anthropology of Muslim Law to an Anthropology of Law in a Muslim Context

In addition, this volume seeks to break with the postulate of cultural exceptionality evident in legal interpretations concerning totally or partially "Muslim" societies. The works on law in these societies seem to focus on looking for the Islamic portion of the law, and to stop there – the multiplication of works on property, *waqf*, *habus*, Islamic finance, and more generally "Islamic law" is a perfect example. Determining to what extent such and such a portion of law, orthodoxically or heterodoxically, is Islamic, and to what extent such and such a portion of law should be explained or not by the historical development of Islamic law, tends to impose its structure on legal phenomena and activities, instead of seeking to discover how they operate. In so doing, research fails to describe the phenomena it should be documenting and, in particular, the ways people understand, and express their understanding of, any given situation, take their bearings with respect to a context and its constraints, and behave and act in a more or less orderly fashion within a similar context delineated spatially and temporarily. Even in situations where an Islamic genealogy can be identified (such as in many countries' family law), *a priori* characterisation of "Islamic law" fails to depict what people actually do in a particular legal context, when they address issues related to family. These are things that can only be investigated by describing people's practices without imposing any pre-established interpretative framework. What, then, of the domains where the relation to Islam cannot even be established genealogically!

Although this book builds on material derived from legal practices observed on Algerian territory, it should be clear by now that its purpose is not to lay bare the secrets of some "exotic" legal universe. On the contrary, it attempts to describe these practices without prejudging what, from a legal viewpoint, may differentiate these societies from other contexts. It does not even postulate the existence of such differences. In other words, this book relates to legal practices in an overwhelmingly Muslim environment, not to Islamic culture observed through the prism of law. Islamic culture is but one of the many components of the context, which is always unique, never uniform, in which legal practices are deployed. To assume that this particular cultural component is fundamental incurs the risk of not paying sufficient attention to other possible components, the things on which the members of the judiciary and legal environment of these societies focus. It also risks overestimating the impact of culture. The corollary of culturalism is non-translatability, which assumes that a concept formulated in Arabic cannot be adequately apprehended in French because its essence can only be accessible in its original formulation. We consider, on the contrary, that every phenomenon, regardless of the language of its expression, remains translatable into another language and accessible to observation and description. This implies, however, that "rather than supposedly reading over the shoulder of an imaginary native a text completed in a culturally standardised form [one reads] line after line the continuous production of a real autochthonous speech" (Moerman, 1987: 5).

It remains for us to justify the use of legal data derived from totally or partially Muslim contexts, while refusing to substantiate cultural differences. First, there are no grounds to consider a given context as more relevant, appropriate or worthy of interest in itself than any other. As this context has been largely overdetermined until now by a reference to Islam, it is not without interest to show when this reference is empirically documented and when it appears as postulated and not demonstrated.

If this book succeeds in demonstrating that similarities or difference between contexts lie in many factors other than that of religion, it will have proved worthwhile, in a general atmosphere where human beings' "common humanity" seems to be denied in the name of conflicts between cultures and ineffably distinct civilisations (and, conversely, where humanity often stops at the frontiers of a "common religion"). At the end of the day, certain specificities might well be attributed to the existence of an Islamic referent, but they cannot be considered to be untranslatable. On the contrary, "their significations can be known and are naturally known: they are governed by grammatical conventions which can be determined and are part of the conceptual equipment of the human species, in spite of the differentiated empirical distribution of their effective usage and of the different types of language games observed in different cultures" (Coulter, 1989: 101).

Law and Property in Post-Colonial and Post-Socialist States

In post-colonial and post-socialist states, policies on property law can be explained partially by the country's particular historico-political background. However, these cannot account for the bulk of local practices (far from it, as we shall see later). In this Introduction, we shall nevertheless depict the major features of Algerian policies in this domain, but only briefly, because the first chapter of this book inventorises and analyses the laws passed since Independence.

A recent volume on colonial law (Bras, 2015) can serve as our starting point. By presenting a close examination of the themes of property, legal literature, judicial personnel and attorneys, this work provides the building-blocks for an anthropology of law in Algeria and shows how profoundly law is a historically situated phenomenon. In the case of colonial law, it is encapsulated in a specific time frame, with a pre-colonial "before", with which there were major discontinuities, and the "after" of Independence, incorporating important aspects of continuity. We can see how greatly colonial law disrupted the local, indigenous understanding of normativity: under the pretence of systematising the pre-existing law, colonial (Muslim) law actually constructed something new. Land law is a very good example of this, since it was based on incompatible tendencies: it founded law on universal principles, while at the same time permitting colonial annexation of land. Colonial doctrine presented Islamic legal norms as those of an imperfect civilisation in need of a civilising process of systematisation. After independence, we can observe how little the political break was accompanied by a legal one; rather, the colonial legacy was reformatted in national terms.

As Robert Young (2001: 57) explains:

> The postcolonial is a dialectical concept that marks the broad historical facts of decolonisation and the determined achievement of sovereignty – but also the realities of nations and peoples emerging into a new imperialistic context of economic and sometimes political domination. The experience of that new sovereignty typically encouraged the development of a postcolonial culture which radically revised ethos and ideologies of the colonial state and, at the same time, reoriented the goals of the independence movement towards the very different conditions of national autonomy.

We cannot understand Algerian society today if we ignore its colonial past. Colonisation and the War of Independence profoundly affected the imaginary and the representations of Algerian society, as well as the policies implemented by the newly independent Algerian state, but also by the POLISARIO Front (the Western Saharan liberation movement) and the Sahrawi Arab Democratic Republic (SADR) (see Alice Wilson's contribution in this volume). Several studies in this book account for the transformations of the ideologies and representations surrounding the issue of property and its legitimacy in post-colonial Algeria, as well as in the specific case of the Sahrawi refugee camps, under the authority of the SADR, in the region of Tindouf.

Since property is closely linked to the processes of constitution of individual and collective identity, it has a singular place in the development of states and their societies. The issues surrounding home-ownership reflect the transformations of such ideologies and of the economies proper to every state and every society. For example, the socialist policies, in particular concerning agricultural land, the establishment of collective agricultural concerns, agrarian reform, etc., implemented by the newly independent state in the 1960s and 1970s, were meant to be a radical departure from those imposed by the colonial state, and thereby to restore the sovereignty of the Algerian people over their land.[6]

6 "'Postcolonialism' commemorates not the colonial but the triumph over it. The 'post' marks

Do we need to go over this again? During the colonial period, Algerian society was profoundly affected by two major policies introduced by the French authorities: the Code of Indigenous Status and an unprecedented dispossession of indigenous land rights. The indigenous regime, a regime of exception applied to the natives, was implemented by the Arab offices in the first days of the conquest (1830), then formalised from the 1870s and confirmed by the act of 28 June 1881. The Code of Indigenous Status enshrined in law the separation between the Muslim populations and French citizens. The Crémieux decree, promulgated in 1870, granted French citizenship to the Jews of Algeria, while the Muslims of Algeria were subject to the justice of the *qadi*s (Muslim judges) in matters of personal status, but also to the French laws and to specific, individual and collective measures (fines, *cantonnement*, receivership) (Ageron, 1979). In the southern territories, the native populations were administered by the military – unlike in the *département* in the north (Valet, 1927; Ben Hounet, 2007).

To this exceptional legislation was added large-scale dispossession of indigenous land rights. Jean Claude Vatin (1983: 125) notes, echoing the overview made by Charles Robert Ageron, that

> between 1871 and 1919 close to one million hectares (897,000) were handed over to the settlers. [...] The Muslims had lost, in 1919, 7 and a half million hectares, which the State and individuals, the major capitalist societies, shared out.

More than 2,700,000 hectares, representing in 1940 35-40% of the arable land in Algeria, were then appropriated by settlers and major European companies (Lapidus 2002: 589).

Both these historical realities, together with the post-colonial and post-socialist developments experienced by Algeria, help to explain, at least in part, the importance of two issues addressed in the chapters of this book: 1) a certain mistrust of the rule of law and the authorities that were supposed to enforce it, along with practices for circumventing it; 2) the importance of conflicts related to land rights, although today the latter only represents a small

---

the many remarkable victories that should not be allowed to fade into the amnesia of history. The postcolonial era in its name pays tribute to the great historical achievements of resistance against colonial power, while, paradoxically, it also describes the conditions of existence that have followed in which many basic power structures have yet to change in any substantive way" (Young, 2001: 60).

proportion of the general economy of property law, as Ammar Belhimer reminds us in the first chapter.

After a period of socialism and collectivism, Algeria engaged in privatisation policies and, especially from the 1990s, introduced a market economy. The role played by the Algerian state in the regulation of this market economy is still substantial and a closer look shows that switching from a socialist-style planned economy to a market economy has been, and still is, an ambiguous move, and a challenge, that affects property law. In this no man's land between socialism and the market economy, the use of law is problematic. Circumventing strategies to avoid and abuse the law have developed. Corruption is on the increase (Hachemaoui, 2013). Have we switched, then, in Algeria – to repeat the question David Stark and Laszlo Bruszt asked concerning Central Europe (1998) – "from plan to market or from plan to clan?".

Presentation of the Chapters

Relations between law and property should not be explained solely by the weight of culture, of the socio-political system and/or of history. The fact that Algeria, and also the SADR, are post-colonial and post-socialist states does not in itself account for all the practices observable *in situ*. The general context and the singular socio-historical conditions are part of the specificity of the Algerian state and its society, but have not asserted themselves everywhere, or always in the same way. Our aim is hence to shed light on the general context and the global issues at play in Algeria, in terms of property law, without presenting them necessarily as a justification for the practices reported in the various chapters of this book. We hope simply to provide the uninformed reader with an overview of some general issues pertaining to property law in this country.

The ethnographic approach we espouse involves specific case studies aimed at emphasising practices, interpretations and justifications in their own contexts, without presupposing the weight of history, of culture, or of the socio-political system. This approach is in line with our criticisms of certain major works relating to legal anthropology and property, and the anthropology of Muslim law, as explained above. The research presented here covers many aspects of the subject of property and law, using different types of fieldwork from many Algerian regions, including the Sahrawi refugee camps near Tindouf. It foregrounds, with the use of cases studies, the ethnographical, praxeological and contextual dimensions of property and law, and thus provides a more realistic view of practices related to law and property in Algeria today. It deals with the issue of legitimate claims to property, which can be invoked in different ways.

Ammar Belhimer (Chapter 1) explains that the legal corpus of independent Algeria has undergone a recent and precarious reformation of private property law. This reformation is still embryonic and not straightforward and goes against the long praised pre-eminence of public ownership as the foundation of justice and social equality. The first constitution of the Algerian state, promulgated on 10 September 1963, did not address the issue of property, whether private or public. Subsequently, the National Charter, and then the constitution of 22 November 1976, referred to state property, to which were ascribed quasi-mythical qualities such as absolute title and inalienability, which were deemed to constitute the highest form of social property. Recent developments reveal a two-fold evolution: the maintenance as state property of the agricultural lands abandoned by the settlers in the aftermath of Independence; and the privatisation of all other immovable assets and economic activities.

Land dispossession processes during French colonisation and legal land policies after Independence led, at least in northern Algeria, to the existence of two distinct agricultural sectors with different modes of appropriation of land resources. The first sector includes Algeria's most fertile lands – the plains – which were seized by the French colonisers and nationalised after Independence. The other sector comprises the peripheral lands of the piedmont and mountain areas, to which most of the Algerian peasantry were relegated. Whereas the historical forms of land appropriation were perpetuated in these peripheral lands, they were prohibited in most of the lands in the plains, first by the French colonisers and then by the Algerian state in line with its collectivisation policy after Independence.

On the basis of a survey of land dynamics conducted in Algeria's Lower Cheliff plain, Hichem Amichi, Marcel Kuper and Sami Bouarfa (Chapter 2) show that the old methods of appropriation of resources have returned in force as far as public land is concerned, after the process of decollectivisation started in 1987. These old forms, previously restricted to the piedmont areas, have become, despite prohibition by the state, the main regulators of access to productive resources in the most fertile areas of Algeria. This chapter analyses the specificities of land appropriation in a post-socialist context by considering two main social categories of Algerian farmers: 1) the beneficiaries of rights to public land use, former workers on state farms and colonial domains, and 2) tenants or sharecroppers, often Algerian peasants dispossessed of their land by French colonisation. The authors discuss the opposition between the right to use the land and the legitimacy gained by working the land. Their analyses are based on their observation of the proliferation of informal arrangements between the two categories of stakeholders who currently work public lands.

The contribution of Tarik Dahou (Chapter 3) illustrates the ambiguities in the ways the law is appealed to, but also circumvented, in the framework of the exploitation of maritime resources (corals) in eastern Algeria. The impact of market economy penetration and of the Algerian state's alignment with international standards for natural resources management is also addressed. One of the issues is the legal mechanisms used regarding concessions on maritime resources in eastern Algeria. Use of natural resources in the Mediterranean is governed by multiple norms, operating at global and local levels. Yet the academic literature on nature conservation does not sufficiently explore the national and local impacts of conservation processes. Since Algeria's ratification of international conventions on bio-diversity (CBD, RAMSAR, CITES[7]), the country has been engaged in re-formulating its national conservation policies and has also been putting considerable effort into fulfilling its international commitments. Changes in legislation regarding coastal areas, as well as new projects extending the maritime border of coastal national parks, illustrate this. The National Park of El Kala (NPEK), one of the most emblematic Mediterranean terrestrial and marine biodiversity sites, is a good illustration of how Algerian actors appropriate nature conservation policies at local and national levels. The example of the NPEK shows how international nature conservation objectives can become blurred at the local level, as attempts to apply international conservation norms produce inequalities and pose threats to biodiversity. Although state legislation permits concessions regarding natural resources within the NPEK, in practice, the exploitation of marine resources is shaped by interactions between public and private networks. The contradictions between state-regulated access rights and exclusions are further exacerbated by the ambiguous relations between the state bureaucracy and local actors. In contrast to world nature conservation recommendations, the nexus of local powers operating in the NPEK has led to intensified commodification of nature, as well as social conflicts over the appropriation of natural resources. Tarik Dahou's analysis focuses on the normative mechanisms and disciplinary techniques used by the Algerian state to govern nature. The comparative study of two marine concessions reveals two dimensions of biopolitics: in the first concession, governed by national legislation, the enforcement of the law is obstructed by the multiplicity of norms and incomplete monitoring, while in

7 Convention on Biological Diversity ; The Ramsar Convention on Wetlands of International Importance especially as Waterfowl Habitat ; Convention on International Trade in Endangered Species of Wild Fauna and Flora.

the second, an “illicit concession”, conservation norms are enforced through disciplinary methods that go beyond the law.

Judith Scheele (Chapter 4) addresses struggles over land and legitimacy in the Soummam Valley. In Algeria, property rights, as experienced on a daily basis, are notoriously slippery. Rights to real estate in particular, even where they are legally defined, always also draw on notions of history, merit and political influence, and are hence not easily governed by law. With the frequent and often violent changes in the legal regime, moreover, clear definitions of property are only rarely achieved, even in contemporary transactions. This is particularly visible in cities, but it remains equally true in the countryside, especially where valuable agricultural land is concerned. Land rights remain deeply political and contextual, as they not only define rights of access and ownership, but also make statements about social and political legitimacy and “sound” definitions of history: in other words, conflicts over property rights are both intensely local and fought out with reference to larger moral frameworks, more often than not that of the Algerian nation. This is perhaps why concrete case studies of these tensions are few and far between. Judith Scheele’s chapter presents one such case study. It describes longstanding conflicts over property rights in one small part of the Soummam Valley in Kabylia, which, while they have their roots in pre-colonial times, have recently led to renewed social protest. After tracing the intricate history of these conflicts, the chapter analyses the terms in which they are fought out locally, before relating them to broader debates within the country as a whole.

Beyond this idea of legitimacy, there emerges the question of how people refer to the law and to local norms. Yazid Ben Hounet (Chapter 5) focuses on land-tenure in steppe-land environments (Naâma Province). He argues that the issue of land-tenure in Algeria has been and remains a problematic and a major challenge because of the policies of dispossession, nationalisation and socialisation that were implemented during the colonial period (1830-1962), and after Independence (1962). The chapter deals with the application of property law concerning land-tenure in Algeria, focusing on the enforcement of the law that gave access to agricultural land (1983) in a steppe-like province in western Algeria (Naâma). It presents and analyses conflicts that have emerged from the enforcement of this law, discusses the issue of agricultural land-tenure and raises the question of law by analysing how people refer to the law in land-tenure disputes. These analyses enable us to understand the operative norms and rules governing agricultural land-tenure, the ways different actors refer to the law (that is, the uses of the law and the role of judicial and/or administrative law enforcement institutions), and the ways they interpret the law.

To gain insight into how individuals are affected by and also utilise multiple legal and normative systems in everyday practice, Nejm Benessaiah (Chapter 6) focuses on inheritance disputes regarding land tenure in the Beni Isguen oasis (M'zab). Historically, the Mozabites of Ghardaia, Algeria, were governed by the *ʿazzaba* (priesthood), who effectively ruled as a theocracy, punishing unsanctioned behaviour through *tebria* (excommunication). Local disputes were resolved according to *ʿurf*, often translated as customary law, consisting of encoded verbal rules or agreements. Resources such as land tended to be subjected to common management, presided over by the family patriarch. A key to successful colonial rule was allowing Muslim communities to continue practising the Islamic faith undisturbed, including the *sharīʿa*. Later, state law became a further complicating factor in power relations between regulatory systems. The multiplicity of legal regimes has even afforded a kind of "forum shopping" by litigants acting opportunistically in their own self-interest, as the author found in the M'zab. While formal modes of local governance were denigrated by the state, informal normative order has also been slowly eroded by conflict with new ideas arriving through the global mass media. This chapter investigates how the presence of multiple systems of law influences the decision-making process of disputants in Beni Isguen, Ghardaia.

In the very specific context of Sahrawi refugee camps, Alice Wilson (Chapter 7) addresses the issue of compensation when property has been lost. Refugees may, if they do not return home, be eligible for compensation for property lost when they go into exile. This chapter considers the question of refugees' eligibility for, and receipt of, material compensation from other refugees in internal disputes that take place in exile. Sahrawi refugees from Western Sahara have been in exile in Algeria since 1976, following the still-unsettled conflict over these territories previously colonised by Spain (Western Sahara) and Morocco's partial annexation in 1975. Sahrawi exiles live in refugee camps in Algeria run as a "state within a state" by an administrative fusion between the POLISARIO Front and the partially recognised authority it founded, the SADR. Drawing on ethnographic fieldwork conducted in the refugee camps from 2006 to 2012, this chapter examines how pre-exile practices of compensation payments in internal disputes virtually disappeared in the early period of exile. This shift reflected practical and ideological factors: in practical terms, refugees were dispossessed and thus divested of property with which to make payments, while POLISARIO focused ideologically on popular justice, which encouraged questions of compensation to be deferred until after national liberation, and discouraged questions of tribes, the social context in which compensation payments had previously been made. Nevertheless, after the ceasefire in 1991, the judicial administration in the refugee camps was professionalised and this, together with a rise in living standards in the camps, had the paradoxical consequence of the limited reappearance of compensation payments in internal disputes, and in the context of tribes.

In this volume, reference to Islamic law only comes to the fore in the last chapter, which focuses on family law and inheritance – more specifically, the practices of transfer of property in situations of *kafāla* (legal fostering). Emilie Barraud explains that, since 1984, Algerian legislation has provided that "adoption (*tabanni*) is prohibited by the *shari'a* and the law" (art. 46). By using a doubly imperative tone and referring to the authority of Islamic law, the Algerian lawmakers intend to underscore the firmness of this official position, and to place it beyond discussion. An outside observer may confirm that "adoption does not exist in Algeria since Islam forbids it". However, ethnologies of elective parenting lead one to nuance this assertion. Adoption as defined in French law has no equivalent in Algerian law, but this does not prevent certain forms of institutionalised social parenthood (such as legal fostering, *kafāla*), as well as illegal adoptions. The Family Code forbids adoption, but has since substituted for it another mode of family integration – the legal fostering, or *kafāla*, of a minor, which is the commitment to maintenance and protection of a minor, but without the latter being endowed with the status of a legitimate child. Thus, under Islamic sanction, the norm would be the absence of adoption. If we allow that the *kafāla* is a form of adoption, the norm would be that the "adoption" of a child is concerned neither with the transfer of the name, which is one of the effects of legitimate filiation, nor with the rules of inheritance attached to that legitimacy. In many cases, however, "conservatory" provisions are made by the parents of children so adopted, in the form of legacies, donations or sales, to "protect" the fostered child. All of these measures are focused on circumventing the Islamic prohibition of adoption, and present new strategies of action.

Throughout the book, legal practices can be explained more by other criteria than by Islamic norms (in particular by the switch from a socialist system to a market economy; the administrative constraints and difficulties encountered by a state in the making, dominated by the annuity economy; and the experience of exile, as regards the Sahrawi refugee camps). Even in the last chapter, the practices of transfer of goods to fostered children (*makful*), although strongly influenced by Islamic law, cannot be solely explained by it – far from it. Family law is often examined in legal studies of Muslim societies, because it was long considered to be the last bastion of a declining Islamic law. Although the rule concerning the inequality of the distribution of inheritance according to the sex of the heirs has been written about extensively, the specific domain of succession has remained largely unexplored. In addition, the a-historical assertion of a casuistic theory has attracted more research than has the ethnographic study of the practices surrounding transfer of goods.

The texts assembled in this volume offer an overview of legal practices regarding property on in Algeria today and enable us to establish comparisons with other contexts in the Muslim world. What are the prevailing practices? What place do Islamic norms in fact occupy in property law in practice today? On what registers and foundations do these practices rest? Rather than giving ready-made answers to these questions, we propose returning each time to the ethnography of legal practices, to remind ourselves that these practices can only become completely meaningful in their own contexts.

References

Ageron, Charles Robert. 1979. *Histoire de l'Algérie contemporaine: De l'insurrection de 1871 au déclenchement de la guerre d'Algérie (1954)*, vol. 2. Paris : PUF.

von Benda-Beckmann Frantz, Keebet von Benda-Beckmann, and Melanie G. Wiber. 2006. "The Properties of Property", in *Changing Properties of Property*. New York–Oxford: Berghahn, pp. 1-39.

Ben Hounet, Yazid. 2007. "Des tribus en Algérie?", *Cahiers de la Méditerranée* 75: 150-171.

Ben Naoum, A. 1993. *Uled Sidi esh Sheykh: Essai sur les représentations hagiographiques de l'espace au sud-ouest de l'Algérie*. PhD thesis, Université de Provence, centre d'Aix.

Bras, J.P. (ed.). 2015. *Faire l'histoire du droit colonial: Cinquante ans après l'indépendance de l'Algérie*. Paris: IISMM-Karthala.

Coulter, Jeff. 1989. *Mind in Action*. Atlantic Highlands, NJ: Humanities Press International.

Durkheim, Emile. 1950. *Leçon de sociologie*. Paris: PUF.

Foriers, Paul. 1982. *La pensée juridique de Paul Foriers*, 2 vols. Bruxelles: Bruylant.

Godelier, Maurice. 1989. *L'idéel et le matériel*. Paris: Fayard.

Hachemaoui, Mohamed. 2013. *Clientélisme et patronage dans l'Algérie contemporaine*. Paris : Karthala.

Kant, Emmanuel. 2003. *Critique de la raison pratique*. Paris: Flammarion.

Lapidus, Ira M. 2002. *A History of Islamic Societies*. Cambridge: Cambridge University Press.

Lévi-Strauss, Claude. 2002. *Les structures élémentaires de la parenté*. Paris: Mouton de Gruyter.

Lucas, P., and J.C. Vatin. 1975. *L'Algérie des anthropologues*. Paris, Maspero.

Martinez, L. 1998. *La guerre civile en Algérie*. Paris: Karthala.

Moerman, Michael. 1987. *Talking Culture*. Cambridge: Cambridge University Press.

Moussaoui, Abderrahmane. 2005. "La pratique de l'anthropologie en Algérie", in

D. Albera and M. Tozy (eds), *La Méditerranée des anthropologues: Fractures, filiations, contiguïtés*. Paris: Maisonneuve & Larose–MMSH, pp. 269-295.

Moussaoui, Abderrahmane. 2006. *De la violence en Algérie : Les lois du chaos*. Arles: Actes Sud.

Stark, David, and Laszlo Bruszt. 1998. "The Privatization Debate: From Plan to Market of from Plan to Clan?", in *Postsocialist Pathways: Transforming Politics and Property in East Central Europe*. Cambridge: Cambridge University Press, pp. 51-79.

Valet, René-Victor. 1927. *Le Sahara Algérien: Étude de l'organisation administrative, financière et judiciaire des Territoires du Sud*. Alger: La Typo-Litho.

Vatin, Jean-Claude. 1983. *L'Algérie: Politique, histoire et société*. Paris: Presse de la Fondation Nationale des Sciences Politiques.

Young, R. 2001. *Postcolonialism: An Historical Introduction*. Oxford: Blackwell.

CHAPTER 1

Land Tenure and Capital Ownership in Algeria

Ammar Belhimer

The legal corpus of independent Algeria has undergone a recent and precarious reformation of private property law, which is still embryonic and not straightforward. It goes against the long-praised pre-eminence of state-held property as the foundation of justice and social equality (Ghaouti, 2014: 10). The first Constitution of the Algerian state, promulgated on 10 September 1963, did not address the issue of property, whether private or public. Subsequently, the National Charter, and then the Constitution of 22 November 1976, referred to state property, to which were ascribed "quasi-mythical qualities such as primacy and irreversibility, the highest form of social property" (Ghaouti, 2014: 10). Recent changes show a two-fold trend: the maintenance of state ownership of agricultural land abandoned by the settlers in the aftermath of Independence; and the privatisation of all other immovable goods and economic activities.

The Agricultural Land Market: From Self-Management to Concessions

Historically won "in blood and in violence", land enjoys a particular legal status. In Algeria, we find the same foundations for the formation and transfer of property, mainly structured around the principles of consanguinity, genealogy and family name, as in the rest of the Mediterranean area (Stahl, 1997). Mainstream (and not only official) historiography on both sides of the Mediterranean suggests, not to say imposes, the blanket idea that the "dispossession of the Algerian *fellahs*" by colonial laws mostly resulted in the transfer of colossal wealth to the newly independent Algerian state, and that it was necessary to cede the land – either totally or partially, definitively or temporarily – to other subjects, especially private subjects, in order to organise its exploitation (Sari, 1978).

The necessary retrocession required by this exploitation led to the creation of a new and ambiguous legal category ("surface rights"). From 1962 to 1975, when the colonial legislation was abrogated, the extant legislation on national state-owned land coexisted with the new legislation. The legal regime for land was governed by a set of texts that corresponded to the newly implemented

 | DOI 10.1163/9789004362116_003

policies. We can distinguish two major periods in this legal development: before and after 1971 (when the agrarian revolution started).

The massive departure of the settlers inspired a first measure for the protection and preservation of "vacant" agricultural properties and of properties placed under the protection of the state: the Ordinance of 24 August 1962 relating to the protection and management of vacant properties.[1] The properties in question covered 2.5 million hectares, that is, 30% of the total useful agricultural surface area, and were a source of employment for close to 100,000 casual workers and 134,000 permanent workers.

This first measure was implemented by texts that extended the area of the state's patrimony to properties that were not vacant, so that their owners too could benefit from the attributes of public state-ownership, that is, inalienability, imprescriptibility, non-transferability and exemption from seizure.[2] Post-colonial Algerian law recommended that properties abandoned by settlers be restored to their former owners, and placed these under the administration of government officials whose mission was to "keep" and to "preserve" the original rights. However, the socialist wave gave little substance to these notions, even if a few restitutions were ordered and effectively implemented. Then the decree of 23 October 1962 prohibited and cancelled all sale and rental contracts, including those concluded abroad since 1 July 1962.[3] The properties affected become vacant again under the ordinance of 24 August 1962 and the conditions and guarantees for this statement of vacancy were defined by the decree of 18 March 1963, which set out a legal remedy. But, as observed by the UN Human Rights Committee, "Those remedies were ineffective, however, since the judges who heard the cases took a long time to deliver their decisions, and new provisions virtually removed all judicial guarantees."[4] The possibility of legal remedy was removed a few months later by a decree of 9 May 1963. Only a process before a commission at the level of the *département* was maintained. To the notion of vacancy were added those of public order and of social harmony, which gave the authorities a quasi-sovereign power of valuation.

---

1 Ordinance 62-20 of 24 August 1962, relating to the protection and management of vacant properties, *Journal Officiel de la République Algérienne Démocratique et Populaire* (JORA) 1962, p. 183. Also see the decrees of 22 and 23 November 1962 and the decrees of 18 March 1963.

2 Decree 63-168 of 9 May 1963, Act 63-27 of 26 July 1963, Decree 63-388 of 1 October 1963, and Ordinance 68-653 of 30 December 1968, relating to self-management in agriculture.

3 Decree 62-3 of 23 October 1962 governing transactions, sales, rentals, leasing arrangements, farmed out movable and immovable goods, *JORA* 1, Friday 26 October 1962, p. 14.

4 Case of Armand Anton v. Algeria, Decision of the Human Rights Committee by virtue of the optional protocol relating to the International Covenant on Civil and Political Rights, on 1 November 2006; 88th session, Communication 1424/2005, dated 24 November 2004.

It was not until 1971 that the promulgation of the ordinance of 8 November brought the introduction of a simple and rapid procedure that noted rights concerning land acquired individually.[5] The modalities of this process were specified in a decree adopted two years later.[6] This ordinance predated the constitutional standards of 1976, which consolidated the new social order, as defined in Articles 13, 14 and 16.[7]

Delimiting the properties concerned, and establishing and issuing certificates was essential for the implementation of the second phase of the agrarian revolution, which enabled 11,000 km² to be allocated to 90,000 peasants. To ascertain, on the basis of official title to the land, private ownership of land that was agricultural or had agricultural potential, the claimant to the property had to present at least one of the four following documents:[8] the deeds issued by the land administration authorities;[9] authentic legal documents;[10] certificates of ownership established and issued in compliance with

5 Articles 76-78 of Ordinance 71-73 of 8 November 1971 governing the agrarian revolution.

6 Decree 73-32 of 5 January 1973.

7 Article 13: "The socialisation of the means of production constitutes the fundamental basis of socialism, and state property represents the highest form of social property." Article 14: "State property is defined as the property owned by the national community of which the state is the emanation. It is irreversibly established on pastoral land, or agricultural land or nationalised land with agricultural potential, on forests, on waters, sub-soil, mines and quarries, natural sources of energy, minerals, natural and living wealth of the continental plateau and of the exclusive economic area. Moreover, state property also irreversibly includes all nationalised companies, banks, insurances and installations, as well as the railways, maritime and air transports, the harbours and communication pathways, mail, telegraph and telephone services, television and radio broadcasting, the main means of land transport as well as the bulk of the economic, social and cultural factories, firms and installations that the state has or may have had realised, developed or purchased. The monopoly of the state is established irrevocably on foreign trade and on wholesale trade." Article 16: "The individual ownership of properties for personal or family use is guaranteed. Non-exploitative private property, as defined by law, is an integral part of the new social organisation. Private property, especially in the economic sector, should contribute to the development of the country and have a social benefit. It is guaranteed in the framework of the law. The right to inheritance is guaranteed."

8 Articles 3-5 of Decree 73-32 of 5 January 1973 relating to the recognition of the right to private property.

9 They result of global investigation procedures laid down in the Act of 26 July 1873 and the partial investigations of the actions prescribed by the Acts of 16 February 1897 and of 4 August 1926.

10 Documents drawn up by notaries or a public administrative authority acting in an official capacity. They include documents of a legislative nature, judicial and extra-judicial documents, notarised deeds, the judgements of former *qāḍīs* before the promulgation of Ordinance 70-91 of 15 December 1970 governing notaries and bailiffs' notaries.

TABLE 1.1 *Legal composition of Algerian land (in 2001). Precarious property : low securitization rate.*

Origine des terres	Nombre d'exploitations	%	Superficie (ha)	%
Melk personnel titré	120 087	11,73	1 090 192	12,89
Melk personnel non titré	252 331	24,65	847 872	10.02
Melk en indivision titré	143 900	14,06	1 294 676	15,31
Melk en indivision non titré	261 005	25,49	2 624 472	31,03
Total Propriété privée	*777 323*	*76*	*5 857 212*	*69*
Domaine privé de l'Etat	181 194	17,7	2 541 876	30,05
Domaine public	5 428	0,53	24 323	0,29
Total domaine national	*186 622*	*18*	*2 566 199*	*30*
Wakf privé	2 211	0,22	24 056	0,28
Wakf public	605	0,06	4 821	0.06
Total Wakf	*2 816*	*0,28*	*28 877*	*0,34*
Non déclaré	1103	0,11	6 392	0,08
Non concerné (Eleveurs)	55 935	5,46	0	0
Total	1 023 799	100	8 458 680	100

Source : Recensement général de l'agriculture 2001

the provisions of Decree 73-32 of 5 January 1973; and/or documents under privy seal.[11]

This process remains incomplete. The table above shows the legal breakdown of Algerian land, according to the data of the Ministry of Agriculture in 2001.

Land rights are still precarious today and this precariousness remains difficult to prove. For historical and sociological reasons, which we have studied extensively elsewhere (Belhimer, 2012), a significant proportion of real estate in Algeria has no deeds. The associated legal texts are circumstantial and provisional and, being adopted in a hurry, they are of limited efficacy and are not easily accessible. The consequences of this are foreseeable: not only does this legal situation make it difficult to increase agricultural productivity, but planning permission will only be granted if the applicant can prove ownership

11 They may provide a certain conclusive force if they have been submitted to a publication procedure in the land registry whereby they become demurrable to the third parties who purchased the goods before 1 January 1971. After recognition of the right to ownership, a report is prepared by the Assemblée Populaire Communale Elargie (APCE) on the basis of which a certificate of ownership is issued to the recognised owners.

of the plot on which the proposed building will be erected,[12] and the absence of deeds also complicates getting a mortgage loan for the development of agricultural land or making other investments.

A conclusive indication of this state of affairs is the evaluation of the registered surface area. For the administration of state-owned land, the end of the registration process, and hence the definitive settling of these real-estate issues, should have taken place in 2014,[13] but representatives of the notaries' guild consider that hardly 20% of its objectives have been achieved.[14] The experts are worried: "A state without a land registry is a blind state."[15] The major current paradox lies in the fact that the legislative corpus governing land tenure refuses to accept the unquestionable reality that property deeds are largely non-existent.

We accordingly find a series of recurrent ambivalences. To borrow a legal expression, there is a consensus recommending formalism for real estate, as reflected in Article 12 of Ordinance 70-91 of 15 December 1970, which regulates the notaries' profession, and repeated *in extenso* in the Civil Law (number 324 bis 1). There it is stated:

> In addition to the Acts which it is imperative by law be drawn up by a notary, the Acts causing the transfer of buildings or of immovable property rights *in rem*, of business assets or of industry, or any part of them, transfers of stocks or of company shares, rural leases, business leases, administrations of business assets or of industrial establishments must,

12 Article 50 of Act 90-25 completed and modified pertaining to land-use planning and town planning states that "the right to build is linked with ownership of the soil".

13 "The general land registry of the country is 45% complete according to the general director of the National Agency of the Land registry (ANC), Mustapha Radi, who goes on to say that the operation will be finalised in 2014", by using in particular Dutch expertise and digital means which help "save time". Chérif Bennaceur has stated: "Still 'delays' have interfered with this operation and must be addressed, since the officials in charge of the National domain and of the ANC are confronted with 'abnormal situations' caused by various factors. … It thus mentions hundreds of cases of difficulties associated with differences in surface areas, the absence of property deeds, anarchic constructions, undeveloped plots transformed into public or private buildings, unlawful occupations especially of the public domain and agricultural exploitations, domain disputes …", *Le Soir d'Algérie*, 18 December 2012.

14 Minutes of the meeting held in the Council of the Nation on 29 October 2012 on land disputes. *El-Moudjahid*, 30 October 2012.

15 Communication of Lamine Cheriet, at the study day on the impact of the land registry operation on the land regime in Algeria, organised by the land expert geometers and the Regional Council of Constantine, on 2 April 2011, reported in *El-Watan*, 3 April 2011.

> failing which they will be invalid, be drawn up by a notary and the fee must be paid to the public officer who has executed or prepared the Act. The payment made for these tasks and remitted into the hands of the public officer who executed the memorandum of association of a company with its amendments should also be taken into account and authenticated, failing which they will be invalid.

Transfers related to real property must therefore be drawn up by a notary, failing which they will be invalid. This provision is a mere formality, since the legal profession has long resorted to "legal subterfuges" (Lahlou-Khiar, 2013) to validate contracts relating to land under privy seal. The courts have sometimes considered authentic documents as proof,[16] and sometimes as an obligation on the vendor, pursuant to Article 361 of the Civil Law,[17] whereby: "The vendor shall do his utmost to transfer the right sold to the buyer and to abstain from any action which might render said transfer impossible or difficult."

The stubborn refusal of the judges in the lower courts to resolve the legal standing of properties without legal deeds has persisted, despite the intervention of a landmark decision of 18 February 1997 by the Supreme Court, including all its chambers.[18] The Supreme Court wanted to make it clear that, pursuant to Article 324 bis 1 of the Civil Law, a contract must be drawn up by a notary so as to be valid, although many courts handling appeal cases steadfastly refused to declare null and void real estate transactions not drawn up by a notary. The decisions made were thus a stopgap measure, in the absence of deeds, and were a means to prove ownership, because they had been published by the land registry office. .

In addition to illegal transactions concerning land assets, the owner of a plot who wants to build on it also faces constraints. As no construction is legally conceivable in the absence of a deed, the result is a proliferation of illegal buildings authorised retrospectively, pursuant to Decree 85-212 of 13 August 1985, which determines the conditions under which the rights of disposal and habitation by the actual occupiers of public or private plots may be settled, when they are objects of acts or constructions that do not comply

16 Supreme Court, Commercial and Maritime Chamber, judgement of 30 April 1989. *Revue Jurisprudentielle* 1991, 4, p.145.

17 Supreme Court, Civil Chamber, judgement of 21 October 1990, *Revue Jurisprudentielle* 1992, 1, p. 84.

18 Supreme Court, judgement of 18 February 1997, including all chambers; commented on by Filali and Lahlou-Khiar (2013). See also Belarbia (2010: 256).

with the rules in force and with the interministerial instruction of 13 August 1985 pertaining to the management of illegal buildings. More recently, Act 08-15 of 20 July 2008 set out the legalisation procedure for buildings, especially those erected without a building permit.[19] It is therefore difficult to contest what Lahlou-Khiar (2013) calls a "juridical imbroglio", after taking stock of the juridical instruments for providing proof of land tenure:

1 *The Notarised Deed*

This is the solution envisaged by Decree 88-352 of 21 May 1983, which instituted a recognition procedure of the acquisitive and establishment prescription of a notarised deed proving ownership of property. It concerns owners who do not have property deeds but who wish to regularise their legal situation, on the essential condition that they hold proof of owner ship as a requester, pursuant to the Civil Law. Article 827 served as a reference for notarised deeds (Benaissa, 2003). Decree 83-352 institutes a vastly simplified procedure, associated with the fact that the notary both issues the deeds and is in charge of most of the administrative processes, which are advantages that have attracted a high level of interest from the people affected.

19 Art. 35 of Act 08-15 of 20 July 2008 fixing the compliance rules for buildings and their completion: When the proprietor or the client of the land tax base on which the building is erected has a deed of property, a certificate of possession or any other deed drawn up by a notary, and when the *dāʾra* commission validates his request, the commission sends his file to the president of the relevant APCE, to establish either a building permit, for regularisation purposes, or a completion permit, or a compliance certificate, pursuant to the provisions of Articles 20, 21 and 22 above. In such a case, the president of the APCE asks the applicant to complete his case, pursuant to the provisions above and to the legislative and regulatory provisions. Art. 36: When the client or the author of the construction has an administrative document issued by a territorial unit, and a building permit, and only when the building is erected in the framework of a housing development, the *dāʾra* commission conducts a land enquiry so as to determine the legal nature of the site. Upon completion of the enquiry conducted by the customs departments, and if the buildings do not comply with the provisions of Article 16 above, the *dāʾra* commission refers to the authorities in charge so as to regularise the land tax base in the framework of the provisions of Article 38 below. If the building is completed, in the sense of the provisions of this law, the owner or the client, after regularisation of the land tax base, is required to file a case to obtain a compliance certificate. If the building is not completed, in the sense of the provisions of this law, the owner or the client, after regularisation of the land tax base, is required to file a case to obtain the completion permit.

The notarised deed is, however, not always accepted by the judiciary when it is flawed: "The absence of opposition to the process of drawing up a notarial deed before the notary during the 4-month period referred to in Article 4 of Decree 83-352, does not constitute an impediment to challenging ownership through judicial process, since the trial judge has the competence to review the content of the Act."[20] Review by a judge has thus led to the discovery of "aberrations of certain notaries" who have established notarised deeds for land belonging to a religious institution *habous*,[21] or have validated unlawful contracts.[22]

2 *The Issuance of Property Deeds by Way of a Land Investigation*

Act 07-02 of 27 February 2007, which instituted a process for recognising real estate property rights and issuing property deeds by way of a land investigation, abrogated the decree pertaining to the notarised deed. It repeats the conditions required for the notarised deed, particularly the recognition of the "acquisitive prescription" (see below).

3 *The Certificate of Possession*

The Act 90-25 of 18 November 1990 pertaining to land strategy, made in the wake of the reforms in favour of economic liberalisation and of political openness, instituted a certificate of possession as a way of proving land tenure. The provisions relating to the certificate of possession refer to the prescriptions in Civil Law pertaining to the conditions of ownership.[23] This document is issued by the president of the Assemblée Populaire Communale Elargie (APCE), upon completion of a quick and simple procedure: a one-year possession of a non-registered plot, without deeds, suffices to claim a certificate of possession, which in turn grants the right to a building permit, to renting out

20 Supreme Court, Civil Chamber, judgement of 18 April 2007, *Revue de la Cour Suprême*, 2007, 2, p. 161.

21 Supreme Court, Civil Chamber, judgement of 22 April 2010, *Revue de la Cour Suprême*, 2010, 2, p. 151.

22 Supreme Court, Land Chamber, judgement of 25 April 4/2001, *Revue Jurisprudentielle*, 2004; special issue relating to the jurisprudence of the land chamber, 2, p. 30.

23 Article 39 of Act 90-25 of 18 November 1990 on land policy: "In the regions where the land registry has not yet been established, any person who in the sense of Article 823 of Ordinance 75-58 of 26 September 1975 (Civil Law) exercises on privately-owned lands without deeds a continuous, uninterrupted, peaceful, public and non-equivocal possession, can obtain the issuance of a possession title designated as 'certificate of possession', which is subject to the registration and land record formalities."

the land, and particularly to using the land as collateral for a mid- or long-term loan.

4 *Acquisitive Prescription*

Article 827 of the Civil Law provides as follows: "He who exercises possession of a movable or immovable item, or on a movable or immovable real right *in rem* without being the owner or the holder, becomes proprietor thereof if his possession continues without interruption for fifteen years." Article 13 of Decree 76-63 of 25 March 1976 relating to the institution of the land register, modified by Executive Decree 93-123 of 19 May 1993, states: "For buildings whose apparent owners are without legal property deeds, but who exercise, according to the indicated written documents in the land registry, a possession whose duration enables them to access the right of ownership by acquisitive prescription, in compliance with the legal provisions set out in this regard, the registration is considered as temporary for a four (4) month period starting on the day on which it took place. This temporary registration becomes final upon expiry of the period defined in the previous paragraph, if no opposition attributing the right of ownership elsewhere has been specified to the real estate guardian, or if past oppositions have been withdrawn or rejected." This provision, and others, testifies to the decisive importance of land records when proving ownership of real estate.

Pursuant to Article 793 of the Civil Law, "The ownership of the buildings and the other rights *in rem* are transferred among the parties present as well as with respect to third parties only if the formalities set out by law and especially the texts governing the land records are adhered to." Article 16 of Ordinance 75-74 of 12 November 1975, establishing the general survey plan and instituting the land register, is also edifying with regard to the significance of land records when proving land tenure: "The voluntary Acts and the agreements tending to constitute, transmit, declare, modify or extinguish a right *in rem*, only become effective, even among the parties, when recorded in the land registry."

5 *Expropriations*

There has been a separation between private property and expropriation since 1989. The Constitution of 1976 had previously created a link between private property and expropriation, with a complementary linking of Articles 16 and 17. Article 16 laid out the principle of the protection of private property and of the related right of inheritance, whereas Article 18 detailed the exceptions to this principle. The drafters of the Constitution of 1989 supported expropriation if it benefited public ownership. Everywhere else, there is a time-honoured tradition that private property and expropriation are addressed in the same provision; expropriation is founded in the interests of the state and not in the private good of individuals. Expropriation is the barometer of the changes at work. Its treatment differs from the way the issue of private property is addressed:

> The more private property is considered to be a sacred right of quasi unlimited and inviolable character, the more expropriation will be made difficult and strictly delimited. Still, a comparative analysis of the Algerian Constitutions of 1976, of 1989 and of 1996 leads to a curious observation, namely that the definition of expropriation has hardly changed, has hardly evolved in spite of the statements concerning breaking away from a Socialist economy. (Ghaouti, 2014: 10)

On the ground, the conditions authorising expropriation have been reduced to a strict minimum, whereas the state gives itself free rein in determining the aims of expropriation. Even the key legitimating element of expropriation, which has the ultimate aim of abolishing home ownership, is totally overlooked. Although Article 20 of the 1989 Constitution introduces a supplement concerning fair and equitable compensation as a prior indemnity, the purpose of public utility always remains glaringly and seriously absent. Consequently, it is essentially the judge's interpretation of this very notion of public utility that constitutes the principal protection of the expropriated citizen.

Act 91-11 of 27 April 1991, although asserting the exceptional mode of expropriation for the public benefit, vastly relied on public interest; paragraph 2 of Article 2 of this Act states: "expropriation is only possible if the purpose is to implement operations resulting from the application of legal instruments concerning town planning, land-use planning and general planning regarding public amenities or works of public interest."

In 2004, the Finance Act 04-21 of 29 December 2004 including the Finance Act for 2005 went one step further by legitimating expropriation not only for a public benefit, but also for the realisation of infrastructures of public interest and of national and strategic scope. The government's Action Programme launched in 2004 had situated as a fundamental axis for the socio-economic development of the country the realisation of infrastructures on a national scale, such as the East-West motorway. Thus, to facilitate and speed up the process, the Finance Act for 2005 introduced its Article 65 provisions, which simply authorise taking immediate possession of properties.

This Finance Act added two new Articles: 12 bis and 12 ter; the latter stipulates peremptorily that: "the expropriating administration may enable immediate possession ...". Pleas introduced by the interested parties cannot halt the execution of this immediate possession procedure.

6 *Joint Possession*

Another obstacle to private property has been joint possession. It is the object of two legal instruments. The framework Land Act 90-25 of 18 November 1990,[24] modified and completed by Ordinance 95-26 of 25 September 1995,[25] concerns restitution to the private owners of land that had been taken over by the National Fund for Agrarian Reform in the framework of its second phase, which determined private property and the nationalisation of the surplus to the benefit of the Fund. Second, there was the Agricultural General Act 08-16 of 3 August 2008.[26]

In the wake of these Acts, we find two regulatory texts. The first was the Executive Decree 97-490 of 29 December 1997, which fixed the conditions for parcelling off agricultural land.[27] The Appendix to the text, pursuant to Article 55 of the Land Strategy Law, takes into account mountainous land (a Finance and Agriculture inter-ministerial decision of 22 February 1989, with reference to Article 81 of the Finance Act of 1989, had classified agricultural land into four areas [very fertile, fertile, of medium fertility, of poor fertility]). Reference is made to the quality of the soil, the irrigation system and other parameters still to be defined, and the "reference surface" according to a table at Article 3 of the Executive Decree. The "reference surface" (from 1 to 20 hectares) varies over six areas, identified according to the regions, the quality of the soils, the level of irrigation and the cultivation practised. Any fragmentation infringing the text annuls the operation. Any transfer occurring amicably or judicially must obey Article 55 of the Land Strategy Law. If it does not, it is deemed invalid and this enables the National Office of Agricultural Land to exercise a right of pre-emption which is enforceable against the heirs.

7 *Inheritance*

In a judgement of 9 July 1984, the Supreme Court rejected citizenship as the basis for rights to inherit, thereby preferring Islamic religious allegiance.[28] According to another judgement of the same jurisdiction, dated 20 June 2001, inheritance is passed to a Muslim on the day of the bequeather's death; no one who converts to the Islamic religion after the bequeather's death is entitled to the inheritance.[29] Such is the case of a foreign wife who has not converted to Islam during her husband's lifetime: she does not inherit after his death. This

24 *JORA* 49, 18 November 1990, p. 1560.

25 *JORA* 27, 18 November 1995, p. 11.

26 *JORA* 46, 10 August 2008, p. 4.

27 *JORA* 84, 12 December 1997.

28 Case 33509, in Hanifi, 2013: 12).

29 Case 244899, *Revue de la Cour Suprême*, 2003, 1, p. 345.

jurisprudential practice is old and founded on Islamic law. In colonial times too, when the spouse was not Muslim, she did not inherit from her husband after his death.

In a judgement of 14 April 1874, the Court of Algiers bore in mind that

> the principles of that (Islamic) religion had greater impact in its effects than other religions, to the extent that any religion, such as for example the Catholic or the Protestant religion, can be adopted without needing to modify Civil Law or citizenship. It is not so when embracing Islam; this religion exerts in itself and through its consequences a direct influence on the person and the rights he/she may claim. (Clavel, 1895, 17; my translation)

The Private Exploitation of State-Owned Real Estate

The collective character of property influences how it can be exploited in specific ways. This gave rise to a new legal category, the right of surface area,[30] which confers on farmers the tenure of constructions and plantations on state land, according to formulae that have not evolved since 1987. The vacant properties inherited from the colonial period have proved to be a poisoned gift for the Algerian state. They were stolen from oppressed and dispossessed peasants, and constituted the best plots. Immediately after Independence, they were exploited collectively before being joined to the national land of the agrarian revolution, which included state-owned estates, and were exploited under joint possession by enlightened individuals or collective production structures. In 1987, in view of the failure of collectivisation, these areas were divided into individual (Exploitations Agricoles Individuelles; EAI) and collective (Exploitations Agricoles Collectives; EAC) agricultural enterprises. This new land-use framework was fixed by Act 87-19 of 8 December 1987, which determined the working methods for state-owned agricultural land, and fixed the rights and obligations of the producers.[31] This gave rise to the constitution of 3,200 collective agricultural estates and 22,000 farming units, including EAIs and

30 Farmers may have "surface rights" on their land, granting them ownership of the buildings and plantations created on state land, according to formulae that have not evolved since 1987 ("Act 87/19 determining how the state-owned agricultural lands are to be worked, and fixing the rights and obligations of the producers", *JORA* 50, 19 December 1987).

31 *JORA* 50, 9 December 1987, p. 1253.

EACS. The subsidiaries of an EAC[32] benefitted from a perpetual right to use of the land, which "must be exploited collectively and as a joint possession, with equal shares between the members of the freely associated collective society. Each producer cannot claim more than one share nor be part of more than one collective society."[33] However, this principle, inevitably implying the impossibility of sharing land and work, "contained the seeds of its own dissolution" (Aït Amara, 2002: 127). The land tenure status and the management rules of the EACS were comparable to those of the *ejidos* in Mexico, which bring together a group of farmers on land distributed by the state: the land so granted can be neither sold, nor rented, nor mortgaged.

This reform gave rise to informal arrangements, marking the beginning of new social relations around state land tenure.[34] Some EACS were shared amicably, and subsidiaries were organised around drillings to remedy the dysfunctions of the collective surface network. A new category of producers appeared, the tenants, who practised open field, then greenhouse vegetable growing (Amichi et al., 2011: 81). Today, more than 70% of EACS are divided and only the citrus-growing EACS are still united. The sustainable presence of citrus fruit trees constitutes a strategic approach that cannot be reconsidered with every agricultural season.

The political goal of the reform was to satisfy the food needs of the country by increasing the production and the productivity of the land. A partial decollectivisation was gradually implemented: a tiny portion (2%) of public land was allocated to families managing EAIs, whereas the socialist agricultural estates (Domaines Agricoles Socialistes; DAS) were broken up into collective structures of three to ten families of former wage-earners (the EACs, 89% of the distributed surface areas). The remaining surface area (9%) was kept for use as pilot public farms, places of experimentation and popularisation. Parallel to these divisions, the level of public support (in loans, equipment) to private farms increased in line with that given to state-owned land (Bedrani, 1987).

The 1987 Act of gave rise to the diversity of today's production systems. It stayed in force up to the adoption on 3 August 2008 of Act 08-16 on agricultural

32 3 to 20 subsidiaries for 9 to 50 hectares.

33 Act 87/19 determining how state-owned agricultural land is to be worked, and fixing the rights and obligations of the producers. *JORA* 1987, 50, 19 December 1987, p. 1253. www.gredaal.com/legislation/foncier/Loi-87-19-mode-exploitation-terres-agricoles-domaine%20national.pdf.

34 These dynamics can be particularly observed in the irrigated perimeter of Ouarizane, situated in the Low Cheliff (65,000 hectares), an alluvial plain in north-east Algeria, with a high salt content.

policy.[35] This law concerned private state agricultural land. The way such land was exploited was no longer through perpetual right of use but through concessions, defined as "an act pursuant to which the licensing authority grants a person the right to exploit the land tenure for a set duration against an annual royalty". It also included "accession to agricultural tenure" for land "developed by beneficiaries in the Saharan and sub-Saharan regions, as well as for non-allocated land allotted to the state as private land". This Act was reviewed and replaced by Act 10-03 of 15 August 2010,[36] which defines the current regime and covers two classes of property: private state lands; and assets defined as "linked with agricultural use, especially constructions, plantations and hydraulic infrastructures".

One year after its adoption, 72% of farmers (157,000 out of the 219,000 identified) had put in an application to comply with the new regulations authorising any person of Algerian nationality to make use of agricultural land belonging to the private state land, on the basis of a specification drawn up for a maximum period of four years. The farmer pays an annual fee to the state, the amount of which is fixed by the Finance Act. The members of the EACs and the EAIs covered by the 1987 Act and holders "of an authenticated Act published in the land registry, or a judgement of the *wālī*" may thus claim eligibility, as may "residents" wishing to "enlarge their farms" and "people with scientific and/or technical abilities who have projects to consolidate and modernise their agricultural unit".[37] These applications must be sent to the National Office of Agricultural Land (the interface for the administration of such land), for the registration and validation of the sheet of specifications. The Office may exercise the right of pre-emption, if the concession right is transferred.

In addition to farming state-owned land, the concession offers "the right to constitute, to the benefit of credit institutions, a mortgage on the immovable right *in rem*". The beneficiary of the concession is also free "to stipulate, to participate in legal proceedings, to sue and to contract pursuant to the Civil Law" and "to execute any partnership agreement". In practice, if authenticated property deeds on the land are not made available or transferred, the Banque de l'Agriculture et du Développement Rural has set a precedent and demanded the possibility of granting mortgages on properties linked to the agricultural concerns (particularly buildings).[38]

---

35 The General Agricultural Act 08-16 of 3 August 2008, *JORA* 46, 10 August 2008, pp. 3-12.

36 Act 10-03 of 15 August 2010, which lays down the conditions and modalities for farming private state-owned agricultural land, *JORA* of 18 August 2010, pp. 4-7.

37 This provision seems to aim at legalising *de facto* concessions to the benefit of the land magnates in the system, since the 1990s.

38 These cases were notified to the *ad hoc* committee in charge of the national consultation

Article 4 of the law gives a wider definition of the concession than previous legislation. Article 13 stipulates that the concession right is "assignable, transmissible and seizable". Its transfer, for free, can take place to the benefit of one of the rights holders of the beneficiary for the remaining duration of the concession in case of incapacity and/or the attainment of retirement age. In case of death, the heirs may, within one year, choose a representative who will exercise the rights and duties (according to the provisions of the Family Code in the case of minors) and waive or transfer their rights. Upon expiry of this period, the Office refers the matter to the competent court.

In the wake of scandals affecting the exploitation of certain estates of the Mitidja, any person who has made land transactions that are prohibited on agricultural land is excluded from concessions. Other exclusions include land where the decision of attribution has been cancelled, and land where the right to farm has been withdrawn after being judicially granted. Four orders of circumstances justify the termination of a concession: deviant use of agricultural lands and/or surface assets; the non-exploitation of various plots for more than one year; sub-letting; and non-payment of the fee for two consecutive years (Art. 29). According to an article in the local press, 11,900 farmers were thus involved in legal proceedings, and 15,000 hectares had been diverted from their agricultural purpose.[39]

The Evolution of Property Rights Other Than in Land

The liberalisation of the economy and the ability of private companies to access certain sectors of activity increased throughout the 1980s: first real estate and distribution, then industry a few years later. A first breach was opened in the socialist sanctuary with the promulgation of the Law on State Property of 30 June 1984.[40] This law was replaced by Act 90-30 of 1 December 1990, due to the fragility of the legal order on which the former relies, especially Article 13 of the Constitution of 22 November 1976, which provides that "state property is the highest form of social property". A Code was projected that was to fill the legal gap resulting from the abrogation of colonial law in 1975. It was presented to the government in 1978, but was only finally adopted by the

on local development and the expectations of the populations during its meetings in the southern *wilayas* in September 2011.

39 "Housing Programmes in Algiers: Strong Pressure on Arable Land", *El Watan*, 3 March 2014.

40 Act 84-16 of 30 June 1984 relating to state-owned properties, *JORA* of 30 June 1984, pp. 678 ff.

People's National Assembly six years later. This text reflects a political discourse, mixing the notions of state and nation, of state property, of local territorial units, and of national state property. Article 1 of the Law of State Property repeats Article 14 of the Constitution, which defines state property as "the property owned by the national community of which the state is the emanation". There is thus a unified representation of national property, based on an organic criterion. As stipulated at Article 7, the *wilāyas* and the municipalities[41] "possess and manage in the name of the national community, the properties making up their respective assets". The state thus holds proprietary rights over the immovable and movable assets on the national territory. The assets of the municipalities and of the *wilāyas*, however, remain governed by the provisions of the communal codes and the *wilāya* codes.

National Property includes public, economic, military, individual and foreign assets. Article 12 of the 1984 law defines the public domain as the collection of "rights and of the movable and immovable assets available to all and to the public, either directly or via a public service, providing they are, by nature or through special arrangements, adapted exclusively or essentially to the particular goal of the said service".

Article 17 specifies that the economic field comprises "the natural wealth as well as the collection of assets and means of production and exploitation, with an industrial, commercial, agricultural and tertiary character, owned by the state and local governments". The economic field thus includes: the natural wealth of the soil and of the sub-soil, especially water resources of all sorts, liquid or gaseous petroleum products, reserves of minerals and metals, or other ores or products extracted in mines and quarries; the natural wealth of the sea and the forests of the national territory, on the surface or beneath it, and on the continental shelf and maritime zones under Algerian sovereignty and jurisdiction.

As for the assets held by socialist entities (institutions, offices, centres, institutes and other bodies of an economic character), they were governed by Article 19, which distinguishes social capital from social assets so as to legislate only on "the assets and rights of all sorts established as a social reserve by the state and becoming part of [these entities'] assets". The assets of these entities are therefore not covered by the principle of state ownership. They could, however, hold and manage dependencies of national property – public or private assets of the state and territorial collectivities – through an allocation, a

41 Algeria is composed of 48 *wilāyas*, 548 *dā'ras* and 1,541 municipalities. The *wilāya* is the largest administrative unit. It consists of a collection of *dā'ras*, each containing several municipalities.

concession or a contract of occupancy. They could do so in two other cases: when they managed a public service that had been assigned to them, and when they were in charge of an operation in the public interest. Consequently, the assets of public companies were subject to legal proceedings, attachment or judicial settlement and, like any other private company governed by the Law of Commerce, their assets could be attached.

Thus, the Act of 1984 set in place, subtly and almost imperceptibly, a permissive property regime in which privatisation was coherent with a new political vision. After the public authorities had launched the debate around the inefficient management of the public sector in 1982, the aim was to substitute the criteria of social efficacy, regional balance and employment with that of financial efficiency (Rahmani, 1996: 96).

The Law of 1984 had hardly taken full effect when the Constitution of 23 February 1989 challenged it by restoring the rules of conventional state-ownership.[42] Act 90-30 of 1 December 1990[43] substituted the notion of state-ownership with public ownership. National public assets were declared "public property", and national private assets "private property of the government". The latter were economic assets previously attached to individual, foreign and military concerns. The state as an owner was hence in fact engaged in mercantile relationships.

Thus, the separation that the 1990 Act initiated between "public property" and "private property" broke with the previous conception of national property. Similarly, the distinction made between "proprietary rights" and "rights of use" means that assets can only depend on the national land regime if they are the property of a civil servant. This measure applies to public institutions as well as to national companies. The administrations enjoyed a special regime: the assets were directly allocated by the state or territorial units and became the property of the public person in question. The assets of the territorial units became dependent on the public domain either by delimitation or by classification. This quality may be lost due to the modalities of Article 34 of the State Property Law.

It should also be noted that the assets of public enterprises are governed by the principle of seizability, thus rendering vain the debate on their alienation when the Acts of 12 January 1988 on the direction of public enterprises were

42 Article 49 of the Constitution of 1989 states: "Private property is guaranteed just as is the right of inheritance. *Waqf* assets and religious foundations are recognised and their purpose is protected by law."

43 Act 90-30 of 1 December 1990, *JORA* of 1 December 1990, p. 1416.

presented to parliament. This led to the introduction of measures to instigate bankruptcy proceedings.[44]

The public domain occupied by public companies was subject to rearrangements. Article 170 of the decree of 23 November 1991 sets out three types of occupancy in the public domain that they may claim: assignment, concession and law. Assignment is a unilateral act through which the proprietary administration makes assets available to a company or to an institution providing the said assets are intended for public service or an operation in the public interest. Concessions are administrative contracts with a general specification sheet. The assets in the public domain may be assigned to a public company pursuant to the provisions of the law: this is the case for activities such as railway transport or electricity/gas distribution.

Privatisation Under Injunction

Act 95-22 of 26 August 1995 relating to the privatisation of public companies[45] established privatisations under injunction and specified the modalities for transferring central and local government assets. According to the Act of 1984, national assets can be acquired by contract, free trade, exchange, prescription and accession, or via expropriation or a right of pre-emption. In the shadow of the public sector, privatisation increased, with the help of a constitutional amendment of 28 November 1996, which went unnoticed, and external adjustment measures. The apprehensions of the private sector waned substantially with this revision, whose Article 24 introduced a new detail concerning the responsibility of the state with respect to citizens by stipulating that: "The State is responsible for the safety of people and goods." Within Chapter IV, dedicated to rights and liberties, the flagship Article 37 guarantees for the first time freedom of trade and industry. Article 122, al. 9 adds: "The parliament legislates ... in the field of the regime of civil, commercial and property obligations." Private property is still not totally independent; it is placed in a sub-group with civil and commercial obligations.

The constitutional revision of 1996 has finally added to the jurisdiction of the legislative power addressed in Article 122 at paragraph 28, relating to the

---

44 Bankruptcy and judicial settlement were only introduced in 1993 by Legislative Decree 93-08 of 25 April 1993, modifying and completing the Commercial Code, Art. 217, *JORA* 27, 1993, p. 3.

45 Act 95-22 of 26 August 1995 relating to the privatisation of public companies, *JORA* 48, of 26 August 1995 p. 3.

rules of transfer from the public to the private sector. Article 37 of the Constitution of 1996 introduces this freedom for the first time: "The freedom of trade and industry is guaranteed. It is exercised in the framework of the law." This provision completes Article 49, now Article 52, and its three paragraphs (see fn. 42 above).

The true foundation of this new law can be seen to lie outside the local corpus, in the external constraint resulting from the diminishing oil revenues since the collapse of the price of oil in 1986. After two earlier and relatively unrestrictive confirmation agreements, the IMF tightened its conditions and in 1994 arranged Algeria's access to its resources (Belhimer, 1997: 202). The agreement of 27 May 1994 foresaw for the period 1995-1998 the dissolution of 88 local public companies and the fixing of a legal framework for privatisation (Belhimer, 1997). This essentially concerned institutional and legislative measures, by preserving the benefit of the first privatisations in the tourism sector. It formalised the creation of a ministry of industrial restructuring charged with the privatisation of public companies, and at the same time the elaboration of a new code of investment, authorising foreign banks to invest in local banks, and it introduced norms governing the sale of public companies. The matrix of this confirmation agreement also set out an amendment to Legislative Decree 93-12 of 5 October 1993 with respect to the promotion of investment, so as "to authorise local or foreign investments in companies up to 49% of their capital" and "the establishment of a base for the transfer of public companies". Executive Decree 94-115 of 28 September 1994 met this requirement of the framework of the confirmation agreement with the IMF.[46] Foreign investment and privatisation go hand in hand in the minds of IMF experts, who tend to read the evolution of laws in the sense of abolishing old discriminations against the private sector. Their purpose was also to grant more rights to national investors so that they could invest in the capital of public companies more easily or buy them out in the case of liquidation. The increased ease of financing, granted for three months at the completion of the year covering the initial confirmation agreement, pursued the same objectives. There was "effective" privatisation of five state-owned hotels (Belhimer, 1997: 216) and a second privatisation programme in the sectors of trade, transport and the agro-food industry was prepared.

46 Executive Decree 94-415 of 28 September 1994 fixing the modalities of application of Article 24 of Legislative Decree 94-08 of 26 May 1994 governing the complementary 1994 Finance Act, in *JORA* 80, 7 December 1994, pp. 3-4.

More fundamentally, Law 95-2[47] established this objective on a lasting basis. The complementary Finance Act for 1994 had already taken the first step by authorising "the transfer to any physical or moral person of the assets forming part of the property of the economic public company, with the exception of the assignment goods and of portions of the public property exploited in usufruct" (Article 24).[48] The decree of 28 September 1994 authorised the General Assembly of Public Companies, at the request of the Board of Administration, including the auditor, to transfer "portions of assets taken individually". As the transfer of assets may constitute an autonomous activity, it may be decided by a general assembly of the holdings or by the Ministry of Investment. In all cases, "the transfer of assets takes place by open competition". These assets are not transferable for two years and the staff of the company have a preferential right and are eligible for a 10% reduction on the set market price.

Even with the IMF's "performance controls" and its periodic inspections, privatisation still constitutes a heavy administrative burden. Previously, Article 125 of Ordinance 94-03 of 31 December 1994 governing the 1995 Finance Act envisaged supporting candidates "in resuming activity after foreclosure or bankruptcy" in the *wilāyas* of Tindug, Adrar, Tamanrasset and Illizi by considering their investments as being "in the public interest". As the transfers, pursuant to the Ordinance, arc paid for in cash, these investments benefit from an enhanced interest rate on the related investment credits, set at 50% of the debiting rate by the credit institutions. The bonus is presented by the credit institution and paid by the Treasury, in accordance with the reimbursement schedule of the loan,[49] whereas the beneficiary of the credit only pays the non-enhanced differential of the interest rate. Public companies are thus privatised through one of the four following modalities: transfer via the financial markets; transfer via calls for tender; over-the-counter contracts; or privatisation by the management. Transfer via the financial markets is set out in Article 25 of the Ordinance. It uses one of the following three techniques: an offer to sell securities on the securities exchange; a public offer of sale at a fixed price; or a combination of both mechanisms. The first quotation is at least equal to the offer price determined by the Privatisation Board. Transfer by a restricted or

47 Act 95-22 of 26 August 1995 relating to the privatisation of public companies, *JORA* 48, of 26 August 1995, p. 3.

48 Legislative Decree 94-08 of 26 May 1994 governing the complementary Finance Act for 1994.

49 Executive Decree 95-29 of 12 January 1995 governing the application of Article 125 of Ordinance 94-03 of 31 December 1994 governing the 1995 Finance Act, *JORA* 4, 29 January 1995, p. 6.

open, national or international, call for tenders takes place on the advice of the privatisation officer. The sale price cannot be lower than the offer price. An over-the-counter contract may be admitted as an exception, if the measures for transfers via the financial markets or via calls for tender have remained without effect at least twice or in two particular circumstances: either the specific transfer of technology or in the case of specific management. Management privatisation is achieved under the same conditions as transfer via calls for tender. Apart from the specific case of employees,[50] the purchaser is compelled to pay the cash value of the privatised capital (Art. 34) and to maintain the activity of the company for an average duration of at least five years (Art. 4). The transferor has obligations intended to protect the value of the capital eligible for privatisation. He is required to perform an assessment "founded on the methods generally admitted in this respect, by taking into account the actual market value" (Art. 5) of the elements of assets and titles to be privatised.

Two bodies are in charge of implementing privatisation operations: the Privatisation Institution and the Privatisation Council. The Institution is designated as "the Officer". The Officer,[51] a physical person, is appointed by the Head of Government. Placed under the latter's authority, he implements the privatisation programme of the companies he is entitled to administer.[52] The Privatisation Council is created with the Institution. It is composed of seven to nine members, also appointed by the Head of Government "by reason of their particular competences in the fields of economic, legal and technological management" (Art. 12, al. 2) for a duration of three years, renewable. The central function of the Council is to assess the companies eligible for privatisation

> according to the appropriate modalities and techniques (…) by taking into consideration the particularities of each case, especially the actual merchant value of the assets, the profits realised, the substantial economic value, the existence of branches, the position of the market, future perspectives and, if necessary, the stock exchange value. (Art. 14)

50 Particular provisions governing share ownership by employees: 10% of the capital is reserved for them in a profit-sharing scheme, and managed by a mutual fund, but there is no associated right to vote or to be represented on the Board of Administration (Art. 36). Employees also benefit from 20% of the capital of the company eligible for privatisation (Art. 37).

51 Executive Decree 96-106 of 11 March 1996 designating the institution in charge of the privatisation, *JORA* 18, 20 March 1996, pp. 13-14.

52 Ibid., Art. 4.

After having suggested, in Article 4, the exclusion from privatisation operations of "healthy" companies, the drafters of the text do not insist on the stock exchange value, preferring to put forward the advantages derived from the old Marxist "commanding heights of the economy", such as the state monopoly on certain activities (position on the market, existence of branches, future prospects, etc.). The Council itself prepares the evaluation reports, or uses experts, and it also fixes a range to determine the offer price of the transfer. The report and the range are approved by the supervision commission. The supervisory body is the Control Commission of Privatisation Operations. It is composed of five members appointed by the relevant ministers and the most relevant trade union.[53] Its role is "to ensure compliance with the rules of transparency, sincerity and fairness governing the process of privatisation operations" (Art. 40). This body approves the experts' report and the evaluation range within one month.

Alleviating the Administrative Burden

Very few candidates have come forward to purchase assets in the framework of the privatisation programme initiated under the regime of Ordinance 95-22. Two obligations discouraged possible purchasers: maintaining the initial activity and the staff employed; and the mode of payment. The Ordinance of 27 August 1997 attempted to remedy the situation via three measures: waiving the obligation to preserve the activity and the staff; payment by instalment; and extending the government's jurisdiction regarding privatisation.[54] Article 2 also waives the obligation to maintain the activity of the company for an average duration of at least five years. However, it mentions that purchaser(s) who commit themselves to "rehabilitate or modernise the company, preserve all or a portion of the wage-earning occupations and maintain the activity of the company may benefit from specific advantages, negotiated on a case-by-case basis". In addition, the purchaser is not obliged to pay cash for the privatised company. Ordinance 97-12 authorises payment by instalments to

53 The Commission is composed of a judge; a president, proposed by the Minister of Justice from among jurists specialised in the fields of business law; a representative of the General Inspectorate of Finances, proposed by the Finance Minister; a representative of the Treasury, proposed by the Minister for the Treasury; a representative of the most relevant employees' union; and a representative of the sectoral ministry concerned (Art. 38 of Ord. 95-22).

54 Ordinance 97-12 of 26 August 1997 modifying and completing Ordinance 95-22 relating to the privatisation of public companies, *JORA* 15, 19 March 1997, pp. 5-7.

the benefit of the employees of the company in question, and extends this possibility to new owners who are not employees. In the latter case, the decision is made by the Government Council on a proposal from the Privatisation Council.

Private Capital Accumulation in the Shadow of Political Power and the Public Sector

In “Capital privé et patrons d’industrie” (Private capital and industry bosses)], Djillali Liabès (2009) delivers an in-depth analysis of the origin of private capital. He endeavours to describe its development strategy, its logic of reproduction, its spheres of accumulation, and the specifics of the relations it has with the state and with political power more broadly. In his view, there are two main periods in “the construction of the concept of the bourgeoisie” in Algeria. From 1967 to 1971 – with the structuring of national private capital – and from 1972 to 1980, a period prior to economic liberalisation, during which “the exploiting bourgeoisie” (as opposed to “the non-exploiting bourgeoisie”) was excluded. Before 1967, the private sector took on forms “affecting all ages” (in the sense that several generations of the same family were involved): a glorified mercantilist form of work from home, family cooperation, manufacture or factories. After 1967, the accumulation of private capital “can be seen in the ‘factory’ process, in the sense that the use of more powerful machines (…) is a response to the expansion of the internal market initiated by the state and the public sector”. The role of the state was essential because “the state accumulation process, especially in industry, follows the factory model by the sectoral and technological location of major industrial projects”. However, the state initiates the protected market, “which allows overcapacities, quality stagnation and possible regression, monopolistic or oligopolistic manipulation of the price structure” and consequently endless renegotiation of hegemony (Liabès, 2009).

In addition to the predominance of the petit-bourgeois element, Liabès identifies a second aspect of the discourse of the Algerian industrial bourgeoisie: its “asserted and claimed apolitism”. Its discourse was eminently industrialist and it took over the state’s modernisation project. Being a business leader became a valued function, a source of personal enrichment but also a means to express one’s resourcefulness. It was through innovation and rational thinking that the bourgeoisie built its new spaces. Without having read Joseph Schumpeter, it claimed an inherited “capital of experience and knowledge relating to organisation, management, leadership and economy”. Liabès (2009: 305) rightly emphasises:

> Starting from (almost) nothing, not having studied in management schools, these industrialists tackled a field that was unknown to them and whose spirit and management methods were quite different from the commercial sector. But quite quickly, these business leaders learnt the trade. This fast apprenticeship has resulted in accumulation strategies implemented via additional investments or the multiplication of investment opportunities.

These features were confirmed by field studies, especially that of Khodja (2007: 100), who provides a picture of the Algerian investor:

> He is a man who wants autonomy from the state, who wants to create his own employment and is helped by his family. He began his career in the private sector of commerce and industry, and seeks to develop this experience, relying on the safe values of the family and the region. He is pragmatic and knows how to grasp opportunities. He is neither an adventurer nor a creator; he copies what exists and succeeds without resorting to consultants.

This Keynesian formulation of the formation of the industrialist class is unavoidable with respect to the predominant role of the state and the proximity of the spheres of power, as a condition for primitive accumulation. The "business bourgeoisie" and the "bureaucratic bourgeoisie" have often been regarded as two aspects of the same source, namely the state as a distributor of annuities, regardless of the forms this takes: access to public markets, political and union aid (aimed at the most oppositional groups), etc. Revolving doors, resulting from political pluralisation, have strengthened the links between the two.

The press has provided an outstanding picture of the "employed boss" in Algeria's national "semi-capitalism":

> Algerian bosses still keep away from politics and do not weigh in with their unstable, volatile and sometimes compromised capital. They are still trapped, between the national bureaucracy and the nation's collective consciousness, which considered them as the bad people, as a result of the egalitarian culture and socialism which prohibits a "flashy" bourgeoisie. In Algerian semi-capitalism, still in its oral stage, a good boss runs after a *wālī* and a bank teller to create his firm, not the contrary. (Daoud, 2004)

Daoud goes on to say:

> A good boss who wants to live his life and support his firm pays for his market and does not take it down. A good boss is generally worn out by his project and is not one who completes it within the deadline. A good boss is someone who manages his environment, not his accounts. He is someone who knows whom to bribe, otherwise he will be a sitting duck. As the market economy in Algeria is still a state business, the good boss is the one who understands its faults, occupies a niche and takes advantage of it, almost surreptitiously.

What place can be given to a bourgeoisie that is not industrious in a prebend economy? What opportunities for accumulation can it find within the narrow administrative framework of the economy? If there are no such opportunities, should the term "big fortunes" not be preferred to "the bourgeoisie"? (Belhimer, 1997: 155-158). It may be considered more appropriate in view of the volume of their informal activities, estimated at 30% of GDP, and the tax evasion generated by these activities (valued at 100 billion dinars in 2004 alone) at a rate as high as 40% (CNES, 2005: 27). The multitude of employers' organisations is a conclusive expression of the wide range of private interests that coexist around a hierarchical distribution of resource revenues.

References

Aït Amara, Hamid. 2002. "La transition de l'agriculture algérienne, vers un régime de propriété individuelle et d'exploitation familiale", *Cahiers Options Méditerranéennes* 36: 127-37.

Amichi, H., G. Bazin, F. Chehat, O. Ducourtieux, J.L. Fusillier, T. Hartani and M. Kuper. 2011. "Enjeux de la recomposition des exploitations agricoles collectives des grands périmètres irrigués en Algérie: Le cas du Bas-Cheliff", *Cahiers Agricultures* 20 (1-2) : 150-156.

Bedrani, S. 1987. "Algérie: Une nouvelle politique envers la paysannerie?" *Revue de l'Occident Musulman et de la Méditerranée* 45: 55-66.

Belarbia, F.-Z. 2010. "Le transfert de propriété Property", *Revue de la Cour Suprême*, special issue, "Jurisprudence de la chambre foncière, 3, p. 256

Belhimer, Ammar. 1997. "Political and Legal Analysis of the Management Strategies of the External Debt of Algeria from 1986 to 1996", PhD thesis, René Descartes University, Paris.

Belhimer, Ammar. 2012. "Le régime juridique de la propriété foncière en Algérie", *Les Programmes du Centre Jacques Berque* 1: 1-16.

Benaissa, A. 2003. "The Evolution of Land Tenure, through Texts, and Modes of Access to Land Tenure", paper presented at the Second Fédération Internationale des Géomètres Regional Conference, Marrakesh, Morocco, 2 May.

Clavel, Eugene. 1895. *Droit musulman : Du statut personnel et des successions d'apres les différents rites et plus particulièrement d'après le rite hanafite*, vol. 2. Paris: Larose.

CNES (Conseil National Economique et Social). 2005. *Eléments de débat pour un pacte de croissance. 26e session plénière, juillet 2005*. Algiers : CNES.

Daoud, Kamel. 2004. *Le Quotidien d'Oran*, 18 December

Filali, A., and Ghenima Lahlou-Khiar. 2013. "Le formalisme dans le contrat", *La Revue Algérienne des Sciences Juridiques, Economiques et Politiques* 3 : 742-754.

Ghaouti, Souad. 2014. "Le traitement de la propriété dans les textes fondamentaux algériens". *La Revue Algérienne des Sciences Juridiques, Economiques et Politiques*, special issue: 9-30.

Hanifi, Louisa. 2013. "L'apostasie dans le droit de la famille algérien", *La Revue Algérienne des Sciences Juridiques, Economiques et Politiques*, 1, p. 12

Khodja, Souad. 2007. "Les investisseurs algériens: De la rupture avec l'aide de l'Etat au retour à la famille et à la région. Méfiance exagérée ou prudence justifiée?", *Revue Algérienne de Management* 2: 90-101.

Lahlou-Khiar, Ghenima. 2013. "La preuve de la propriété foncière", *La Revue Algérienne des Sciences Juridiques, Economiques et Politiques* (special issue: "La propriété et le droit"): 155-170.

Liabès, Djilali. 2009. *Capital privé et patrons d'industrie en Algérie*. Algiers: ENAG éditions.

Rahmani, Ahmed. 1996. *Les biens publics en droit algérien*. Algiers: Les Editions Internationales.

Sari, Djillali. 1978. *La dépossession des fellahs*. Algiers: SNED.

Stahl, Paul Henri. 1997. *La Méditerranée : Propriété et structure sociale XIX et XXe siècles* [Encyclopédie de la Méditerranée, série Temps présent, 8] Saint-Rémy-de-Provence : Edisud.

CHAPTER 2

The Legitimacy of Tilling the Land versus Land Use Rights: Algerian Farmers' Land Appropriation Processes on Public Land

Hichem Amichi, Marcel Kuper and Sami Bouarfa

Introduction

"…We are not peasants! It is those who inherited land from their parents who are true peasants … they grew up to love the land, they know its value … they will never abandon their land." Such statements routinely rounded off our interviews with farmers who had had usufruct of public land for several decades. These "assignees" of public land often raised the question of land use legitimacy when we discussed the phenomenon of informal land leasing and sharecropping arrangements, which has been widespread since the 1987 Algerian land reform, but is strictly prohibited by law. The distinction these assignees made between the "true peasants" and themselves was particularly striking, and revealed the deep unease that these beneficiaries of the public sector had developed in their relationship with the land. This led to our first question: How should we explain the particular relationship these assignees have with public land? Driven by our curiosity, we went in search of the "true peasants", according to the definition provided by the public sector assignees. We met them in the piedmont, where the majority live. This land, which overlooks the irrigated plain that is public land, is cramped and often unproductive. After much hesitation and when a certain degree of confidence had been established, the interviewees began to express their opinion. Very rapidly in the ensuing discussion the word "lessees" emerged, as opposed to "assignees", the formal beneficiaries of the public sector. This distinction was based on the representations of the two social categories: on the one hand, lessees, who were perceived by the interviewees to be young and hard-working, but who had no formal access to public land, and on the other, the assignees, who were considered older and lazier farmers who enjoyed the many advantages guaranteed by the state, especially access to the best land in Algeria.

So, how can the presence of lessees on public land be explained, given that leasing has been strictly prohibited by all the land reforms adopted since Independence? The proliferation of informal land leases raises many ques-

 | DOI 10.1163/9789004362116_004

tions. Chaulet (2010: 277) has questioned the legitimacy of working the land and the rights to the use of public land in the Mitidja plain in Algeria:

> … The existence of lessees pits the legitimacy of working the land against the land use rights in the Mitidja. Do the lessees have the right to be there? Why are they paying to work land that is the property of the state? Because they come from far away and they were not there at the right time? And what do they pay for exactly? The land use rights of assignees? The right to remain in the Mitidja for a while?

These questions are not confined to Algerian public land, but by and large apply to all situations where land was managed directly by the state, through agrarian reforms. This mainly concerns socialist countries, which adopted centralised land management by creating large-scale state farms run by state employees. In the global context of economic liberalisation, these countries engaged in a process of decollectivisation in the 1980s. This led to new configurations of farms that were smaller and on which farmers had the freedom to grow and market their produce, according to market economy principles. In some countries, the land remained the property of the state but was conceded to assignees with the obligation that they farm it themselves. The transition from a centralised agricultural model to a capitalist model led to the withdrawal of the state from several domains, notably the financing of and technical support for agricultural activities. This resulted in the formation of a social category of farmers who had access to land but did not have the financial means to cultivate it. The beneficiaries of these reforms developed several strategies, often through informal transactions, to continue their agricultural activity. Such situations have been reported in the literature on Romania, for example, which introduced a vast land privatisation policy (Amblard and Colin, 2009). Similar situations emerged in countries outside the former socialist bloc, as in Mexico, for example, in the case of the *ejidos*, which provided access to the landless (Colin, 2003; Cochet, Léonard and Tallet, 2010), and in India in the context of the green revolution (Byres, 1981).

The case of public land in Algeria, where centralised state-led policies in the public agricultural sector were tried out, confirms the general observations of assignees who find difficulties working land for which they obtained land use rights (Amichi, Bouarfa and Kuper, 2015; Imache et al., 2010). The Algerian case also illustrates the appearance of lessees on such land, and the proliferation of informal contracts linking the two categories of land occupancy. Lastly, it confirms observations in various situations in India, Mexico and Romania about reverse tenancy configurations by which the power relations between landowners and lessees turn to the advantage of the latter, due to changing technology and the practice of high value-added agriculture (Singh, 1989; Amichi, Bouarfa and Kuper, 2015; Colin 2013). However, these analyses do not generally answer the questions raised by Chaulet (2010), nor do they investigate the complicated and sometimes antagonistic relationships between these actors. Public land in Algeria is a particularly interesting historical example of competition between different actors over land access, which makes the relationship with the land complicated and sometimes leads to conflict. Historically, this competition particularly concerns two social categories belonging to two different agricultural sectors, formed during the French colonial period and renewed after Independence. One category consists of assignees, who benefited from land use rights to former colonial land that was nationalised after Independence. They obtained these rights because they had been labourers on colonial farms and on post-Independence state farms, and were present during the successive land reforms after Independence. The other category consists of lessees, who obtained access to public land through informal arrangements after the 1987 land reform. The lessees are often descendants of Algerian peasants who had been dispossessed of their land during the French colonial period. A sense of injustice persists among these lessees, who consider they have a legitimate right to legal access to this land. This feeling is reinforced by the fact that the lessees saw public land abandoned or neglected by some assignees, who were unable to cultivate it.

Previous divisions of agricultural land in Algeria have led to a wide spectrum of land rights and social relations. Land tenure systems are complex pluralistic systems that have been influenced by pre-Islamic customs, Islamic land law, the various occupations of Algeria (especially under the Ottomans and the French), and the diverse land reforms adopted after Independence (socialist and liberal periods) (Bessaoud, 1999). In his historical study of land tenure systems in North Africa, Bouderbala (1999) analyses the diversity and the superimposition of land property regimes in the region. He clearly distinguishes between land rights, which are delimited by formal law, and actual land use practices, which are implemented by farmers who do not always have all the means they need to farm the land. These land use practices cover various forms of contracts and associations. The aim is to reduce risk, and the agreements are adapted to suit the precarious situation of the majority of farmers (ibid.). The contracts and arrangements can be understood in the framework of legal pluralism, which considers land use rights as plural and not limited to a dichotomy between formal and informal sectors and between private and public resources. We use this approach in our analysis and argue that the range of land use rights is not fixed and bounded. On the contrary, significant interactions occur between formal and informal rules, thereby rendering them functional and dynamic, and allowing their adaptation to local environmental, social and economic conditions (Kuper, Amichi and Mayaux, 2017).

Legal Pluralism to Apprehend the Diversity of Land Rights

The analytical framework of legal pluralism allows us to grasp the wide range of rights of access to land by admitting that there is "more than one legal order or mechanism within one socio-political space, based on different sources of ultimate validity and maintained by forms of organization other than the state" (von Benda-Beckmann, 2002). Several other sources can in fact exist in addition to the state, including local customs, social norms and international frameworks for natural resources management. These sources are not exclusive; on the contrary, they are often intertwined and overlapping and, through their interaction, give meaning to, and regulate the social universe or specific social domains (ibid.), in our case access to land, as shown by Bouderbala (1999). The concept of legal pluralism has been, and continues to be, a subject of debate, particularly with regard to the question of what constitutes "law" (Merry, 1988; Tamanaha, 2000; Dupret, 2007; Berman, 2013). However, the interdiscursive relations in law and society help us understand that these different sources belong to the same "comprehensive social system" and cannot be conceptualised independently (Luhmann, 1988: 18). In addition, legal pluralism enables us to take a dynamic approach to property rights and land use (Meinzen-Dick and Pradhan, 2002). Lastly, the "unresolved relationship between rule systems with different sources of legitimacy" may undermine both the authority of state entities and the performance of customary institutions (Benjamin, 2008: 2256). Understanding the different forms of legitimacy is, therefore, at the heart of any analysis of property rights and land use.

Our analysis of the agricultural dynamics on public land in Algeria did not, therefore, start with a study of the rules set by the state to manage public land but rather focused on the actual practices of the actors present on that land, without regard to their legal status. More specifically, we envisaged relationships between actors through the concept of "legitimacy", in order to understand the process of appropriation or dis-appropriation of land by actors. This allowed us to answer the following two questions: How do actors justify their presence on public land? What is their relation to the state? We then focused on the state's view of the diversity of actors, particularly after the recent adoption of the 2010 land law.

To understand the processes of land appropriation through which actors build their legitimacy, we conducted 100 interviews with a variety of actors (assignees of collective farms, tenants, lessees) present on public land. We were interested in three main points concerning these actors: i) their personal agricultural trajectory, ii) their agricultural practices, and iii) their interactions with the other actors and their relationship with the state.

Our investigations were conducted on public land in the municipality of Ouarizane in the Lower Chéliff plain in north-western Algeria. The Ouarizane municipality comprises 6,000 hectares divided into two distinct geomorphological units: piedmont and plain. The land in the piedmont, which is very fragmented and uneven, is mostly private. The land in the plain, which is more suitable for agriculture, is mostly public. The way the land is distributed is the result of a historical construction, which was especially brutal during the period of French colonisation. The colonisers dispossessed the indigenous peasants who occupied the plains, and pushed them towards the piedmont. When Algeria became independent in 1962, the unequal distribution of land was not reviewed. The colonial land was nationalised and has remained public to this day, while the fragmented land in the piedmont remained privately owned.

Diversity of Land Property Rights on Public Land: The Product of an Eventful Agrarian History

The agrarian history of Algeria is particularly eventful due to a series of foreign occupations. Each occupation shaped procedures for land access and created a wide range of land property regimes. Public land is currently characterised by the superimposition of land use rights, which allows various actors to cultivate the land. To understand the range of land property regimes, we need to understand the particular history of the different types of land and the conditions that led to the formation of these rights. We distinguish three main periods during which land property rights changed profoundly. The first is the period marked by the law of the Ottoman Empire, particularly regarding the management of tribal land. The second is the French colonial period (1832-1962), during which Algerian agriculture was divided into two main sectors after a long and violent process of land dispossession. The third is the period after Independence (since 1962), during which the agricultural sector has been the subject of a series of agrarian reforms (socialist and subsequently liberal).

Under the Ottoman Empire, collective land appropriation in Algeria underwent significant deterioration, leading to the diversification of land rights. The principle was that "unoccupied land" should come under the authority of the Dey, as the ruler of the Regency of Algiers, or one of his representatives. The Ottoman authorities could take control of the land and hand it over to someone else to use and make productive. Collective tribal (*ʿarsh*) land was considered unoccupied and became the largest part of the public land controlled by the Regency. This land was managed in two different ways: 1) directly by the Dey, or his hierarchical agents, called *beylik* land; and 2) indirectly by military or Ottoman officials in return for services provided to the Dey, called *azel* land. Both types of land were worked through the use of forced labour exacted from neighbouring tribes or through *khammes* (sharecroppers), who received ploughs, draft animals and seed from the state, and were paid one-fifth of the yield for their work. With each generation, public land expanded, as land was confiscated from rebel tribes or from tribes that were suspected of rebellion. Parts of the confiscated land that were not farmed either by *khammes* or tribesmen was sold through land markets to private individuals from among the Ottoman Turks living in the country. In this way, an important class of landowners was created.

The territorial extension project during the French colonial period was based on the legislation left by the Ottoman Empire. The colonists routinely tried to support their land policy by presenting it as consistent with the pre-colonial system and Islamic law (Bouderbala, 1999). The first option chosen was based on a state view of Islamic land law, presented by Dr Worms in 1846 (Worms, 1846), supporting the idea that, in Muslim countries, the land belongs to the sovereign and individuals have a right of use (Ageron, 1970). According to this doctrine, it was considered normal that the French state, which succeeded the Ottoman Empire, should take possession of the land. This doctrine provided the foundation for the "policy of *cantonnement*" of Marshal Randon, the governor of Algeria from 1851 to 1858, in accordance with which, in addition to *beylik* land, the land belonging to Ottoman officials (*azel*), the tribal land (*ʿarsh*) considered vacant, *ḥabus* land (land under the control of religious establishments), and lastly woods and forests were taken into the ownership of the state (Bouderbala, 1999). This policy exchanged the existing right of use granted to indigenous tribes who had usufruct, for a right of ownership to a small portion of the land they had formerly used (Merle, 1998). On the *ʿarsh* land, this policy justified the repression and dispossession of the indigenous population. Thus, the state-owned land reserve increased continuously, as the French army advanced across Algerian territory.

The state-owned reserves turned out to be insufficient for French colonial ambitions and it became necessary to acquire land by purchase. Francisation of Islamic land law was accelerated by the adoption of the 1873 Warnier Law, which allowed the establishment of private property on *'arsh* and *melk* land (private land managed under Muslim law). This law opened the way for the market and for private colonisation. Indigeneous people who were using undivided land were issued – within the framework of the Warnier Law – with titles stipulating their land quotas; undivided collective property was thus transformed in favour of growing individualism. The massive dispossession of peasant land by military, legal and economic means, the forced displacement of populations, obliging nomads to settle, and especially the destruction of tribal unity, led to the disintegration of Algerian rural society. This resulted in the formation of a rich, mechanised "sector" on some of the best land in the plain, held mostly by the European, and in part Algerian, bourgeoisie, and, at the same time, the massive impoverishment of the peasantry, relegated to the most marginal lands in the mountains and the piedmont.

After Independence, the colonial land was nationalised to form the public agricultural sector. A succession of reforms during the first three decades after Independence (1962-1987) brought agricultural production under state control, following the collectivist doctrine. The creation of state farms on nationalised land characterised the first three post-Independence land reforms. The "agricultural self-management" reform of the 1960s, based on the Yugoslav socialist model, determined how these state farms were managed. The "agrarian revolution" of the 1970s consisted of confiscating the land of large landowners and transferring it to those "who are tilling the land". And lastly, in response to disappointing performances, the agrarian reorganisation at the beginning of the 1980s divided the socialist state farms into smaller units in order to better organise agricultural production. These agricultural policies reproduced the colonial model of agricultural development on public land based on large farms with employees and significant use of mechanisation. Private land, mostly located in marginal areas (piedmont, mountains) was not affected by these reforms. The old forms of production were maintained on this land, notably the practice of sharecropping and tenant farming, and a large proportion of the land remained undivided.

The 1987 land reform, adopted in the context of economic liberalisation, handed over the use of public land to small groups of assignees (3-10 assignees on 10-50 hectares), who were supposed to work the land collectively, but who were free to choose their farming system as a function of market demand. Paradoxically, this reform broke down the barriers between the two sectors, as actors from the two sectors established informal land use arrangements. These arrangements were made between two social categories: on the one hand, the assignees, who obtained the right to use public land, and, on the other hand, the lessees, who were descendants of the Algerian peasantry living in the piedmont area. In the following sections, we analyse the relations between these two social groups and their access to public land and, by extension, their relation to the Algerian state.

'Heroes of the Past': A Complex Relationship between Assignees and Public Land, Closely Linked to Their Relation to the Algerian State

The formation of the social category of assignees is intimately linked to the agrarian history of public land. The core of these actors is formed by former workers on the colonial farms who were then "recruited" by the Algerian state because of their knowledge of the farms and their agricultural skills, but also because they were already in situ. After Independence, new employees were recruited to strengthen the workforce on state farms. Despite the official designation of these farms as "self-managed", for about 25 years these workers were considered, and considered themselves, to be state employees. Their way of working the land, the supply of agricultural materials, the marketing of produce, and their salaries depended entirely on the state.

The 1987 land reform, which took place in the context of economic liberalisation, brutally ruptured this link. The land was granted to the workers, who became assignees, and was to be worked collectively in small groups of 3-10 assignees. Their incomes no longer depended on the state but rather on the product of their labour and market forces. The state continued to support the assignees financially during the first years after the reform but to a very much more limited extent than in the socialist period, and this support was drastically reduced as state revenues fell. The drought that coincided with the formation of these groups in the early 1990s resulted in a severe economic crisis.

When they faced these difficulties, a deep sense of abandonment by the state spread among the assignees. During our interviews, the assignees told us that they had not been informed about the consequences of this reform. The initial enthusiasm and euphoria that accompanied the early years, when the former workers officially gained access to land use rights, quickly gave way to survival strategies. These strategies consisted of reaching agreements with private actors who suggested informal partnerships through sharecropping arrangements or rental contracts. The assignees adopted these informal agrarian contracts in order to be able to continue working their land, and they sometimes had off-farm activities to supplement their income.

The sense of abandonment changed the historical legitimacy that had justified the presence of the assignees on public land up to 1987. The past legitimacy had its origin in the assignees' contributions to the preservation of the agricultural productive potential of the land for many decades after the departure of the French colonists. The first years after Independence were even considered as a "heroic period" in which the workers continued to work the land, initially even in the absence of formal instructions or a legal framework (Chaulet, 1984). After many decades of toiling in often difficult conditions on this public land, they believed they were fully justified in enjoying access to it. After the withdrawal of the state from 1987, the discourse of the assignees changed towards one in which they justified their strategy of informally leasing out the public land by regarding the rent as a financial compensation for all their efforts. They believed the "stipend" they received for leasing the land was necessary compensation for the difficulties they had faced when left to work their land on their own, which they associated with their abandonment by the state.

Despite the difficult economic situation of most of the assignees, another form of legitimate access to public land still concerns a considerable number of them. It is characterised by their strong attachment to the state, despite the latter's withdrawal. Such assignees still hope to witness a state comeback, in which the state would play a strong role in the management of public land. Abdelkader, a 78-year-old assignee, clearly illustrated the link to the public land that he developed, which is deeply rooted in the relationship he continues to maintain with the state. He referred to his pride in working land that once belonged to French settlers:

> I still remember the day when I worked as a seasonal worker on a colonial farm. I collected onions with a group of young people from my village. At the end of the day, the settler paid us for the day. He paid us so little that we took our courage in both hands and asked for a rise. The settler told us to give him back what he had given us, so he could give us a bigger sum. As soon as we had given him back the money, he drove off to his farm. We were left with nothing after a hard day's work. Imagine how proud I am today to work on part of the land that belonged to the settler who exploited us, thanks to the Algerian state!

The Emergence of the Lessees or Revenge on History

In contrast to the assignees, the social category of lessees had always felt abandoned and marginalised by the state. This category of Algerian peasantry did not benefit from public land after Independence, despite their massive participation in the national war of liberation. Although the official texts noted the need to distribute former colonial land under agrarian reform to all the peasantry whose land had been despoiled by French colonisation, they were not in the right place at the right time.

These peasants saw in the 1987 land reform a historic opportunity to reoccupy public land as lessees. Their involvement in public land did not happen as a result of political support, but rather through their own work. The legitimacy of the presence of lessees on public land was based on two fundamental points. The first dates back to the colonial period, when their parents were dispossessed of their land by French settlers. According to these lessees, it means a great deal to them to have access to this land today. The second point is the legitimacy provided by their investment in "tilling the land" – hence their title, "true peasants". They have the necessary capital to practise the intensive market-oriented agriculture favoured by today's agricultural policies, and they are also capable of adopting agricultural innovations, because of their sound knowledge of agricultural practices and their open-minded attitude to technical innovations arriving from elsewhere. For example, it was some lessees who first adopted drip irrigation in the area, and introduced new horticultural varieties. More generally, they are renowned for their entrepreneurial agricultural practices.

The lessees' legitimacy, based on their work, continues to increase with their economic success, in contrast to the economic decline of a large proportion of the assignees. This success is illustrated by the expansion of the amount of land rented out, which increases every year, and by the growing intensification of their farming systems. For example, a lessee in the Lower Cheliff started by leasing three hectares in 1993, rising to about 80 hectares in 2010. The legitimacy of the work of the lessees in "tilling the land" currently overrides the formal right of assignees to use public land as decreed by the state. This supremacy is particularly illustrated by the reversal of the balance of power between the two categories (reverse tenancy). Tenants have taken control of the entire agricultural production process, while the assignees merely lease out the land and have become invisible as farmers. The most extreme form of this configuration is when the assignee rents out his land to a lessee and then works for the lessee as a labourer on his own land (Imache et al., 2010).

However the social category of economically upwardly-mobile lessees represents only a small proportion of the descendants of the Algerian peasantry relegated to the piedmont. Only a minority of this peasantry had the financial capital and the know-how to invest in public land. This social category of lessees was then joined by another type of lessee with a different historical background. Since 2000, with increasing government subsidies for agriculture, investors with an urban background have become interested in agriculture, and more particularly in public land. These investors come from other sectors (particularly from construction and trade), and consider agriculture as a new way of diversifying their investments and at the same time taking advantage of public subsidies. In this more market-oriented environment, public subsidies do indeed encourage investors, who are considered by public policies to have more legitimacy and to be capable of developing high value-added agriculture.

Functional Coexistence between Assignees and Lessees through a Wide Range of Agrarian Contracts

Despite the apparent competition between assignees and lessees over the use of public land, in practice there is coexistence, which takes the form of a variety of informal contracts and arrangements. These ensure a working relationship between the two categories of actors by, on the one hand, allowing the assignees to avoid completely abandoning public land and thus enabling them to maintain their relationship with the state and obtain annuities, while, on the other, allowing the lessees to gain access to fertile land with high production potential.

These agrarian contracts offer a wide range of possibilities and are very flexible, as they are continually adapted to changing conditions (Boudjellal et al., 2011). They enable cooperation between two actors who often do not have the same productive resources. The arrangement generally consists of assignees with land, and sometimes access to irrigation water, contracting with lessees who provide the capital and sometimes access to irrigation water too, and who often possess considerable technical agricultural skills. Depending on the extent of the participation of each party in the production processes, these agrarian contracts are adjusted and negotiated before the beginning of the season.

The most common agrarian contracts on public land today are concerned with sharecropping and renting. Both were completely prohibited on public land after Independence, when the state stipulated that direct farming by the owner or by the farmer who had the usufruct of the land was the only permissible use of public land. However, sharecropping and renting contracts continued to regulate the use of private land in the piedmont, where the state was less present.

The flexibility of these agrarian contracts is due to their ability to adapt to changes both in access to the productive resources specific to each partner to the contract and in the socio-economic environment, which determines agricultural production. We distinguish two types of adaptations in these contracts (for more details on these arrangements see Amichi et al., 2012, and Amichi, Bouarfa and Kuper, 2015). The first is a modification in the procedures for execution of the contract, particularly regarding profit sharing, but without fundamentally challenging the type of contract in place. In the Lower Chéliff, this is illustrated by sharecropping, which shifted from a sharecropping arrangement of one-third to two-thirds, to half and half. This change in the distribution of net income from agricultural production to the sharecropper (i.e. the sharecropper receives half the net income instead of the one-third in the previous contract) is justified by the greater involvement, financial or otherwise, of sharecroppers in the production processes (more participation in financing or in the supply of water, etc.). In the case of land rents, adaptation shows up in increases in the length of the contract from one season to a year or even several years.

The second adaptation is a change in the type of contract, which is due to a major change in relations between the actors. The end result is often renting rather than sharecropping, for example. In Lower Chéliff, there has been a change from sharecropping contracts to rental contracts in a context in which the value of the land, the major input by assignees, gradually depreciated in comparison with water, capital and technical and economic expertise, primarily the contribution of the tenants. This development was influenced by the increasing difficulties assignees had in mobilising capital and obtaining access to water, alongside an increase in the lessees' ability to mobilise capital and their increasing access to groundwater. More fundamentally, this relates to what is referred to in the literature as "reverse tenancy", i.e. the lessee is increasingly the dominant partner in the sharecropping arrangement.

The flexibility that characterises the rental and sharecropping arrangements is lacking in the framework for public land management proposed by the state, in which very few alternatives are offered to assignees. The discrepancy between the state framework and the real-life conditions of the actors encourages them to look for solutions elsewhere.

Pluralities of Legitimacy on Public Land: What Place for the State?

When we analysed the ongoing relationships between the actors on public land in more deta\il, we observed some competition between two social categories – assignees and lessees – but that competition is part of and contributes to the diversity of legitimacies "of being present" on public land. These legitimacies concern interaction and change.

We have shown that the legitimacy of the presence of the category of the assignees on public land changed tremendously after the 1987 reform. This legitimacy was originally based on their permanent presence on the land during the colonial period, and from Independence until the withdrawal of the state, when it shifted to a legitimacy justified by the need to benefit from a land rent, associated with a strong sense of abandonment by the state. This feeling, which is experienced by a large proportion of the assignees, explains why today they do not wish to see their children take over their farms. This attitude was also reported by Claudine Chaulet among assignees in the Mitidja plain. She was struck by the cold "even icy" responses of assignees: "It is out of the question that our children should work the land as we did. We have suffered enough, they should get out" (Chaulet, 2010: 33).

However, a previous study by our team, (Amichi et al., 2012) has shown that there are some exceptions, and that assignees may have other relationships with public land. Two other main forms of legitimacy were not fundamentally changed by the withdrawal of the state at the beginning of 1990s. First, some of the assignees do not consider themselves to be "real" peasants. For them, the withdrawal of the state was rather an opportunity to leave the farming sector. This resulted in the definitive transfer of their land use rights to private actors in return for remuneration, which allowed them to become involved in other economic sectors. Second, and in contrast, another category of assignees remains attached to the state and continues to assert its pride in remaining there and working the land themselves, despite all the difficulties. These assignees hope for the state's return and want to pass on their land use rights to their children.

Likewise, lessees too have developed different relationships with the land and with the state. We identified two main types of legitimacy. First, lessees from the piedmont legitimise their presence on public land by their ability to develop it through productive agriculture. This legitimacy was nourished by a strong sense of historical revenge and a desire to regain the land of their ancestors who were dispossessed by colonialism. The legitimacy of these lessees was constructed on a land ownership process that takes place outside the state framework and even against the original wishes of the public authorities and results in a relative distance from the state. Their presence on public land is mainly justified by their labour and capital investments and so they do not feel indebted to the state. The refusal by the majority of lessees to benefit from state subsidies reveals their desire to maintain their independence vis-à-vis the state.

In contrast, the other type of legitimacy of the lessee is based on proximity to the state. This is a new category of lessees who come from urban backgrounds and generally have little knowledge of agriculture. They are attracted by the productive potential of public land and also by the possibility of receiving subsidies from the state through its agricultural development programmes, which began in the 2000s. These entrepreneurs consider agriculture to be simply another sphere of activity that will allow them to make a profit. The more liberal state thus favours the presence of agricultural entrepreneurs rather than assignees, who are categorised as belonging to the distant past of a state-led socialist agricultural model.

The diversity of legitimacies that justify the presence of the various actors on public land, thereby maintaining a relationship between these actors and the state, brings us to the question of the relations the state wishes to cultivate with these actors. What kind of legitimacy will the state support, and in favour of what kind of agricultural model? What is certain is that the state wishes to intervene to regulate existing informal practices concerning public land. The adoption of the land law of 2010, which represents the first stage in the return of the state, provides some clues as to state strategy.

The return of the agricultural state through increased subsidies from the 2000s onwards, and through the adoption of land reform in 2010 expressed a desire to "put some order" into the public agricultural sector. This inevitably reduces the diversity of actors present on public land. In a way, it is about restoring the legitimacy of the state, which was undermined by the development of different types of legitimacy that sometimes ran counter to it. The choice of an agricultural concession as a model of management of private land, instead of the perpetual use granted to beneficiaries since 1987, demonstrates the state's strategy, based on two axes. The first axis is to forge a new alliance with the category of lessee-investors considered to be economic actors capable of meeting the challenges of the intensive agricultural desired by the state. Support for this category of actors is revealed in the favourable agricultural subsidy system supplied to the minority of rich farmers and private investors who have contacts within the local administration, and by the possibility for these investors to share a land concession with the assignees through a partnership, as introduced by the new law of 2010. For the first time since Independence, this measure thus makes it formally possible for actors other than former workers on state farms to farm public land.

The second axis of state strategy consists in not brutally disrupting its historic link with one of the social bases closest to the central government in rural areas, the assignees. The concession model does not challenge the presence of assignees on public land, but it leaves the way open for them to leave. A compensation system is implemented for certain assignees in the form of state subsidies, but these are marginal compared with the subsidies that benefit investors. These marginal compensations make it possible to keep the assignees "ticking over" through state aid. In this way, the state supports the legitimacy of the investors to occupy public land in return for their capital investment in a progressive way, without antagonising the assignees. But if the progressive character of the substitution of legitimacy ensures that the state will face limited resistance from the losers (assignees and lessees in the piedmont), it does not necessarily ensure the disappearance of the other types of legitimacy. For example, some of the assignees who have developed a strong attachment to public land and some of the lessees of the piedmont, who have been present on public land since the 1990s, will not easily give way to new investors whose legitimacy now has state support. New forms of resistance can thus be expected to emerge, which in turn will give birth to new forms of legitimacy.

Conclusion

Our work showed how four social categories of actors came to co-exist on public land in Algeria, through the emergence of multiple forms of legitimacy. The former workers on colonial and state farms were initially rewarded for their know-how, their loyalty and simply "for being there", before being discredited as farmers with little entrepreneurial spirit after the more liberal reforms of 1987 (Bedrani, 1987). However, the assignees still consider themselves closely linked to the state, either as annuitants by renting out the land to those able to develop it, or as small-scale market-oriented farmers hoping the state will return. Even in the latest land reform of 2010, their presence is not questioned. These assignees engaged in sharecropping arrangements, first with peasants from the piedmont who have a historical legitimate right to the land, although not recognised by the state, and later with entrepreneurs encouraged by state subsidies. These different legitimacies depend on a wide range of sources, but are part of one and the same eventful agrarian history and hence of the same "comprehensive social system" postulated by Luhmann (1988). In our view, the state has contributed not only to developing the legal framework governing agriculture on public land, but also to the construction of the plurality of the legitimacies of the different social categories of public land and the informal and extremely dynamic practices of land use there. This explains the many hesitations in the often contradictory land reforms undertaken, which favour one category of actors without completely abandoning another. The relationship between the different systems of rules, which are based on different types of legitimacy, remains unresolved, thereby providing a certain degree of freedom for informal arrangements, but also depriving certain categories of farmers who are keen to cultivate the land with state support.

References

Ageron, C.R. 1970. "Les Algériens musulmans et la France (1871-1919)", *Revue Historique* 243 (2): 355-365.

Amblard, L., and J.-P. Colin. 2009. "Reverse Tenancy in Romania: Actors' Rationales and Equity Outcomes", *Land Use Policy* 26 (3): 828-836.

Amichi, H., S. Bouarfa, and M. Kuper. 2015. "Arrangements informels et types d'agriculture sur les terres publiques en Algérie: Quels arbitrages?", *Revue Tiers Monde* 221: 47-68.

Amichi, H., S. Bouarfa, M. Kuper, O. Ducourtieux, A. Imache, J.L. Fusillier, G. Bazin, T. Hartani, and F. Chehat. 2012. "How Does Unequal Access to Groundwater Contribute to Marginalization of Small Farmers? The Case of Public Lands in Algeria", *Irrigation and Drainage* 61 (1): 34-44.

Bedrani, S. 1987. "Algérie: Une nouvelle politique envers la paysannerie?", *Revue de l'Occident Musulman et de la Méditerranée* 45 (1): 55-66.

Benjamin, C.E. 2008. "Legal Pluralism and Decentralization: Natural Resource Management in Mali", *World Development* 36 (11): 2255-2276.

Berman, P.S. 2013. "Le nouveau pluralisme juridique", *Revue Internationale de Droit Economique* 27 (1): 229-256.

Bessaoud, O. 1999. "L'Algérie agricole: De la construction du territoire à l'impossible émergence de la paysannerie", *Insaniyat* 7: 5-32.

Bouderbala, N. 1999. "Les systèmes de propriété foncière au Maghreb: Le cas du Maroc", *Cahiers Options Méditerranéennes* 36: 47-61.

Boudjellal, A.A., Y. Bekkar, M. Kuper, M. Errahj, A. Hammani, and T. Hartani. 2011. "Analyse des arrangements informels pour l'accès à l'eau souterraine sur les périmètres irrigués de la Mitidja (Algérie) et du Tadla (Maroc) = Analysis of local arrangements to access groundwater in the Mitidja (Algeria) and Tadla (Morocco) irrigation schemes", *Cahiers Agricultures* 20 (1): 85-91.

Byres, T.J. 1981. "The New Technology, Class Formation and Class Action in the Indian Countryside", *The Journal of Peasant Studies* 8 (4): 405-454.

Chaulet, C. 1984. *La terre, les frères et l'argent: Stratégie familiale et production agricole en Algérie depuis 1962*. Alger: Office des Publications Universitaires.

Chaulet, C. 2010. "Postface", in *La Mitidja 20 ans après: Réalités agricoles aux portes d'Alger*, ed. A. Imache, T. Hartani, S. Bouarfa, and M. Kuper. Versailles: Editions Quae: 277-278.

Cochet, H., E. Léonard, and B. Tallet. 2010. "Le métayage d'élevage au Mexique: Colonisations foncières et dynamiques d'une institution agraire dans l'histoire contemporaine", *Annales de Géographie* 676: 617-638.

Colin, J.-P. 2003. *Figures du métayage: Etude comparée des contrats agraires (Mexique)*. Paris: IRD éditions.

Colin, J.-P. 2013. *Marchés fonciers et concentration foncière: La configuration de "tenure inversée" (reverse tenancy)* [Les Cahiers du Pôle Foncier 3]. Montpellier: Pôle Foncier.

Dupret, B. 2007. "Legal Pluralism, Plurality of Laws, and Legal Practices", *European Journal of Legal Studies* 1: 1.

Imache, A., T. Hartani, S. Bouarfa, and M. Kuper. 2010. *La Mitidja 20 ans après: réalités agricoles aux portes d'Alger.* Versailles: Editions Quae.

Luhmann, N. 1988. "The Unity of the Legal System", in *Autopoietic Law: A New Approach to Law and Society*, ed. G. Teubner. Berlin, New York: Walter de Gruyter, 12-35.

Meinzen-Dick, R.S., and R. Pradhan. 2002. *Legal Pluralism and Dynamic Property Rights* [Capri Working Paper]. Washington DC: International Food Policy Research Institute.

Merle, I. 1998. "La construction d'un droit foncier colonial: De la propriété collective à la constitution des réserves en Nouvelle-Calédonie", *Enquête, Anthropologie, Histoire, Sociologie* 7: 97-126.

Merry, S.E. 1988. "Legal Pluralism", *Law & Society Review* 22 (5): 869-896.

Singh, I. 1989. "Reverse Tenancy in Punjab Agriculture: Impact of Technological Change", *Economic and Political Weekly* 24 (25), 24 June, A86–A92.

Tamanaha, B.Z. 2000. "A Non-essentialist Version of Legal Pluralism", *Journal of Law and Society* 27: 296-321.

von Benda-Beckmann, F. 2002. "Who's Afraid of Legal Pluralism?", *The Journal of Legal Pluralism and Unofficial Law* 34 (47): 37-82.

Worms, M.-G. 1846. *Recherches sur la constitution de la propriété territoriale dans les pays musulmans, et subsidiairement en Algérie*. Paris: Franck.

CHAPTER 3

Rights of Access or Rights to Bypass? Maritime Concessions in Algeria

Tarik Dahou

> I want to insist right away on reserving the possibility of a justice, indeed of a law that not only exceeds or contradicts 'law' (*droit*) but also, perhaps, has no relation to law or maintains such a strange relation to it that it may just as well command the '*droit*' that excludes it.
>
> JACQUES DERRIDA, "FORCE DE LOI: LE FONDEMENT MYSTIQUE DE L'AUTORITÉ", PRESENTED AT THE COLLOQUIUM *DECONSTRUCTION AND THE POSSIBILITY OF JUSTICE*, OCTOBER 1989, CARDOSO SCHOOL OF LAW.

Algeria's concern with biodiversity conservation has grown since the 1980s and 1990s, when the country signed several international conventions.[1] Following the Barcelona Protocol (1995), the Algerian state adopted a "Blue Plan" for the Mediterranean and started to update its existing regulatory arsenal.[2] These changes expressed the state's commitment to protect its coastal ecosystems, and constituted the basis for the extension of coastal national parks in the east of the country to their contiguous maritime areas. The extension of the National Park of El Kala (NPEK), one of the largest coastal wet lands in the Mediterranean region, hosting two-thirds of its endemic marine species, illustrates this policy. The NPEK is listed in the Ramsar Convention and figures among UNESCO's biosphere reserves. However, the exploitation of natural resources in the NPEK is not currently carried out in compliance with international and national norms of conservation. Furthermore, contrary to the express commitment of the Algerian state to protect the heritage value of

1 These include: the Convention on Biological Diversity (1995); the Ramsar Convention on Wetlands (1982), and the Convention on International Trade in Endangered Species of Wild Fauna and Flora (CITES) (1983).

2 This included the creation of a national seashore commissioner, and a law on the shoreline (Law 02-02 of 5 February 2002 on the protection and improvement of the coastline).

 | DOI 10.1163/9789004362116_005

these resources, the enforcement of these norms leads to the establishment of private access rights.

When states ratify international conservation conventions, they are supposed to adhere strictly to a set of norms, and are expected to transmit these down to the local level. Yet the enforcement of international norms also depends on the ability of the various segments of central administrations and local authorities to press for their implementation in the local territories (Camau and Massardier, 2009). Even though international laws define a rational management of nature, local state agents and authorities can reshape rights of access to resources. As a consequence, external regulatory principles often become the subject of national and local power struggles. Adopting the historically grounded perspective of political anthropology, this article examines how environmental norms are interpreted, appropriated and implemented at the local level using the NPEK as a case study. The difficulties involved in enforcing laws in the context of a plurality of legal norms and actors have been well documented in political science literature. Here, I consider the trajectory of the government of men and nature that goes beyond the legal-rational framework in order to study how the nation state and local actors appropriate international environmental norms, and how they transform such norms through their own methods of government and social practices.

In this article, in the light of Foucault's insights on biopower (1994 and 2003),[3] I examine the manipulation of rules, irrespective of their legality or legitimacy, and how this manipulation is linked to discipline. In his treatment of power and its diffusion, Foucault (2003) explains that the enforcement of norms relies both on regulatory processes and on disciplinary techniques that go beyond rationalised state intervention, and calls this twofold process "normalisation". Anthropologists who are inspired by Foucault in their analysis of environmental policies have either examined the continuity between norms and disciplines (Agrawal, 2005) or emphasised historical discontinuities (Murray Li, 2007). However, these approaches do not pay sufficient attention to the intricate relationships between pre-modern (sovereignty and coercion) and modern (rationalisation and normalisation) forms of govern-

3 The work of Escobar (1995), who transposed Foucault's thought to development studies, led to the emergence of a critical scholarship on environmental policy and interventions. These works adopted governmentality as a framework of analysis and used Foucauldian notions of power/knowledge to understand inequality in access to natural resources. However, the notion of biopolicy has not been sufficiently explored, even though it has been used in the study of biomedicine (Rabinow and Rose, 2003). This notion may be useful in environmental studies, especially in the government's analysis of nature from a historical and comparative perspective, since it helps bring to the fore localised processes of power.

ment, and their impact. Through the case of the NPEK, I explore the contradictions between modern forms of normalisation and pre-modern forms of discipline, as well as their political consequences in particular historical contexts.[4]

I focus on how legal rules concerning the management of nature, intertwined with disciplinary techniques, help "normalise" the use of resources along the shoreline of the NPEK. I also explore how this process is closely linked to the history of resource use and appropriation in this maritime territory. I argue that the "normalisation" of environmental action is not just an issue of law enforcement. Rather, it assumes a process of accommodation to disciplinary techniques involving interpretation and negotiation, even in a coercive context. To examine the links between these two dimensions of biopolicy, I shall focus on two maritime concessions granted by the Algerian state for resource exploitation. The first concession is governed and legitimised by law; deviations from the legal norm may be explained in terms of gaps in the law (Lascoumes and Le Bourhis, 1996). The second is an illicit concession, where an asymmetrical relationship exists between the actors, driving them beyond the boundaries of law within more strictly disciplinary relationships. Tackling Algerian biopolicy in this way enables us to understand the appropriation of resources in relation to legal institutions and coercive methods. The rights of access to marine resources are the result of power relationships, dependent on successive forms of state government – privateers, colonial state, socialism and liberalism, which are all structured by military power.

From Privatisation to the Farming Concessions of Lakes and Lagoon

The NPEK is composed of several lakes and a lagoon with exceptional fauna and flora. This biodiversity was the main justification for its creation in 1983. The total surface area of Lake Tonga, Lake Oubeira and the El Mellah Lagoon is vast: close to 5,600 hectares (7% of the NPEK, which covers 76,438 hectares). The residents of the Park (currently more than 100,000 people) have long been using these bodies of water for food and commercial fishing. In the following section, I shall summarise these various modes of exploitation and the evolution of rights of access to aquatic resources.

4 Even though relations between sovereignty and normalisation are characterised by heterogeneity in Foucault's thoughts on biopower, he clearly envisaged their interactions and overlapping in the limited case of state racism (Genel, 2006).

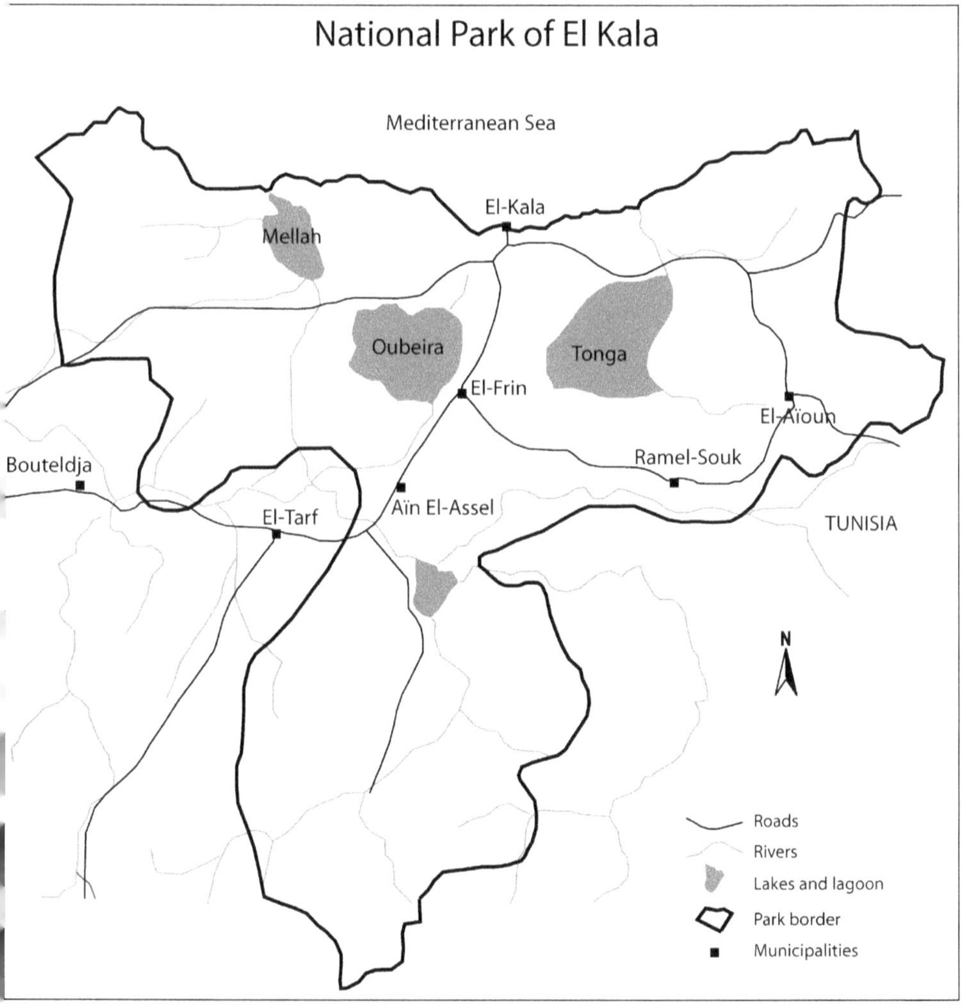

MAP 3.1 *Map of the NPEK*

From Private to Public Management

Since Independence, the residents of the *wilāya* (a unit of the central administration at local level) have been increasingly drawn to the lakes and the lagoon for fishing. This movement, which initially started under French colonial rule, focused first on the El Mellah Lagoon (860 hectares), due to its high productivity and the high market value of its marine species. Linked to the sea, it has a rich marine biomass and many species of fish, thanks to the water inflows.

The commercial exploitation of the lagoon for fishing started in the 1920s, when a (French?) settler made improvements to the channel linking the lagoon to the sea in order to increase fishing productivity. Although local labour was used, this concession was privately managed, since the entrepreneur was the only person entitled to exploit the resources.[5] At that time, a dyke system at the mouth of the lagoon was created and even now this helps capture fish, depending on water flow according to the seasonal variations in temperature and water salinity. The channel has also been cleaned to limit silting from the adjacent dune.

After Independence, the management of the lagoon was nationalised under the socialist regime, which promoted agricultural co-operatives and public companies. The management of the fishing activities in El Mellah was transferred to the Algerian Fisheries Office, which managed the fishing traps at the mouth of the lagoon as well as net fishing carried out by the resident communities on the banks. The Office assumed the management of the channel, as this was considered a strategic area affecting the lagoon's biodiversity and ecosystem balance.

In 1979, the management of the lagoon was transferred from the Fisheries Office to the National Algerian Fishing Company (ENAPECHES). The aquaculture unit of El Kala was created in 1982 to develop the lagoon and Lake Oubeira. The residents continued their fishing activities and took part in the commercial exploitation of thc lagoon and in net fishing, as wage-labourers. This type of fishing was quite productive (at least 60 tonnes per body of water per year; see Cataudella, 1982) and depended on a well-trained labour force. The local people caught the fish with the assistance of their children, and the women practised livestock husbandry. ENAPECHES also undertook the development of Lake Oubeira. In this fresh water lake of 2,200 hectares, specialised fishing groups from the aquaculture unit started fishing for eels, after catching mature specimens in the lagoon. In contrast, ENAPECHES never undertook the development of Lake Tonga.

The state employed more than 60 people in fish production. After ENAPECHES went bankrupt in the late 1990s, most of the employees were laid off, but continued to fish commercially, supplying local markets, with the help of their families. Fishing complemented the income of the people living alongside these three bodies of water.

The Establishment of the Domain Concession

During the 1980s, following the drop in oil prices, the Algerian government signed loan agreements with the IMF, with a privatisation component, although the fishing infrastructure that belonged to ENAPECHES was not

5 See <www.faosipam.org/htm/Uploads/aquaculture_algerie.pdf> (accessed 2 March 2013).

transferred till 2005. At the time, the exploitation of the El Mellah Lagoon and Lake Oubeira was granted to a private entrepreneur through a domain concession.[6] The entrepreneur, a member of the Algerian parliament,[7] became the sole holder of fishing rights for a period of twenty-five years. Commercial exploitation of fish on Lake Tonga was also granted to him, but only for a 3-hectare surface area and for a five-year period.

Since these bodies of water were part of the integral protection zone of the NPEK and subject to the statutes of the Ramsar Convention, the concessionary domain was granted under specific conditions intended to protect the ecosystems from the environmental damage associated with commercial exploitation.[8] The terms of the concession agreement for El Mellah Lagoon and Lake Oubeira[9] stipulated that fish catches must not exceed one-third of the total biomass. There were also other restrictions, aimed at maintaining the lake's ecological balance, such as maintenance of the channel and control of the intrusion of exotic species in aquaculture. These measures were to be implemented in a commercial concession involving both fishing and shellfish farming.

The private beneficiary of the concession of the El Mellah lagoon obtained the access rights for 5,000,000 Algerian dinars (approx. € 50,000) and he pays an annual fee of 1,350,000 Algerian dinars (€ 13,500). These costs seem extremely low considering the duration of the concession, even if the concession-holder is required to mitigate the environmental impact of his activities in order to guarantee sustainable exploitation. There are, however, other constraints on the entrepreneur's activities in the concession. The entrepreneur is required to make investments to develop infrastructure for prawn and clam farms. This is especially tricky as it involves negotiating zoning decisions with the various administrative departments that are responsible for the

6 These bodies of water and maritime spaces are part of the public domain. This means that exploitation rights can only be transferred through a concession. This involves a *process* by which the public domain is excluded from a general use to the benefit of a physical or legal person granted rights to a particular use.

7 In the Maghreb (Hibou, 2011; Catusse, 2008), and in the sub-Saharan states (Dahou, 2004), political liberalisation has been accompanied by economic privatisation and state clientelism.

8 *Official Journal of the Democratic and Popular Algerian Republic* (*JORADP*). Conventions and international agreements – law and decrees, ordinances, decisions, notices, communications and announcements. Executive decree 03-280 of 24 Joumada Ethania 1424 corresponding to 23 August 2003 defining the mode of issuance and of establishment of the national concession for the exploitation of lakes Oubeira and Mellah (*wilāya* of El Tarf).

9 Art. 23, *JORADP*, 2003.

improvement and follow-up of the concession (Department of Fisheries, Department of Land Use Planning, Department of the Environment, the NPEK and the *wilāya*).[10] The entrepreneur started to move the sand at the dune adjacent to the lagoon, even though the dunes are protected by coastal law and the zoning plan of the Park. This raised local fishermen's concern that he was selling sand to the construction industry, especially as a former sand pit situated in the Park was recently closed for infringement of coastal law.

According to the terms of the concession agreement, if the development of the site was monitored by the state, the entrepreneur was not required to hire local labour. This meant that only a small number of wage-earners[11] were hired for surveillance of the area against poaching. They earned 10,000 dinars per month (€ 100), without health insurance. Some of them are involved in net fishing, but fishing is prohibited to residents, including for food needs. The inhabitants criticise the private concession for excluding them from fishing and for paying them low wages. They complain about the poor maintenance of the channel and note that the sand silting at the dykes threatens the ecological balance. They also denounce night-time clandestine exploitation of the sand at the dune. The inhabitants claim that such practices constitute land grabbing, and that they need to be granted access to the lagoon for fishing, and to the coastal shores to develop recreational activities dedicated to tourism. The state administration was also concerned about the suspect practices by the concession holder. The Department of Fisheries notes that the entrepreneur did not comply with its requests to build decantation basins to help limit the organic pollutant spills into the lagoon. For the entrepreneur, lack of compliance was highly profitable, given the low acquisition cost of the concession. The latter was, in turn, related to the local political elite's success in influencing the officials of the *wilāya* of El Tarf.

In the Oubeira concession, the conditions concerning infrastructure (e.g. the creation of a breeding centre for various juvenile species) were not respected either. The commercial exploitation of eels is regulated by the Convention on International Trade in Endangered Species (CITES), which has cited eels as a threatened species since 2007.[12] CITES requires the drafting of a management plan based on scientific data to regulate commercial fishing so that the renewal of fish stocks is not compromised. However, in areas belonging to the concession, the exploitation of eels, as well as other fish, has taken place without restocking.

---

10 Art. 55, *JORADP*, 2003.

11 See <http://www.fao.org/fishery/countrysector/naso_algeria/fr> (accessed 2 March 2013).

12 See <http://www.cites.org/fra/cop/14/prop/F14-P18.pdf> (accessed 2 March 2013).

Fishing in Lake Oubeira is done from small boats, and is only permitted to the beneficiary of the concession. The entrepreneur employs wardens from the *douars* (a group of housing and administrative units) bordering the lake, who allow only subsistence-oriented fishing. As at the lagoon, only a few residents are hired, mainly for eel fishing, and the fish are exported to Italy. The entrepreneur prefers to rely on a network of fishermen from whom he buys eels at a price independent of market variations, for only 50 dinars (€ 0.50) per kilogram. The concession holder has been able to appropriate most of the benefits derived from fishing by using a non-contractual form of outsourcing.

Appendix 2 of CITES, which requires a management plan for eel export, came into force in 2009. At that time, due to the new difficulties involved in exporting, the entrepreneur abandoned the concessions on Lake Oubeira and Lake Tonga, but he did not make the required investments. The state did not draft the required management plan, nor did it exert sufficient pressure on the entrepreneur to oblige him to carry out the necessary infrastructural work. For five years, the entrepreneur benefitted from exclusive access to the lakes in exchange for the payment of the low fee. He disengaged himself when CITES came into force, without having to pay any compensation for his failure to invest in infrastructure (farming equipment and a breeding centre).

The legitimacy of this concession in the NPEK, where the inhabitants are working for low wages, is questionable. Research has shown that in 2009 the average monthly income of rural households residing around these bodies of water was € 500, as the local economy is characterised by a low percentage of wage-earning jobs. In comparison, despite the sub-optimal exploitation of the El Mellah Lagoon and the non-compliance of the entrepreneur, the annual turnover of his concession can be estimated at between € 500,000 and € 1,000,000.[13] Given that the concession was granted on condition of its rational and sustainable exploitation, it is clear that the concession holder was blatantly avoiding implementing the conservation requirements.

The switch from public to private management took place via the granting of a public domain concession. The allocation of resources was carried out through a hybrid regime, combining exploitation and conservation, which leaves the entrepreneur great freedom to define the forms of exploitation. The business norms adopted by the entrepreneur excluded former holders of rights to use of the territory, and moreover did not guarantee the restoration of the ecosystem.

---

13 As the entrepreneur does not divulge the precise turnover of his business, the lower value given here is taken from his own production statements and the higher value is based on previous data, from the time of the national company (Cataudella, 1982).

The politico-administrative context also helps explain the dynamics of this exclusive appropriation. The appropriation of aquatic resources is shaped by complex local power relations. The granting of an exclusive concession to an entrepreneur who is a member of parliament raises the question of his connections with the representative of the administrative authority, the *wālī* (head of the *wilāya*), who is the ultimate decision-maker in domain concession allocations. In Algeria, given the lack of decentralisation, public choices at the local level are often made in negotiations between elected officials and the representatives of central authority (Hachemaoui, 2003), without any formal participation by local people. However, the decision-making process does not rule out local actors' deployment of various strategies in relation to the norms. For the exploitation of the lagoon, the concession-holder is bound by the standards of commercial aquaculture recommended by the Fisheries Departments. By contrast, the residents, who have been evicted and whose access to space and resources are limited, try to expose the concession's conservation problems to the National Park Administration in order to reclaim the management of the site for recreational purposes. These examples show the complexity of the local power relations involved in the appropriation of aquatic resources.

In addition, the multiplicity of norms that apply to different conservation spaces within the NPEK makes it difficult for decentralised administrations to adequately control the conservation area and make sure that the norms are respected. As different parts of the conservation area have different statuses and are regulated by different norms concerning resource use, with no clearly established hierarchy, there are multiple contradictions which in turn lead to gaps in the law (Lascoumes and Le Bourhis, 1996). These gaps are likely to encourage the non-sustainable management of resources by the entrepreneur. The variety of interpretations of the norms and the difficulties in controlling their application offer many opportunities for actors to enforce the law, differentially or asymmetrically, which go beyond the simple circumvention of the norms ("law-bending"). The differences in the frameworks of interpretation of the law enable partial enforcement of the norms and their alignment in accord with particular interests. The example of the management of the dune highlights the diversity of administrative actors and the multiplicity of norms that apply to this space; which makes it difficult to control the activities of the entrepreneur. Similarly, the CITES norms are difficult to implement in the absence of relevant scientific data, and this offers entrepreneurs an opportunity to withdraw from the concession, without paying any compensation. The multiplicity of norms and the political and financial power of the entrepreneur, enable him to manipulate the authorised modes of exploitation and to break free from the norms of sustainable exploitation of the ecosystem. Far from being fictitious, the multiplicity of norms and their uses in local power relations enable the appropriation of resources to be steered towards a private form, in defiance of the public-interest character of conservation.

From Coral Exploitation Concessions to Coral Contraband

Fishing activities, long practised in El Kala, intensified under colonisation with the arrival of French trawlers and the creation of a fish cannery. Even though industrial activities and state exploitation of the lagoon were later brought to an end, some of the local population are still engaged in fishing, particularly in the port of El Kala and its gulf.

Intensification of Fishing and Old Exploitation of Coral

The boom in fishing is the principle reason behind the extension of the NPEK into the marine zone. In the *wilāya* of El Tarf the number of sailors and boats has doubled within a decade. The fishing sector has acquired a crucial importance in this *wilāya*, with low employment and income levels. Jobs are rare in the NPEK and are overwhelmingly seasonal. Even though investment in the fishery sector is not as high as in other regions in Algeria, the area has experienced a considerable expansion of commercial fishing. While fishing has increased in the gulf of El Kala (in the 2000s, production went up from 1,500 to over 3,000 tons[14]), the fleet remains artisanal and old. This restricts fishing to already intensely exploited coastal areas. The fishermen have been warned about over-fishing the traditional capture areas and the declining production, but the average income for fishermen is close to € 400 per month for trawler fishing, and less than € 300 for small-scale fishing and artisanal sardine fishing (Chakour, 2011), so the warnings have little effect.

In spite of the Ministry of Agriculture's[15] public discourses on the preservation of the coastline of El Kala, the Ministry of Fishing encourages rent-seeking, including its recent public policy of financing new sea trawlers. Overfishing of the nearby spawning grounds by the trawlers leads to a decline in fish stocks. According to the fishermen, illicit fishing has had negative impacts on the ecosystem and the fish resources. The trawlers respect neither the limits of the zones nor the periods of biological rest. These practises not only lead to a reduction in the operating margins of the local fishermen, but also contribute

14 Data collected from the Fisheries Directorate of the *wilāya* of El Tarf in 2008.

15 The Ministry of Agriculture is responsible for the National Parks, and the Ministry of the Environment is in charge of the coastline.

to the labour force's shift from artisanal fishing to the more lucrative coral fishing.

El Kala has long been identified as one of the most important coral fields in the Mediterranean region. It was first exploited by the Arabs, then by privateers. European interest in this area steadily intensified as the value of the coral used in jewellery increased. From the thirteenth century onwards, the Genoese controlled coral exploitation. In the sixteenth century, the Regency of Algiers granted this area as a coral concession to France (Masson, 1964: 30-130). Since then, fishermen working with the Marseille Company have settled in El Kala, and continued to take coral, using the St Andrew's cross (an instrument formed of a wooden or iron cross to which nets are fastened).

The control of this area is closely connected to military power struggles. The Regency of Algiers leased coral exploitation to foreign powers in exchange for financial resources, but these concessions could be revoked, depending on alliances and the profits they produced (Masson, 1964: 30-130). In the seventeenth century, the privateers, having broken free from the Ottoman Empire, imposed less favourable conditions on the company. The resources, which have long been the object of concessions established by the state, were at the centre of power struggles and market relationships on an international scale. After the colonial conquest, coral harvesting became a lucrative trade for European fishermen. Italian fishermen who settled in eastern Algeria used to pay a fee to dredge the reefs of El Kala using the St Andrew's cross, taking the coral back to Liguria and Campania. Colonial scientists had recommended fallow systems for sustainable exploitation, but the colonial administrators preferred to establish economic incentives for locally moored small boats (Lacaze-Duthiers, 1864). French naturalisation laws aimed at populating Algeria with European settlers and the development of a local coral channel enabled the Italians to settle in El Kala.

After Independence, particularly at the end of the 1970s, diving, which intensified harvesting, and rising prices justified the centralisation of coral production in the hands of the Algerian Fishery Office. In the mid-1980s, following the failure of public companies and the collapse of oil prices, national entrepreneurship was promoted on the basis of a concession system. In 1992, a decree prohibited the export of coral. In 1995, a set of legal safeguards[16] aimed at helping the reefs recover quickly was adopted within the concessions. Coral

16 According to Decree 95-323 of 21 October 1995, the concessions are temporary and revocable, and fishing quantities are limited by quotas that can be reviewed on the basis of the landing controls carried out by the Fisheries Departments, coastguards and customs officials (Cazalet and Alliouche-Kerboua, 2011).

harvesting was limited by a quota system and subjected to a set of rules. Only diving was authorised, and a dozen concessions were granted to local entrepreneurs from El Kala or from Algiers, who cooperated with Italians for their know-how. These concessions were renewed until the prohibition on fishing that accompanied the project to establish a marine protected area at the beginning of this millennium. In the absence of data on coral stocks, official appraisals suggested a moratorium on coral harvesting (Bouazouni, 2004; Grimes, 2005). This was a prevention measure unparalleled in the entire Mediterranean region.

Bottom coral exploitation was governed by various regulations, ranging from sustainable fishing allowing resource renewal to total prohibition. In 1995, with the Barcelona Agreement, the idea of coral conservation to preserve biodiversity gained momentum. In 2010, a number of conservation-oriented NGOs, concerned with the intensive exploitation that threatened this fragile sedentary species, red-listed by the International Union for Conservation of Nature, attempted to include it in CITES. However, the expected change in international regulations failed to come about, and individual countries continue to have total freedom in their management of coral fishing. Thus, today, while some state actors advocate unlimited coral fishing, others are for the application of quotas or the introduction of protected zones.

Algeria switched from exploitation to protection without assessing the impact of the concessions on the resources. In 2001, coral fishing was suspended[17] along the whole Algerian coast, pending a future decision to resume harvesting. This moratorium put an end to the concessions but has not abolished all forms of exploitation.

Continuity in the Rules of Appropriation

An illegal network of coral fishing and commercialisation then developed in El Kala, in spite of the presence of coastguards in this border area. Coral harvesting was carried out by small boats and fishing with the St Andrew's cross. This was considered safer than diving and did not require large investments. Resorting to this older method is nevertheless more destructive, since the cross, by tearing off the coral, may prevent its recovery. In addition, the use of this method means that a high percentage of the coral collected is lost on the seabed. Lastly, it affects the biodiversity of the seabed by scraping the rocky surfaces. Despite its prohibition, however,[18] this method is used intensively,

---

17 Decree 01-56 of 15 February 2001.

18 Decree 04-187 of 7 July 2004, which fixes the list of prohibited fishing equipment, includes the St Andrew's cross.

since fishermen equipped with a GPS can hide the St Andrew's crosses in the sea.

This illegal exploitation in the El Kala maritime zone is connected with the traffic in coral to Italy via Tunisia, where coral is shipped to the bay of Naples. For a contraband activity, the intensity of these operations is exceptional: at least 300 small boats registered in the port of El Kala are involved. Coral harvesting has replaced fishing for other species, especially in the zones where the main fields of red gold (coral) are located – due to the huge number of crosses hidden in mid-water. As increasing numbers of fishermen as well as inhabitants of El Kala and neighbouring villages have switched to this illegal sector, the seabed is becoming increasingly damaged. The value of coral varies on the world markets (its price can reach € 5,000/kg), while the local price after collection is around € 700, so the price differential has stimulated the boom in illegal trade routes and the use of unscrupulous methods.

Coral exploitation in this zone involves diverse actors, including civil servants, who finance and arm the boats and hire a labour force, which is exposed to the inherent risks of this activity. There are even boats that are funded by staff of the Chamber of Fisheries, which is made up of civil servants and fishermen's representatives and is responsible for regulating the fisheries sector. Both private and public sectors are involved, as the maritime administration also benefits through corruption. The involvement of members of the local and central administration (the armed forces, which directly include the coastguards, are attached to the Presidency) leads to the perpetuation of this traffic.

The study revealed that the modalities of coral appropriation that have become permanent in the long run have been primarily influenced by the international markets, except during a period of state-led exploitation from the late 1970s to the 1990s. This exceptional management regime was related to the emergence of a local jewellery industry, and included close monitoring of the collection of coral. Apart from this break, a regime of concessions controlled by the central state and in favour of private operators exporting the red gold has remained the rule. Starting with the period of piracy,[19] through the colonial period and until now, a regime of concessions situated outside of the law has persisted, despite the prohibitions concerning fishing and collection methods. This intense and visible form of exploitation is created by a concession regime that depends on the leniency of the coastguards, the indirect beneficiaries of the traffic.

---

19 This corresponds to the medieval period, from the fifteenth to the eighteenth century, during which the Mediterranean powers clashed over resources and commercial routes by delegating the use of violence at sea through the granting of letters of marque.

Exploitation continues regardless of the sustainability of the species. Even though diving extraction and quota systems included conservation-related criteria, they were only short-lived from the historical perspective of the long trajectory of the exploitation of this maritime territory. Paradoxically, past forms of private appropriation are resurfacing, with the revival of old fishing techniques, precisely at a time when the conservation laws regulating the public status of this resource are most stringent against private exploitation. This continuity in the forms of appropriation of coral is significant, especially in the face of the assertion of the public character of the resource through the legal moratorium that forbids its collection. The historical trajectory of concessionary regimes in the area can help us understand how the present modes of appropriation are affected by the long-term influence of the international configuration of resource extraction.

Here again, the application of international norms of conservation is paradoxical. This case is, however, quite different from the example of legal gaps discussed above. The norms prohibiting coral exploitation have never been subject to debate among state sectors or local authorities, or challenged and altered as a result of their confrontation with other norms. They represent nothing more than a threat of sanction, which may be bypassed by corruption. The history of coral exploitation shows that forms of appropriation can acquire a permanence that makes it possible to bypass the legal regimes of access to resources, despite the fact that the maritime space is part of the public domain. Conservation norms evolve within local power relations, in relation to a complex game of negotiation between heterogeneous actors and a variety of norms. These conservation norms are reinterpreted within a framework of state-society relationships and commodification processes, each with their own histories that shape their disciplinary, rather than regulatory character.

Different Models of Concessions on Natural Resources

Management practices in the conservation areas analysed in this article rely on a variety of different modes of granting of exploitation rights by the state. Sometimes exploitation rights are granted via a legal path, as in the case of the concessions for the bodies of water within the NPEK. In other cases, exploitation rights are granted illegally, as in the case of coral harvesting in maritime areas. In this same territory, the action of the state alternates between favouring legal and illicit forms of concession. However, all these forms of concession lead to privatisation of the resources, regardless of the apparent public character underpinning ecosystem preservation. To grasp the rationale behind the government of nature, these different forms of concessions must be analysed together.

From Imposing the Law to the Difficulties of Its Enforcement

In the case of the management of El Mellah Lagoon, Lake Oubeira and Lake Tonga, the granting of the domain concession complies with the international conventions that define the protected status of the NPEK. These conventions provide the criteria for exploitation and investment that are supposed to allow the preservation of the ecosystems. Nevertheless, the entrepreneur's non-compliance with the international criteria raises the question of the legitimacy of the concession and the adequacy of the monitoring by the state administration.

Even though careful monitoring of the concession is required by the international criteria, state departments find it hard to carry out this task. This is because the Department of Fisheries, in particular, on the one hand depends on the entrepreneur's data for producing figures and, on the other, lacks the scientific knowledge and financial and technical means to assess the environmental conditions. Neither does the Department rely on the academic work that has been produced on the basis of local studies. In the absence of an independent evaluation, the entrepreneur can easily ignore the depletion of the species and ecosystems that he is supposed to maintain. In this context, limiting the exploitation to 30% of the biomass is an impossible task if the biomass is unknown, be it at the beginning or during the exploitation. In addition, the concession agreement allows the introduction of a high-yield exotic species for shrimp farming.[20] The situation is thus further complicated by the fact that no prior impact assessment on the ecosystem of the introduction of this new species was required.

Similar problems exist in eel conservation measures. As mentioned earlier, since the coming into force of Appendix 2 of CITES, a management plan is required to farm eels for export. However, the Ministry of Fisheries has never used any academic expertise, even though Algerian universities have been conducting biological research focusing on eels in this area. Having no information (or opting to ignore the existing research) on the status of the eel population, the Ministry can hardly define for concession-holders the sustainable production criteria that would favour eel reproduction. The norms guiding the management of the concession might include all possible safeguards, but the lack of scientific data prevents verification of whether these safeguards are respected, and thus undermines the application of the norms.

---

20 Art. 35: Breeding species. The sole species to be bred are as follows. Prawn: *Penaeus japonicus*. Clam: *Ruditapes decussarus*" (*JORADP*, 2003).

As indicated earlier, the infrastructural works (decantation basins and fry rearing centres) required by the concession agreement may have helped to preserve the ecosystemic conditions necessary for the reproduction of aquatic species. From the perspective of the Fisheries Department, these investments could have been treated as a condition imposed on the investor to compensate for the extremely low fee required for a total monopoly over resource exploitation. However, the local administration has ignored the investor's lack of attention to these issues. The result is a privatisation of natural resources, without any concern for their preservation.

According to the law, the entrepreneur has to meet the requirements imposed by the state – which derive from the international conventions. The legal principles help justify the management of the site according to the international criteria of sustainability, and legitimate the concession. But in practice, the entrepreneur does not respect international conservation norms, nor is he concerned with local equity. Furthermore, the administrative control of the concession depends on the existence of scientific data, which government offices are reluctant to seek.

An Illicit Concession

"Illicit concession" is an oxymoron that perfectly fits the way coral is exploited. Despite the existence of a legal norm that forbids the collection of the coral, its exploitation occurs in public view, and with the consent, and sometimes even the active participation, of various public administrators. The intensity of these illicit practices can be linked to the actions of the state. While the exploitation of eel seems to focus on stock regeneration, the prohibition of coral fishing gives rise to a network of actors, ranging from the regulatory authorities of the fishery sector to the maritime control forces concerned with the capture of illegal rent. Coral exploitation has reached such a height that its heritage status has vanished into thin air, and it has become a commodity traded far away by illicit transnational networks.

Controlling space at sea is always difficult, as boundaries and routes are less visible than on land. However, the manipulation of the law is mainly sensitive to power dynamics. The fishing prohibition norm has redirected the coral rent towards fishermen and smugglers, and led to the redistribution of the control and allocation of this rent among different segments of the administration. The law of prohibition has given the coastguards a monopoly over the control of the maritime domain and has deprived the fisheries authorities of their role of overseeing the exploitation of coral. While these authorities used to have regulatory power over concessions, such power now lies only with the coastguards in charge of enforcing the conservation norm (Cazalet and

Alliouch-Kerboua, 2011), which has taken the form of a strict prohibition. As a result, the smugglers need only to bribe the coastguards, since the latter are the only public body legally entitled to supervise maritime practices. The coastguards' monopoly is based on a particular conception of maritime sovereignty. The military guarantees that maritime borders and fishing areas are respected, but it also controls how marine resources – as part of a public domain – are appropriated, and has the sole prerogative of enforcing the fishing code.

This hegemony of the Navy over maritime spaces is an important element of Algerian maritime policy. Its exercise of power in national maritime space contradicts the official texts stipulating possible collaboration with civil servants from the Fisheries Department. This hegemony cannot be questioned, partly because of the uncertainty maintained by the Ministry of Fisheries concerning the state of existing coral stocks.[21] The governance of maritime resources is divided between several ministries in Algeria, but the Navy, representing the military, holds the greatest power by virtue of Algeria's national sovereignty claims. The rule of prohibition strengthens this monopoly and brings the government of nature back into the remit of the military, thereby establishing ambiguous links between the state and society.

On the Government of Men and Nature

In both of the cases studied, resorting to conservation law leads to situations where natural resources are privatised without concern for their renewal. In the case of the domain concession, the entrepreneur adopted a short-term rent-seeking strategy, altering the ecosystems from which multiple groups (diverse publics) derive benefit. The case of the marine space illustrates how official and non-official rationales interact to create "illicit" regimes of access to coral. Modes of appropriation are transformed through the illicit extraction of the resource – in which state actors are complicit – and the outcome is exclusion (particularly of fishermen), and the privatisation of maritime spaces and resources. In both cases, the state legislates, and invokes international legitimacy, on the basis of the norms of conservation. Thus, the two cases are two sides of the same coin, and represent aspects of the government of men and of nature in the NPEK.

Both the prohibition of coral fishing and the granting of exploitation rights on the lagoon and the lake as a domain concession, while not simultaneous, are part of government techniques, through which local actors try to establish clienteles by distributing rents and attempting to limit any contestation of

21 The results of a study led by this Ministry in 2005 to assess coral stocks have never been disseminated.

their action. Even though the state authorities did not foresee such a boom in coral exploitation, they nevertheless considered it to be in their political interest to leave young people to become involved in this lucrative activity. Thus, allowing illegal activities was a deliberate decision, in a region hit by unemployment, where the privatisation of resources has evicted the local inhabitants from their fishing grounds. The state authorities banked on reducing resistance to the concession by letting the young inhabitants of the lake areas take part in the illegal coral harvesting. This contributes to the local economy, as, according to our estimates,[22] the coral collection sector generates between € 1,000,000 and € 4,000,000 per year – excluding the profits from trade.

Today, the situation is inextricably tangled: the profitability of fishing is reduced due to intense coral fishing, and the public authorities are reluctant to tackle the dilapidation of marine resources that results from such practices. In 2008, when the state wanted to address the problem directly by forbidding recreational boats from acquiring a GPS (since it helps locate the St Andrew's crosses hidden at sea, and enables clandestine activities), young men tried to set fire to the harbourmaster's office, and injured some coastguards. The prohibition of the GPS was lifted immediately, but disciplinary methods thereafter took more arbitrary forms. Those who refused to pay bribes were prosecuted by the military tribunal – but the charges were finally dropped.

These power struggles arise from changing state-society relationships. They reflect a mode of governance that is often incoherent and steered by social conflicts. Coral exploitation is a conflictual field, not only among the various categories of local actors – for example, between outsiders and insiders involved in this black economy – but also among the governmental offices that control maritime spaces, and the smugglers. The state authorities manipulate the official and non-official rules, sometimes having recourse to legal norms to regulate official practices, and sometimes reinforcing or bypassing these norms in order to discipline the non-official practices more successfully.

The local enforcement of international conservation norms is heavily dependent on government techniques. Arun Agrawal (2005) mobilises the Foucauldian concept of governmentality to explain the mechanisms through which regulatory policies on natural resources are being appropriated at the local level. He sees the decentralisation of natural resource management as a path towards a possible "subjectivation" of conservation policies by local actors, who gradually adhere to these policies through the delegation of

22 These estimates are based on our own investigation of the average fished quantities, the collection price and the average number of outings.

resource management to forest councils. However, this approach exaggerates the coherence of government through a rationalisation of the norms, and thus does not take into consideration conflicting subjectivities. Tania Murray Li's (2007) argument, also following Foucault, focuses on the incomplete forms of power emerging from the governmentality of sustainable development. This approach allows her to take into account the historical constitution of the government and its chaotic evolution, and to overcome the limits of governmentality. However, even though Murray Li is aware of the specificities of the articulation of sovereignty with governmentality, when she considers the historical context, she does not explore the local impact of that articulation in terms of overlapping legal and illegal regulations. The Foucauldian notion of biopolicy is more relevant here for examining the interactions between modern (regulation and conduct of the self) and pre-modern (law and coercive disciplines) forms of government. It enables us to study more closely how they are interwoven in particular historical and local contexts.

In his analysis of biopower, Foucault (1994 and 2003) has shown that power is embodied through mechanisms of regulation, and that these mechanisms are always combined with disciplinary methods. This perspective reveals the private, if not occult dimension of government. Biopolicy, as a theoretical framework, encompasses both public and private mechanisms for governing men and nature. For Foucault, the normalisation of behaviour through rational processes comes in addition to the disciplinary methods (coercive or/and consensual), which may be private as well as public. State-society relations around the maritime policy in El Kala are shaped by a biopower that regulates the interactions between population and nature through market and conservation norms (specific to aquaculture and maritime fishing), as well as through disciplinary techniques (via coral fishing prohibition and the militarised maritime police). Access to maritime resources is shaped through processes that cannot be reduced to the strict application of conservation law. Access is part of a biopolicy, reflecting the dynamics of power relations, contestations of these relations, and their unintended effects. The resulting form of government does not fit with the dichotomy of rule-makers and those subject to the rules, since the access to and exploitation of marine resources are granted through both legal and occult concessions, depending on the shifting conflicts and alliances between public and private actors.

Scales of Norms and Public-Private Relationships

The domain concession of approximately 4,000 hectares of a coastal wet zone to a private operator is probably unique in the Mediterranean region, especially in a protected area. The norm allows for a transfer of resources from the public domain to an entrepreneur, thereby excluding the local inhabitants from using these resources. Invoking a rational management plan, the state claims to comply with international conservation norms and criteria of efficiency, as long as the exploitation has been transferred to a single agent.[23] Under this condition, having recourse to law may legitimate a private concession, even though it becomes difficult to prove the concession holder's lack of compliance with conservation principles. In the case of coral exploitation, invoking the conservation norm (the moratorium) enables the distribution of illegal income among various actors. This illegal concession, which involves networks of both public and private actors, excludes other fishing practices. The aim is the establishment not of free access, but of private access, regulated through power struggles manipulated by the public authorities.

Considered within the historical perspective that includes the pre-colonial and colonial periods, this case suggests that the state has recourse to the law (sometimes with conservation justifications [Davis, 2007]) in order to grant exclusive concessionary areas to its clients. In addition, this specific form of recourse to the law is also consistent with the move towards a "discharge" government (Hibou, 1999).[24] However, it should not be forgotten that, from this perspective, the state devolves its responsibilities together with the delegation of political power. Nevertheless, in this case, due to the public domain status of the maritime areas, the state remains the exclusive owner of marine resources and controls the distribution of benefits down to the most local scale, even through a process of "privatisation of the state" (Hibou 2004).

The historical trajectories of the government of men and of nature through law and illicit rules play a part in the definition of rights of access as the contemporary conservation regimes. Hidden behind the conservation rationale, public actors are still able to influence the relationships between maritime actors and their environment, and to govern by creating inequalities. In this case, conservation law acts as a reference for power relationships between actors. The strict application of law for a more equitable use of nature is not sought after. Conversely, the differential enforcement of the law helps to build an asymmetrical framework of reference among the public actors, as well as between public and private actors.

The conflicts taking place at different levels move the boundaries, not only between land and sea, but also between public and private (Dahou, 2009), inducing a transformation of public goods into privately appropriable goods,

---

23 Interviews with members of the Fisheries Department in 2009 and 2010.

24 Hibou borrows this term from Weber to explain the devolution of economic and political powers to private agents to govern remote areas.

similar to the situation experienced during the piracy and colonisation periods. In spite of the public property character of marine resources, appropriation tends to take private forms, initiated by the state to govern its maritime spaces. As a result, property rights become increasingly vague and the state becomes unable to clarify the property status of environmental goods without relinquishing its biopower.

References

Agrawal, Arun. 2005. *Environmentality. Technologies of Government and the Making of Subjects.* Durham NC: Duke University Press.

Bouazouni, Omar. 2004. "Parc national d'El Kala: Étude socioéconomique du PNEK". Projet régional pour le développement d'aires marines et côtières protégées dans la région de la Méditerranée (MedMPA), PAM, PNEK, PNUE, RAC-SPA. <http://medmpa.rac-spa.org/pdf/Rapports/Algerie/etude%20socio-economique_El%20Kala%20ALG.pdf> (accessed 10 August 2017).

Camau, Michel, and Gilles Massardier. 2009. "Revisiter les régimes politiques", in *Démocraties et autoritarismes: Fragmentations et hybridation des régimes*, ed. M. Camau and G. Massardier. Paris: Karthala-IEP, 7-39.

Cataudella, Stéfano. 1982. *Analyse et développement d'une exploitation lagunaire extensive. Exemple du Lac Mella –Algérie.* Projet Régional de Développement de l'Aquaculture en Mediterranée, FAO, Tunis. <ftp://ftp.fao.org/docrep/fao/009/af018f/af018f.pdf> (accessed 6 September 2017).

Catusse, Myriam. 2008. *Le temps des entrepreneurs: Politique et transformations du capitalisme au Maroc.* Paris: Maisonneuve et Larose.

Cazalet, Bertrand, and Kamel Alliouch-Kerboua. 2011. "Expertise juridique portant sur le projet de création d'une aire marine protégée sur la partie marine du Parc national d'El Kala (PNEK)". GEMALIT, programme GouvAMP WP2.

Chakour, Saïd-Chaouki. 2011. "*Rentabilité de la pêche, rente halieutique et marché du poisson à El Kala*". GEMALIT, programme GouvAMP WP1.

Dahou, Tarik. 2004. *Entre parenté et politique: Développement et clientélisme dans le Delta du Sénégal.* Dakar/Paris: Enda Graf/Karthala.

Dahou, Tarik. 2009. "La politique des espaces maritimes en Afrique: Louvoyer entre local et global", *Politique Africaine* 116: 5-22.

Davis, Diana K. 2007. *Resurrecting the Granary of Rome: Environmental History and French Colonial Expansion in North Africa.* Athens: Ohio University Press.

Escobar, Arturo. 1995. *Encountering Development: The Making and Unmaking of the Third World.* Princeton NJ: Princeton University Press.

Foucault, Michel. 1994. *Histoire de la sexualité*, vol. 1: *La volonté de savoir.* Paris: Gallimard.

Foucault, Michel. 2003. *Society Must Be Defended: Lectures at the Collège de France (1975-1976)*. Reprint. London: Picador.

Genel, Katia. 2006. "The Question of Biopower: Foucault and Agamben", *Rethinking Marxism* 18 (1): 43-62.

Grimes, Samir. 2005. "Plan de gestion de l'aire marine du Parc national d'El Kala". Projet MedMPA, PNUE, PAM, CAR-ASP. <https://www.scribd.com/document/159865292/Plan-de-Gestion-de-l-Aire-Marine-Du-Parc-National-d-El-Kala> (accessed 10 August 2017).

Hachemaoui, Mohammed. 2003. "La représentation politique en Algérie: Entre médiation clientélaire et prédation (1997-2002)", *Revue Française de Science Politique* 53 (1): 35-72.

Hibou, Béatrice. 1999. "La 'décharge', nouvel interventionnisme", *Politique Africaine* 73: 6-15.

Hibou, Béatrice. 2004. *Privatizing the State*. New York: Columbia University Press.

Hibou, Béatrice. 2011, *The Force of Obedience: The Political Economy of Repression in Tunisia.* Cambridge: Polity Press.

Lacaze-Duthiers, Henry. 1864. *Histoire naturelle du corail: Organisation, reproduction, pêche en Algérie, industrie et commerce*. Paris: Baillière et fils, Librairie de l'Académie impériale de médecine.

Lascoumes, Pierre, and Jean-Pierre Le Bourhis. 1996. "Des passe-droits aux passes du droit: La mise en œuvre sociojuridique de l'action publique", *Droit et Société* 32: 51-73.

Masson, Paul. 1964. *Les compagnies du corail: Étude historique sur le commerce de Marseille au XVIe siècle et les origines de la colonisation française en Algérie-Tunisie*. Paris: Fontemoing Éditeur.

Murray Li, T. 2007. *The Will to Improve: Governmentality, Development and the Practice of Politics*. Durham NC: Duke University Press.

Rabinow, Paul, and Nikolas Rose. 2003. "Foucault Today", in *The Essential Foucault: Selections from the Essential Works of Foucault, 1954-1984*, ed. P. Rabinow and N. Rose. New York: New Press, 1-30.

CHAPTER 4

Dignity and Honour: Struggles over Land and Legitimacy in the Soummam Valley

Judith Scheele

"As a social phenomenon", notes Baudouin Dupret (2010: 324), "law cannot be reduced to the mere dispositions of a legal code", although the latter remains of course "an integral part of it". This is particularly true with regard to land rights in Algeria, which are notoriously complex, confused and contested (Nemouchi, 2011: 134). Colonial land law was a tool primarily forged to serve settlers' interests, and was in practice mostly applied to those parts of the country that were seen as agriculturally valuable (Aït Amara, 2002: 134). National independence in 1962 was followed by two decades of far-reaching nationalisations, often based not on a legal framework but rather on the acceptance of the *fait accompli*, as nationalist credentials and labour came to determine access to land (Chaulet, 1987: 71, 73). Piecemeal privatisation started in the 1980s, against a background of much political upheaval and as part of a world-wide "liberal thrust" (Aït Amara, 1992: 192), but it has yet to be completed, leaving legal situations on the ground uncertain and open to negotiation. This changing legal framework on the national level is refracted through regional patterns of land tenure and local power structures (Parks, 2011: 2). On the ground, property rights and possession do not always coincide, and legal property rights might be documented in a plethora of mutually exclusive "superimposed" title deeds, alongside other claims (Nemouchi, 2011: 134). The question is thus which one of these title deeds or "ancestral rights" is to be publicly recognised, and in what circumstances? Decontextualised, legal titles and claims have little validity, heuristic or otherwise; and the legal status of a given estate only ever provides part of the answer to who will actually enter (or remain) in possession.

This is partly so because attitudes to the law itself are inherently ambivalent: as part and parcel of the Algerian national framework and an indispensable sign of statehood, it provides a guideline to be invoked by all. Yet it is also tainted by its close association with the French colonial state, from which much of its conceptual framework – and in particular the original land registers and notarial documentation it relies on to establish initial rights of ownership – is drawn. Law is thus never sufficient to establish legitimate possession, for it also needs to make room for political and moral claims that

 | DOI 10.1163/9789004362116_006

inform Algerian political life more widely. Meanwhile, much possession – in the ever-growing urban *bidonvilles*, for instance – is held without any legal title at all, but in the hope that the local administration will eventually legalise the *status quo* rather than risk social upheaval. This chapter, based on fifteen months of anthropological fieldwork in 2002, 2003 and 2004, and repeated visits since then, analyses one case of contested property rights, the case of a large agricultural estate in the Soummam Valley in Kabylia, a Berber-speaking area north-east of Algiers. It shows the various layers of legitimacy that can be invoked to claim ownership, from "ancestral rights" and *aḥbās* (endowments, singular *ḥubus*) via those obtained by "martyrdom" in the struggle for Independence, to rights based on agricultural labour and the "general interest". In public rhetoric at least, law is here ultimately subordinated to considerations of general morality and politics.[1]

Protest

In December 1998, several large agricultural estates in the Soummam Valley were legally returned to their former owners, mostly families who had been influential under the French and who had been expropriated at Independence.[2] One of these estates was the former *domaine autogéré* Akloul Ali, 959,77 ha of arable land at the bottom of the valley just east of Akbou, which was returned to the Ben Ali Chérif family. This restitution was contested; four meetings, held during 1997 and 1998, had been necessary to prepare for it, and even as the decision was taken, the representatives of the Peasants' Union (UNPA) and the Chamber of Agriculture voiced their disagreement, the former on the grounds that he did not recognise the validity of the title deeds presented, the latter because he was opposed to the expulsion of the farmers currently working the land.[3] This disagreement found a wider echo: in 2003, the *Assemblée Populaire de la Wilaya* (APW) de Béjaïa registered its opposition to the restitution, after *Front des Forces Socialistes* (FFS) members of the Assembly had circulated a paper entitled "Conspiracy against the Revolution", declaring the restitution to

1 Fieldwork was funded by the Arts and Humanities Research Council (UK), and the African Studies Centre at the University of Oxford. My greatest thanks are due, however, to my hosts, interlocutors and friends in Ighil Oumsed.

2 Decree 15-89 of 30 December 1998.

3 "Procès verbal de réunion de la commission de wilaya chargée de l'examen des dossiers de restitution des terres nationalisées, objets de donation au fonds national de la révolution agraire ou mises sous protection de l'Etat", 1 June 1998.

be illegal.[4] Similarly, the local population was outraged, especially as the new owners started selling parts of the land, from 2004 onwards, at a price (2000 DA/m²) judged to be only a fifth of its real value.[5]

The population of the village of Laâzib in particular, right in the middle of the contested estate, claimed that the land should rightfully be theirs. They filed several complaints against specific land sales, all of which were rejected or remained unanswered.[6] They were joined in their struggle by representatives from neighbouring villages, formerly belonging to the *ʿarsh* Illoula Ousammeur on whose territory most of the returned land lies. In 2008, the *zāwiya* (religious centre, plural *zawāyā*) in Chellata, with which the Ben Ali Chérif family is historically associated, also contested the restitution, claiming that the estate said to belong to the Ben Ali Chérif family was in fact *ḥubus*, and hence belonged to the *zāwiya*.[7] In 2004, as representatives of the new owners attempted to demarcate their property, they were met with violent resistance by the local population. As a result, twelve local inhabitants had to appear before the judge in Béjaïa in October 2005, sparking a demonstration in front of the court building to protest their innocence and to reiterate local claims to the land.[8] This was but one in a long series of public demonstrations and protests. Up to the present time, protesters routinely block the (very busy) national road (RN 26) leading from Béjaïa to Bouira, to draw attention to their claims. Some of these roadblocks last several days.[9] Protesters also repeatedly organise demonstrations in Akbou and in Béjaïa, drawing several hundred participants, and some institutional support on the local and regional level.[10]

---

4 "Délibération n. 19/2003 de l'APW, portant demande en annulation d'un acte de restitution de terres nationalisées", 16 November 2003; and K. Medjoub, "Terres restituées ou complot?", *El Watan*, 29 November 2003. The FFS is one of the two regional parties. It constitutes, alongside the governing *Front de Libération Nationale* (FLN), the most important political force in the Akbou area.

5 Hamid Aït El Djoudi, "Lâazib (Akbou): Restitution des terres", *El Watan*, 28 October 2004.

6 G.K. and T.M., "'Un contentieux juridique et historique': Terrains des héritiers de l'ex-bachagha à Akbou", *El Watan*, 12 August 2007.

7 Takerabet Mokrane, "La zaouïa de Chellata entre en lice", *El Watan*, 3 April 2008.

8 Taos Yettou, "Rassemblement de citoyens d'Azib", *La Dépêche de Kabylie*, 2 October 2005.

9 Arezki Slimane, "Les contestataires ferment la N 262, *L'Expression*, 4 August 2008; Takerabet Mokrane, "Commune d'Akbou: Les terres de la discorde", *El Watan*, 13 August 2008.

10 Takerabet Mokrane, "Les protestataires reviennent à la charge: Terres restituées aux Benalychérif (Akbou)", *El Watan*, 11 July 2009; B. Mouhoub, "Le Aarch de Chellata réclame les terres de ses ancêtres", *La Dépêche de Kabylie*, 5 July 2011; Menad Chalal, "'Qui a restitué les domaines de Ben Ali Chérif ?' se demande l'ONEC d'Akbou", *Béjaïa-Aujourd.hui.com*, 27 February 2013.

The argument put forward by the protesters comes in three parts. The disputed land used to belong to the surrounding villages, they argue, and was only taken from them as punishment for the villagers' involvement in the 1871 insurrection.[11] Mohammed Saïd Ben Ali Chérif, former *bachagha* and soon-to-be *caïd* (both were titles in the French colonial administration of Algeria, although the title of *bachagha* goes back to Ottoman times) received it in recognition for "services rendered" to the French colonial state.[12] This means that although his – and thus his heirs' – possession of the land might be legal, inasmuch as it conforms to the legal system of the time and is backed up by legal documents, it is certainly illegitimate, as all claims that he might have are based on his "betrayal" of the Algerian nation:

> We can neither keep quiet nor accept that Decree 15-89 of 30 December 1998 [...] be a second decree of sequestration, as on 25 May 1871! The same decree of sequestration that at that time turned citizens into bandits and outlaws, is now resuscitated and updated to feed the heirs of a *bachagha* who has sucked our parents' blood to the last drop [...] It is the duty of the Algerian state to clean out the leftovers of colonialism among us.[13]

Local villagers, on the other hand, have no title deeds because, as victims of the colonial regime, they were never in a position to have their claims recognised. The pre-legal nature of their claims, however, makes their "ancestral rights" or even "natural rights", according to one of the protesters,[14] more rather than less morally binding. Thus, one of the placards brandished by the protesters in 2005 read: "The colonial justice system (*justice*) has confiscated our ancestors' right; it is up to us now to take it back through the Algerian justice system."[15]

Secondly, Ordinance 95-26, passed on 25 September 1995, on which the restitution is based, explicitly states that no restitutions can be effected to former owners whose actions during the War of Independence were "dishonourable".[16]

---

11 In 1871, as the French army was occupied fighting the Prussians, large parts of Kabylia rose in an uprising against colonial rule. This uprising was brutally quashed, and resulted in the sequestration of roughly a fifth of tribal and communal lands in the area (see below).

12 Hamid Aït El Djoudi, "Restitution de terres contestée à Chellata", *El Watan*, 2 September 2006.

13 Arch Illoula Oussameur, "Lettre ouverte à son Excellence le Président de la République", *La Dépêche de Kabylie*, 7 August 2006.

14 Bachir Sadi, "Les habitants de quatre villages ferment la RN 26", *La Dépêche de Kabylie*, 3 August 2008.

15 Yettou, "Rassemblement de citoyens d'Azib".

16 Medjoub, "Terres restituées ou complot?".

"Dishonourable", however, is not a precise legal category, particularly as the "fake *mujāhid*" (freedom fighter) haunts the Algerian political landscape as much as the unrecognised hero dying in poverty.[17] Moreover, this caveat only applies to actions carried out during the War of Independence, and not before, and hence jars with local perceptions of historical culpability. As the conduct of the Ben Ali Chérif family during the war was uncertain and ambiguous,[18] protest against the restitution hence focuses on the role they played beforehand: that of grand colonial *seigneurs*. Indeed, a website run by Tamurtiw ("My land/country"), one of the associations that is most committed to the struggle against the restitution, features copies of a large number of historical texts that bear witness to the lavish lifestyle of the Ben Ali Chérif family at the time, their contempt for the local populations and their close and cordial relations with the French colonial overlords.[19] In other words, their ancestor's former status as *bachagha* is cited to show that, morally, the Ben Ali Chérif family were on the wrong side, and this is sufficient cause to delegitimise whatever they might have done during the war itself. The local habit of referring to the Ben Ali Chérif family in the singular bears witness to this moral telescoping of history, which also makes it possible to extend the War of Independence back in time. As could be read on another placard: "The restitution of the lands despoiled by the *bachagha* Ben Ali Chérif is a betrayal of the gallant martyrs of the 1830-1962 revolutions."[20] It hence needs to be resisted as a matter of national pride and loyalty, in the face of the growing disenchantment that characterises Algerian society more generally:

> To return the lands of Laâzib to the *bachagha* is an act that denies the sacrifice of our gallant martyrs… We are here, not to ask for visas to go somewhere else, but on the contrary, we ask for the land of our ancestors to be given back to us. Our motto is: our land is not for sale, and the fatherland is to be defended.[21]

17 This also explains why the "silence" of the ONM (the National Organisation of Mujāhidīn) is so often pointed out, as they have the last word in such matters – at least officially. See K. Medjoub, "L'ONM, la grande muette", *El Watan*, 3 April 2008.

18 The family left for Tunisia during the early stages of the war, keeping everybody in doubt over their true allegiance: see "SLNA Famille Ben Aly Chérif", Archives Nationales d'outremer (ANOM), Aix-en-Provence, box 93/4244.

19 See <http://chevally.unblog.fr/> (accessed 13 March 2014).

20 Yettou, "Rassemblement de citoyens d'Azib". The French armed force occupied Algiers in 1830; Independence was proclaimed in 1962.

21 Toufik Kadri, vice-president of the Illoula *ʿarsh*, cited in Sadi, "Les habitants de quatre villages".

A third line of argument is based on the use to which the land is put: good agricultural land is covered in concrete, the protesters claim; it is exploited by the "real estate mafia" (*mafia du foncier*), and "sold off" at derisory prices.[22] "Fertile land has been reduced to aridity."[23] Or, in the words of Hamid Amarouche, representative of the Illula *'arsh*: "The Algerian Revolution got rid of the French colonist; now a new kind of colonist appears – the Algerian colonist with his money."[24] An unnamed protestor was more precise, identifying the culprits as the "new bourgeoisie who hardly care about the citizens' struggle, to satisfy their egos while stamping on the laws of the republic".[25] Meanwhile, local *communes* are starved of land, as is the case in particular for Akbou, which has grown exponentially over recent years, and has increasing metropolitan ambitions.[26] Accordingly, from 2007, the protesters changed their strategy, from asking for a full restitution of the land to demanding that it should be turned over to the public domain and used "in the general interest".[27] Productive use in the interest of all, in an egalitarian republic, is thus opposed to individual greed and passive investment, either by bourgeois profiteers or by former colonial officials raised in luxury: a placard held by protestors proclaimed: "We Algerians represent the future, and you, French *bachaghas*, represent the past."[28]

Legal and moral arguments, however, do not exhaust the rhetoric used: while the protesters insist on their desire to find a legal solution to the problem, and underline how they have appealed to all the judicial and political institutions that they could access, they tend to conclude with veiled threats: "We find it extremely difficult to temper the ardour of the thousands of citizens whom we represent."[29] "If nobody listens to our grievances, our movement might radicalise"; and "If the public authorities do not react to repair this injustice, we will occupy the land, whatever happens!" (Mokrane, 2008b).[30] And

22 Takerabet Mokrane, "Akbou: Besoin d'une réserve foncière", *El Watan*, 19 June 2007.

23 G.K. and T.M., "'Un contentieux juridique et historique'".

24 Quoted in Sadi, "Les habitants de quatre villages".

25 Mokrane, "Les protestataires reviennent".

26 Mokrane, "Akbou: Besoin d'une réserve foncière"; Takerabet Mokrane, "Une ville carrefour à promouvoir: Commune d'Akbou", *El Watan*, 12 February 2007; Takerabet Mokrane, "Développement à Akbou: La ruralité à l'assaut de la ville", *El Watan*, 4 February 2009.

27 Tahar Hamadache, "La Soummam après le soulèvement de 1871: Réalités, malentendus et enseignements", *El Watan*, 9 July 2008.

28 Yettou, "Rassemblement de citoyens d'Azib".

29 Takerabet Mokrane, "Laâzib (Akbou): Contestation contre la restitution des terres", *El Watan*, 12 April, 2009.

30 Mokrane, "Commune d'Akbou".

demonstrations are indeed accompanied by at times violent attempts to stop people from working and building on the disputed land.[31] In a statement published in 2008, the Ben Ali Chérif family hence complained:

> Since the legitimate restitution of our property, we have been prevented from developing it by a few citizens on the fringe of the law who have readily used intimidation and physical threats towards us and the employees we have recruited, and sabotage all attempts to work the land. We have had these facts confirmed by bailiffs many times over without however impeding the agitators' provocations and manoeuvres. My family house where we were born and have lived is still occupied and we cannot access it.[32]

It does seem that the local security forces and political institutions at least tacitly support the protesters, or in any case find it difficult to intervene. And so far, in the absence of any legal response to the protesters' claims, this "hands-on" approach seems to have been the most efficient way of furthering their grievances, indicating the limits of an exclusively legal approach to questions of land tenure in contemporary Algeria (Parks, 2011: 228). "Law", "politics" and morality hence seem to be inextricably intertwined, leading not to "legal pluralism", but rather to the predominance, at least in popular rhetoric, of the political and moral over the legal, which, due to its colonial antecedents, is inherently suspect.

History

> We know little about real estate law before colonisation, even less about the constitution of private property. The image we have rests on the perception and juridical categories devised by colonialism to apprehend local land tenure. (Aït Amara, 1992: 187)

Kabylia is mostly known for its longstanding independence from any kind of state-rule, its relative inaccessibility, emphasis on small private property, and (relative) economic and political egalitarianism.[33] This, however, only

31 "Une maison incendiée", *La Dépêche de Kabylie*, 3 August 2008.

32 "La famille Benalychérif met les choses au point", *Algérie-Politique*, 1 May 2008.

33 The classic treatise on Kabyle property law is Hanoteau and Letourneux (2003: vol. 2, 160-313). Although in practice, this "egalitarianism" should be treated with caution, it has

describes part of the region: in the few broad valleys that cut through it – the Sebaou and the Soummam, essentially – different social and political structures developed that were an integral part of the Kabyle economy (Lacoste, 1984), but which are less often cited as typical. These valleys, under Ottoman control from the early eighteenth century onwards, not only housed Ottoman auxiliary tribes, often recruited from elsewhere, but also acted as an outlet for local notables eager to invest their surplus wealth beyond the boundaries of the tribal institutions that controlled agricultural land in the mountains. Such investment relied on some degree of cooperation with the Ottoman state, which in turn offered opportunities of enrichment to educated families who were acting as intermediaries with the Ottomans: "The use of land in the plains and low hills is thus essential to understanding both the nature of the traditional Kabyle economy and the ways in which political fiefdoms, independent of the tribal organisation, were constituted" (Mahé, 2001: 50).

In the Soummam Valley in particular, Ottoman administration relied exclusively on influential religious families to collect taxes, rewarding them with estates (*ʿazībs*) in the valley (Mahé, 2001: 53), populated by workers mostly imported from elsewhere, or shed by the tribal system.[34] With the French conquest, many of these families succeeded in maintaining their high status, and offered their services as intermediaries to the new colonial overlords. The Ben Ali Chérif family are a good example of this: prestigious scholars claiming sharifian and Moroccan origins, they were associated with their *zāwiya* in Chellata, near a high mountain pass leading to Greater Kabylia, but they also came to own vast agricultural lands and an *ʿazīb* in the valley – the village of Laâzib or ʿAzīb Ben Ali Chérif, which is at the heart of the current protest.[35]

Although many of the "*grandes familles*" co-opted by the French were involved in the 1871 insurrection against French rule – most famously the insurrection's first instigator, El-Mokrani – the then *bachagha* Mohammed Saïd Ben Ali Chérif was declared innocent, some say because otherwise he threatened to inculpate the French colonial army (Julien, 1964: 497), and amends were

become an integral part of the "Kabyle myth" and of the Kabyle self-image and hence internal historiography.

34 On black colonies in the Kabyle valleys, mostly associated with Ottoman rule and agriculture, see Aucapitaine (1860a) and Robin (1873); on the "shedding" of people by Kabyle villages through exile and poverty, see Scheele (2014: 184-185).

35 It seems that, under Ottoman rule, the family owned a house and *ʿazīb* near the current *daïra* (prefecture) of Akbou, which was expropriated and destroyed after the 1871 insurrection. Laâzib Ben Ali Chérif, further down the valley, was then granted them in compensation: see Hamadache, "La Soummam après le soulèvement de 1871".. For a description of the Chellata *zāwiya*, see Aucapitaine (1860b).

made for land initially confiscated from him.[36] About a fifth of the property of the local tribes, however, was sequestered. Confiscations were particularly extensive in the agriculturally valuable Soummam Valley.[37] "In fact", as Mahé (2001: 206) comments wryly, "the geography of the insurrection and that of state colonisation based on sequestrations intended to punish it, hardly matched": the real aim of sequestration was to further colonisation through expropriation. This had far-reaching consequences on the ground:

> Before the insurrection, the tribes of the [Akbou] *cercle* were among the rich tribes of Algeria. The insurrection and its effects have noticeably changed this situation of prosperity. The Akbou *cercle* has paid two and a half million [francs] of war contribution, and a considerable amount of land has been given up to colonisation [...] Usurers have speculated on the local populations' obligation to settle immediately, and have made them sign costly agreements, which means that they paid in actual fact much more than the sums indicated above [...] Today, they still have to settle accounts, and bailiffs seized various properties of bankrupt debtors.[38]

Expropriated land was handed out to European colonisers, in particular refugees from Alsace-Lorraine, which had just been lost to the Prussians (Akbou was initially called Metz). This agricultural colonisation was a spectacular failure, however, as colonists were left with little help, had no knowledge of agriculture, and succumbed in large numbers to malaria.

In Akbou, set up in 1872 on 3,255 ha divided into forty-two concessions, only nine of these were left by 1901 (Mahé, 2001: 586), as locals bought their land back wherever they could, and as small agricultural properties were sold to large owners established in the valley. Some of these are still remembered by contemporary inhabitants, or by the current toponymy: the name of the village of "Biziou" refers to a former French colonist, and people still recall the

36 Hamadache, "La Soummam après le soulèvement de 1871".

37 Twelve "colonial centres" were established in the Soummam Valley, where 29.1% of confiscated land was situated, although it only housed 12.6% of Kabylia's overall population at that time (Mahé 2001: 209).

38 "Rapport sur la situation matérielle, morale et politique des tribus du cercle d'Akbou, 10 August 1875" (ANOM 62K8). Among the Illoulen Oussammeur, 9,915 ha, i.e. two-thirds of the total tribal land of 14,872 ha, were sequestered, of which 2,150 ha (almost 15%) were declared land reserved for colonisation. In order to regain their sequestered land, the tribe as a whole paid 400,000 francs (ca £950,000 in terms of buying power in 2004 (INSEE, 2005). See also "Rapports annuels du cercle d'Akbou, 1873-1879" (ANOM 62K8, 70K7).

colonist of al-Firma, who was, or so the story goes, accused of spying for the Germans during World War I. If a large part of the land that is today contested might indeed have been given to the Ben Ali Chérif family immediately after the insurrection, some of it at least was bought much later, as part of the gradual tendency towards agricultural centralisation: the title deeds on which the current restitution was based were established between 1919 and 1941.[39] This was a time when property rights in the valley were changing fast, with the local population attempting to participate as much as they could. Thus, in 1924, seventy-one villagers from Ighil Oumced, one of the villages of the Illoulen Oussammeur, grouped together to buy an important piece of land from the "Ben Ali Chérif consortium", a small part of which was indeed part of what they considered to be their "ancestral land", but most of which was situated on the territory of the adjacent tribe, the Ouzellaguen.[40] Despite the large number of buyers, the land was not shared out equally, but according to socio-economic divisions internal to the village, which became more pronounced as some families succeeded better than others in entering the colonial economy. Remittances from emigrants were key here, as was cooperation with the French administration, albeit on an incomparably smaller scale than had been the case with the Ben Ali Chérif family (see also Scheele, 2009: 80-83, 154). "Ancestral rights" were thus partly redistributed according to market conditions, but this in no way reduced the moral and political attachment to village land.

In contemporary lore, however, this long history of official sequestration, European colonisation, internal village stratification and land sales has been erased from memory, to be replaced by a more general moral outrage at expropriation and violation committed by the Ben Ali Chérif family. Older women in particular place great emphasis on the betrayal of the trust with which, as the leading religious family of the area, they used to be invested.

> When the French came, we were all ignorant, and we were worried. Ben Ali Chérif said: "I will protect you and your land, just tell the French that I own it all, and they will not touch it." We would be working in the fields in the valley, and the French officer would come riding past, and every time he saw somebody he would stop and ask: "Whose land is this?" And as instructed, we would say: "It belongs to Ben Ali Chérif!" The French officer was not stupid: he would say, "Are you sure? And what about the sky, does Ben Ali Chérif also own the sky?" And we would say: "He does,

39 A. Saïd, "Les terres wakf au centre d'un conflit", *L'Expression*, 29 May 2006.

40 "Contrat de vente", 14 August 1924, Cadastre du Département de Constantine, Constantine.

by the grace of God." The French officer would shrug and write it all down. Afterwards, Ben Ali Chérif took the paper and kept it. This is how we lost our land.[41]

The *Zawāyā*

The longstanding resentment against the Ben Ali Chérif family is thus aggravated by a sense of betrayal, and their failure to live up to the model of religious and political protection that might, in the past at least, have legitimised their privileged position. Yet while, for some of the old women telling these stories, the Ben Ali Chérif family's religious status is a mitigating factor, for most, it rather aggravates matters: in everyday rhetoric, often informed by a Berberist vision of history, marabout families are easily accused of being outsiders, promoters of "superstition", bourgeois exploiters of the peasantry (the "simple Kabyles"), as well as collaborators with the various colonial powers, particularly the French. This is made worse by the fact that at least a few of the formerly leading marabout families have managed to convert their cultural, educational and economic capital into modern education and access to state institutions. Among protesters in the Soummam Valley, resentment against the Ben Ali Chérif family, marabouts or even religious figures as a whole, colonial "feudal structures", and the rising new middle classes are thus all wrapped up into one feeling of outrage.[42]

For several decades, this anti-maraboutism was echoed in official state rhetoric on Islam, which, influenced by its own brand of reformism, viewed traditional religious families with some suspicion. Hence, religious endowments and property held by absentee or non-working owners were among those nationalised in 1971 for the benefit of the agricultural revolution. While the surface of land thus nationalised was minimal compared with the former colonial estates, and while many of the "*grandes familles*" managed to find legal loopholes to avoid expropriation, this was nonetheless a symbolically powerful gesture.[43] From the 1990s onwards, however, public rhetoric changed

41 O.H., interviewed in Ighil Oumced in November 2003.

42 Hence, when, in support of the claims of the Ben Ali Chérif family, a group if villagers in Laâzib underlined the many government positions that members of the family had occupied in independent Algeria, this exacerbated rather than lessened local resentment against them: see "Halte aux diffamations contre Ben Ali Chérif", *La Dépêche de Kabylie*, 29 November 2003.

43 During the Agrarian Revolution, 400,000 ha (or 7.2%) of privately held land was expropri-

considerably. Prominent government figures visited regional *zawāyā*, paying tribute to their spiritual influence and pledging their support, and organised with great pomp a conference on the *zāwiya* tradition at the prestigious Club des Pins in Algiers (Hadj Ali, 1992, see also Scheele, 2007) – perhaps thinking that the *zawāyā* and all they stand for might act as a panacea against more radical political forms of Islam. As part of the official recognition of the role played by *zawāyā*, legislation was passed in 1991 that made it possible for religious institutions to recuperate land that had been expropriated in 1971.

This, of course, posed the question of who the rightful heir to the *zāwiya* tradition is, and what exactly this entails. Historically, *zawāyā* drew their income from gifts and donations, and landholdings constituted as endowments, which, put together, amounted to a sizeable portion of arable land in Algeria. French colonial law, however, converted *ḥubus* land into state property. One common way of avoiding this, and hence of protecting the *zawāyā*'s income, was to formally turn *aḥbās* into private property while maintaining their collective use, by establishing French title deeds mostly to the benefit of the religious family running the *zāwiya* in question. Although this was often done with the agreement of local assemblies, over time, the memory of such transfers faded, especially among those who now held individual title deeds and could claim former *ḥubus* land as private property.[44] This is what the religious association of Chellata was hinting at, when they asked for the restitution of the disputed land not to the Ben Ali Chérif family – whose title deeds are thus presented as mere legal expedients to avoid expropriation, echoing the local legend recounted above – but to the *zāwiya*, which they said they represented.[45] Not only did this open the question of who is in fact entitled to represent the *zāwiya*: former tribal or village councils, religious associations, contemporary teachers and scholars in cases where the *zawāyā* are still functioning, or the Ministry of Religious Affairs that is nominally in charge of them (and that might thus have a vested interest and the necessary political influence to make some of these claims heard).[46] But it also implied the instability of *all* colonial title deeds as based on an initial ruse or act of violence, a breach of moral contract: "notarised agreements dating from the colonial period are invalid and

ated, alongside 600,000 ha of communal or *ḥubus* land (Aït Amara, 1992: 189), compared with 2.3 million ha nationalised at independence (Côte, 1985: 42).

44 For examples of this process elsewhere in Kabylia, see Saïd, "Les terres wakf"; Lyès Menacer, "La bataille judiciaire des associations religieuses: Bradage des terres wakf de certaines zaouïas en Kabylie", *El Watan*, 1 April 2007.

45 Mokrane, "La zaouïa de Chellata".

46 Menacer, "La bataille judiciaire des associations religieuses".

should be annulled", in the words of the president of another religious associations, involved in a similar conflict.[47]

This implicit attack on the legitimacy of all legal documentation might explain the violence with which the Ben Ali Chérif family reacted to the *zāwiya*'s claims: roughly a third of the only public statement they seem to have made with regard to the restitution is taken up with refuting them. This is done, not in legal terms, but rather by vilifying the spokesperson of the association, their former ally, who, "motivated by sordid interest and a malicious and ungrateful spirit, makes defamatory remarks about us and claims to want to start a procedure that rests on no serious or credible foundation", and who, in any case, cannot claim to represent the *zāwiya* without the Ben Ali Chérif family's preliminary agreement, or so they say.[48] Ironically, perhaps, we find here a similar language of the betrayal of trust – this time by a client of a patron, rather than vice versa – to that used in local legends of expropriation, recounted above.

Independence

For most people, however, the days of patronage, gratitude and trust are definitively gone. As Independence was declared in 1962, the first action to demonstrate on the local level that a "revolution" had really taken place was the expropriation of the Ben Ali Chérif family's extensive land-holdings and their conversion into a public domain:

> During the war, after Ben Ali Chérif had left, his workers managed the land, all by themselves, as if he had never gone away. After the war, the army took over the land, and ALN officers were installed as administrators. They did not stay for long; then Boumediène came, and the land was turned into state property. It was managed by people from outside, administrators, but the people who were working on it were the same as before.[49]

The former colonial house at al-Firma, used by Ben Ali Chérif as a secondary residence, was occupied by members of the three families who had managed and worked the domain. A small part of the land formerly owned by the Ben

47 Ibid.
48 "La famille Benalychérif met les choses au point", *Algérie-Politique*, 1 May 2008.
49 A.M., interviewed in al-Firma in January 2004.

Ali Chérif family was taken over by various villagers immediately after the war, or even during the troubled period before the ceasefire.[50] They were rarely those who claimed former ownership. The division of Ben Ali Chérif's property and the constitution of the public domain, where villagers had hoped for a restitution of their family lands, clearly symbolised the new power structures that were to dominate post-Independence Algerian society: power was passed on to those who had "made" the new country-to-be, rather than to others who might have been the former owners of the land, but who during the war had become guilty by omission.

At Independence, former colonial properties accounted for a third of agricultural land in the country, producing more than half of its agricultural output (Côte, 1985: 42). Their counterpart was a large and largely property-less agricultural workforce, amounting to 550,000 landless peasants, of whom 120,000 were employed on colonial farms and 70,000 on Algerian-owned farms, and 360,000 were described as "floating day-labourers" (Aït Amara, 2002: 131). Initially, it was the 120,000 workers who had been employed on colonial farms on a regular basis who spontaneously took over their management, often even during the War of Independence, and then more openly after Independence was declared. Colonial property was nationalised in October 1963, and the existence of what came to be known as "self-managed estates" (*domaines autogérés*) was recognised by law.

> The initiative came from the permanent workers on farms, more precisely from those working on large farms in regions of high colonial density. These workers were often of faraway and diverse origin, settled randomly and far from their kin according to employment opportunities, responsible only for nuclear families, with no experience. They had no choice but to defend their way of life, their jobs, and their right to stay, to take root in the name of their past, present and future labour. (Chaulet, 1987: 71)

Or, as the open letter to the Algerian President, drafted in the name of the Illoula *ʿarsh* in 2006, puts it with regard to Ben Ali Chérif's former domains: "At Independence, the land that we are claiming was put under the protection of the state [...] and is worked by Algerians like us [...]. This is good, because we are brothers.".[51]

50 Côte (1985: 42) notes that, during the War of Independence and without leaving any legal trace, the colonial sector shrank from 2.8 million ha in 1954 to 2.3 million ha in 1962.

51 Oussameur, "Lettre ouverte".

This openly declared tolerance, however, hides tensions on the ground. As indicated by the French colonial census, the inhabitants of most villages in the valley – including Laâzib – are diverse.[52] In popular lore, they have come "from everywhere", and contain a large number of "Arabs", "kabylised" by having picked up the language. Marital alliances between former colonial and mountain villages are not so much rare as easily forgotten, especially in public rhetoric,[53] and people resident in the *ʿazībs* are commonly described as lacking retinue and decorum, and general awareness of the finer points of Kabyle sociability. Their destiny is too inevitably bound up with the colonial occupation: either docile labourers, or footloose and unstructured immigrants, they are easily seen as "collaborators" with the powers that be and hence as not fully-fledged members of Kabyle society. The fact that the Ben Ali Chérif family had some success in garnering support for their claim to restitution among the inhabitants of Laâzib is seen as a proof of this, or at least of their gullibility.[54] Although today, the inhabitants of Laâzib are at the forefront of the struggle against the restitution of land to the Ben Ali Chérif family, according to the president of the association Tamurtiw, based in Laâzib, it took him a lot of time and effort to be accepted, and to make it clear to the mountain villages that it was in everybody's interest to pull together.[55]

And in fact, claims to the land voiced by former colonial farm workers and mountain villagers are contradictory, as they rest on two different and mutually exclusive notions of ownership: one based on work – Chaulet's "past, present and future labour" – and the other on "ancestral rights". The former has become a political slogan – the land belongs to those who work it – that has been too often repeated to be forgotten, whatever might have happened to the Agricultural Revolution, and the latter is based on uncertain but nonetheless morally powerful readings of history. Neither has any real underpinning in the contemporary Algerian legal framework, which, in Aït Amara's (1992: 186)

52 "Tableau de Recensement de la Commune d'Akbou, 1931-1958", Archives de la Daïra d'Akbou, Akbou.

53 "Registres de mariages de la commune d'Akbou, 1898-1963", and "Sijill al-zawāj, 1985-2003", Archives de la Commune d'Akbou, Akbou.

54 Farouk Ben Ali Chérif is said to have promised villagers from Laâzib that their land would be returned to them if they supported restitution. After he died, his brothers refused to honour his promise (see El Djoudi, "Lâazib"). For support for the Ben Ali Chérif's claim within Laâzib, see "Halte aux diffamations contre Ben Ali Chérif", *La Dépêche de Kabylie*, 29 November 2003. The president of the Tamurtiw association that is at the forefront of the struggle against the restitution, claims to have received death threats from his fellow villagers.

55 T.K., interviewed in Laâzib in March 2008.

words, since the 1990 law on real estate "re-establishes the situation inherited from the colonial [not the pre-colonial] period", but they are both based on powerful moral principles that are immediately recognisable to all. And this is indeed the crux of the matter: if the only generally accepted legal framework is morally tainted – and how could it be more tainted than by its intimate association with colonialism – debates over legitimate rights have to go beyond the legal, and hence include local history and the moral status of the individuals concerned. As long as villagers in the valley and in the mountains fight as underdogs against "traitors" and morally corrupt "*bachaghas*", colonial or contemporary, no internal contradiction can invalidate their struggle. Yet this moral emphasis also means that, in legal terms, this struggle remains strikingly inefficient.

The moral inadequacy of national legal frameworks characterises debates over access to land more widely in Algeria, where most (legally sanctioned) property really *is* theft, or at least can be considered thus (to rephrase Parks, 2011: 313). At Independence, the only properties that had nominal title deeds were those held either by European colonialists or by people close to the colonial state, as otherwise they would not have had access to the colonial legal system. In any case, only a small percentage – a seventh or an eighth – of "indigenous" properties came with officially recognised documents (Aït Amara, 2002: 134).[56] While such questions were largely muted immediately after Independence, with impending privatisation of land from 1987 onwards, the Algerian countryside was marked by a renewal of social struggles over land (Chehat, 1992: 9). Pressure for legal change preceded legislation: Aït Amara (1992: 190) notes that restitutions of nationalised land started "on the sly" from 1983 onwards, forcefully encouraged by former owners. Restitutions to former owners led to (the resurgence of) local conflicts, many of which were decided not by legal but rather by extra-legal means: "In many cases and without waiting for the implementation of legal procedures, the owners resort to pressure and threats to proceed to the eviction of beneficiaries and to recover their land" (Aït Amara 2002: 133).

The 1990s in particular, when insecurity was rife, are generally seen – whether correctly or not – as a period when this new way of establishing property rights was inaugurated, as violence related to land could pass unnoticed in the general climate of fear and insecurity (see also Parks, 2011: 222-225). "Terrorism", as one newspaper article concludes, "hidden under the banner of Islam, has played its part as the armed wing (*bras armé*) of the

56 This, of course, does not include privately drafted contracts following Islamic law, but they seem to be largely absent from contemporary debates.

counter-revolution."[57] Hence, the only violent death that took place in the 1990s in Laâzib was, in local explanations, connected not to Islamic terrorism, but rather to the struggle over the Ben Ali Chérif estate.

These struggles over land feed into two major socio-political worries in contemporary Algeria: "anarchic" urbanisation and the ongoing agricultural crisis. Both are seen as signs of socio-economic inequalities that have grown exponentially since Algerian economic policies took a liberal turn in the late 1980s, and have led to a radical fall in living standards for most, and to the very visible rapid enrichment of the privileged few. Since the beginning of privatisation – a process that is still ongoing – the price of land has been rising steadily, making family agriculture increasingly unviable (Aït Amara, 2002: 136). At the same time, cities and even minor urban centres are expanding fast. As there is no legal protection of agricultural land, whoever owns a piece of land can build on it (Nemouchi, 2011: 135) and green fields are increasingly turned into brown. Agricultural land has come to be seen as a long-term investment for urban wealth, while rural means of production are centralised in the hands of a few wealthy entrepreneurs (Amichi, 2009: 11; Nemouchi, 2011: 142). This further aggravates the country's extreme reliance on food imports, by now little tempered by state subsidies, which drive up the cost of living.[58] Although recent legal reforms encourage privatisation, they often came after the fact (Aït Amara, 2002: 133; Amichi, 2009: 10; Nemouchi, 2011: 141) and are thus only part of the story: much of this property boom and the "rurbanisation" that marks the Algerian landscape has taken place by extra-legal means, as *de facto* occupations and constructions – "put up at night by the light of burning tyres", or so the story goes – are recognised by state institutions (Nemouchi, 2011: 138). In the general "confusion" (*flou*; Nemouchi, 2011: 134) that characterises Algerian property rights, the law, although invoked by all concerned, is thus often neither here nor there.

57 C.P., "A Draa Ben Khedda les anciens des domaines autogérés résistent depuis 20 ans à la restitution des terres confisquées en 1963, aux descendants des collaborateurs du colonialisme", *Alger-Républicain*, 13 November 2012.

58 As early as 1985, a fifth of the income generated by hydrocarbon exports was spent on food imports (Chehat, 1992: 9), and between 40% and 95% of basic foodstuffs were imported (Côte, 1985: 44). In 2011, 75% of food consumed in Algeria was imported (Vitraulle Mboungou, "Importation des produits alimentaires: Les pays les plus dependants", *Afrique-Expansion*, 12 April 2011); food imports were worth 9.5 billion dollars in 2013 (K. Remouche, "Sécurité alimentaire : L'Algérie en situation précaire", *Liberté*, 12 February 2014).

Conclusion

The appeal to various normative frameworks by protesters in the Soummam Valley cannot be described as "legal pluralism". None of the people involved doubt that Algerian national law provides the framework for legal debates, and even reference to the *sharīʿa* – as made by the *zāwiya* in Chellata with regard to former *aḥbās* – is effective only inasmuch as recent national legislation makes it possible to recognise such claims. Nor is law irrelevant to the debate: precise references to the texts of specific laws are an important part of everybody's rhetoric, several demonstrations were carried out in front of the law court in Béjaïa, and protesters have filed a large number of complaints with the relevant legal institutions and insisted on meeting with a number of members of the judiciary.[59] Legal texts judged to be relevant have been made publicly accessible by the associations involved. They are discussed in great detail and, where they seem to provide grounds for protest, they are cited *ad nauseam*. Moreover, much is made of the fact that buildings are put up "illegally" – i.e., without a building permit – on the disputed land.[60] Yet these references to the law are merely part of a larger appeal to overarching moral claims that may or may not be backed up by the law, and the law is only cited when it suits these claims. Elsewhere, it is easily dismissed as unjust, or quite simply ignored. The law, then, is subjected to moral and political concerns that are external to it. This reflects the inherent ambiguity of national legislation in Algeria: as the framework of the Algerian state, defined as the natural expression of the revolutionary Algerian people, the law ought to be just, but in fact, as a relic of colonial history, forcibly relying on colonial precedents and documentation, it is morally tainted, and hence to be rejected. Nonetheless, the protestors do not attempt to act against the law itself. No claims are made that condemn recent legislation as wrong; rather, the claimants aim to draw attention to the particulars of their case, which they say has been misinterpreted by local administrators. Similarly, in their frequent appeals to the "president of the Republic" or "the authorities", the protestors seem to hope for the intervention of a political power that is above the law and that is therefore morally just.[61]

While this might be understood as a naïve position – after all, in a modern state, the law is the law, and is applied regardless (in theory at least) – in

59 Yettou, "Rassemblement de citoyens d'Azib"; Mouhoub, "Le Aarch de Chellata réclame les terres".

60 El Djoudi, "Restitution de terres contestée".

61 See, for example, Oussameur, "Lettre ouverte": Sadi, "Les habitants de quatre villages"; Bachir Sadi, "Des terres aux Ben Ali Chérif", *La Dépêche de Kabylie*, 4 July 2009.

contemporary Kabylia, this is by no means a foregone conclusion. Since the "Black Spring" of 2001 in particular, the local potential for political disruption and social upheaval is well known, and makes negotiations on the ground complex and long-winded. The Ben Ali Chérif family might be the legal owners of the disputed estate, but this legal right has not been of much practical use to them, as any attempt to take actual possession of the land has been met with violent resistance by the local population – who are protected, it seems, by local power-holders who cannot reverse legal decisions taken on the national level, but who can effectively block their implementation on the ground. Hence, an attempt to open a private clinic in Laâzib has resulted in failure, as the building works simply could not be carried out.[62] Similarly, a villa built on some of the disputed land was burnt down before it was even completed, while the security forces were "discreet" or "shone by their absence".[63] The only people who have been able to make use of the disputed land are well-connected dignitaries with a strong power-base on the regional level – many of whom, or so people whisper locally, obtained land not through sales but as "gifts" granted before the restitution was passed, in order to "facilitate" it – or local entrepreneurs with enough money to keep everybody happy. This negotiability of rights on the ground is characteristic of the Algerian political system more generally, which, although it looks notoriously centralised to the outsider, is regionally specific and based on a fragile and constantly changing equilibrium between different local and regional social groups, while the national government has little power of enforcement on the local level. "State institutions", notes Bob Parks (2011: 309), "can only project enforcement where they are strong enough to co-opt or re-wire local elites; in Algeria, this capacity has always been variegated across space and across time". This can cut both ways: throughout Algeria, similar restitutions of colonial properties have been made, more successfully, even before the relevant law was passed,[64] whereas in other regional settings, no amount of legislation will make it possible to go against a consensus in the "almost hermetically sealed local political-economic arenas" (Parks, 2011: 306). As one of the protestors in the Soummam Valley put it, theirs is after all a "revolutionary struggle", a "matter of dignity and honour"[65] – and revolutions do not necessarily stop to respect the law.

62 G.K. and T.M., "'Un contentieux juridique et historique'".

63 Mokrane, "Commune d'Akbou".

64 C.P., "A Draa Ben Khedda"; see also Parks, 2011: 225.

65 Sadi, "Des terres aux Ben Ali Chérif"; Mokrane, "Laâzib (Akbou)".

References

Aït Amara, Hamid. 1992. "La terre et ses enjeux en Algérie", *Revue des Mondes Musulmans et de la Méditerranée* 65: 186-196.

Aït Amara, Hamid. 2002. "La transition de l'agriculture algérienne vers un régime de propriété individuelle et d'exploitation familiale", *Cahiers Options Méditerranéennes* 36: 127-137.

Amichi, H. 2009. "Évolution des systèmes agraires collectifs : De la décollectivisation aux nouveaux arrangements. Cas du bas Cheliff, Algérie", in *Economies d'eau en systèmes irrigués au Maghreb*, ed. T. Hartani, A. Douaoui and M. Kuper. Montpellier : Cirad.

Aucapitaine, Henri. 1860a. "Colonies noires de Kabylie", *Revue Africaine* 4: 73-77.

Aucapitaine, Henri. 1860b. *Zaouia de Chellata: Excursion chez les zouaoua de la Haute Kabylie. Extrait des mémoires de la Société de géographie de Genève*. Geneva: Imprimerie Fick.

Chaulet, Claudine. 1987. "Les ruraux algériens et l'état", *Revue des Mondes Musulmans et de la Méditerranée* 45: 67-79.

Chehat, Foued. 1992. "Déterminants et premiers effets de la réorganisation de l'agriculture algérienne", *Economie Rurale* 207: 7-10.

Côte, Marc. 1985. "Campagnes algériennes: Un héritage colonial difficile à assumer", *Méditerranée* 55/3, 41-50.

Dupret, Baudouin. 2010. "Droit et sciences sociales. Pour une respécification praxéologique", *Droit et Société* 75: 315-335.

Hadj Ali, S. 1992. "Algérie: Le premier séminaire national des zaouias", *Maghreb, Machreq, Monde Arabe* 135: 53-62.

Hanoteau, Adolphe, and Aristide Letourneux. 2003 [1872-3]. *La Kabylie et les coutumes kabyles*. 3 vols. Paris: Bouchène.

INSEE (Institut national de la statistique et des études économiques). 2005. *Valeur d'achat du franc français 1900-1963*. Paris: INSEE.

Julien, Charles-André. 1964. *Histoire de l'Algérie contemporaine: La conquête et les débuts de la colonisation, 1827-1871*. Paris: Presses Universitaires de France.

Lacoste, Yves. 1984. "Rapports plaine-montagne en Kabylia", in *Unité et diversité du Tiers-monde*. Paris: La Découverte, 470-539.

Mahé, Alain. 2001. *Histoire de la Grande Kabylie, XIXe-XXe siècles*. Paris: Bouchène.

Nemouchi, Hayette. 2011. "Pratiques sociales et problèmes fonciers en Algérie", in *Régulation foncière et protection des terres agricoles en Méditerranée*, ed. M. Elloumi, A.-M. Jouve, C. Napoléone and J.C. Paoli. Montpellier: CIHEAM, 127-143.

Parks, Robert P. 2011. "Local–National Relations and the Politics of Property Rights in Algeria and Tunisia". PhD dissertation, University of Texas at Austin.

Robin, J.N. 1873. "Notes sur l'organisation militaire et administrative des Turcs dans la Grande Kabylie", *Revue Africaine* 17: 132-140, 196-207.

Scheele, Judith. 2007. "Recycling Baraka: Knowledge, Politics and Religion in Contemporary Algeria", *Comparative Studies in Society and History* 49 (2): 304-328.

Scheele, Judith. 2009. *Village Matters: Knowledge, Politics and Community in Kabylia, Algeria*. Woodbridge: James Currey.

Scheele, Judith. 2014. "Community as an Achievement: Kabyle Customary Law and Beyond", in *Legalism: Community and Justice*, ed. F. Pirie and J. Scheele. Oxford: University Press, 177-200.

CHAPTER 5

Land Appropriation, Tenure and Legal Practices in a Steppe-like Environment (Algeria)

Yazid Ben Hounet

The Algerian Agricultural Land Ownership Act (*Accession à la Propriété Foncière Agricole* – APFA), Act 83-18, was adopted on 13 August 1983. It concerns lands belonging to the state and located in Saharan or steppe-like areas, as well as public land that may be used for agriculture. Any physical person of Algerian nationality enjoying his/her full civil rights and any legal person with the status of a cooperative registered in Algeria, may, under this Act, acquire farmland or land intended for agriculture in the specified areas for the symbolic price of one dinar. The transfer of property rights was subject to a five-year resolutive condition (barring an "act of God"), relating to development of the land in compliance with a programme drawn up by the purchaser and endorsed by the administration. The APFA's legal framework, *istiṣlāḥ arāḍī* in Arabic (land development), corresponds to and implicitly reproduces a traditional Muslim legal form of appropriation, namely the improvement (*iḥyā*) of land (Denoix, 1996): anyone who improves or reclaims land by cultivating it or restoring it, or by making it useful, becomes its owner.

In 2008 – 25 years after it was passed – the APFA was suspended following the formulation of the government's new land policy, which became law after adoption by the People's National Assembly in the summer of 2010, and modified the conditions for working agricultural land.[1] This new text maintains *ad vitam aeteram* the state as landowner, while farmers and herdsmen are now authorised to use the land as a concession.[2] There were several reasons for

1 Act 10-03 of 15 August 2010 on the conditions and modalities of farming the state's private agricultural lands was published in the *Official Journal* 46, on 18 August 2010.

2 This new law aroused fear of land-grabbing (farmland being cornered by foreign companies or states). It also worried the National Union of Algerian Farmers (UNPA). According to the daily *Le Jeune indépendant* in an article of 16 September 2010 ("Opening up the agro-industrial sector to multinationals: Several transnational companies are interested"): "The minister of Agriculture and of rural development, Rachid Benaissa, [was] considering a series of foreign candidates for farming land in the country. Since 2006, foreign farmers have been authorised to invest in [...] the Sahara, steppe-like and mountainous areas." The new law was designed precisely to regulate these temporary authorisations.

 | DOI 10.1163/9789004362116_007

these new measures. The APFA had not, as will be shown below, come up to expectations, and in particular it did not lead to a substantial increase in agricultural output. The state, and particularly the State-held Lands Department (Ministry of Finance), sought to support agriculture by preserving state property and giving big (and especially foreign) agribusinesses opportunities to expand their activities in Algeria. This change in legislation on agricultural land was a consequence of the government's economic policy. Since the 1990s, the government had wanted to move toward a market economy while retaining certain benefits of the nationalisation and socialisation of the country's assets and resources (Belhimer, 2012). Concessions thus replaced land-ownership. Over the past thirty years, Algeria (particularly its Saharan and steppe-like areas) has experienced various forms of appropriation of agricultural land, as private property or as temporary concessions.

In this article, I shall focus on the APFA and, more broadly, on the legal issue of land tenure in Algeria. The process of private appropriation of agricultural land under the APFA will be presented and analysed, along with some of the conflicts it sparked. This will lead to a discussion of the ownership of agricultural land, specifically in relation to the law. The legal issue of property rights depends heavily on the economic and political balance of power.[3] The issue of land tenure and its transfer will be our starting point for describing how the APFA was applied and interpreted by both the authorities and the people. Disputes and their settlement enable us to see which norms are invoked. The analysis of a property dispute shows us which rules are enforced in a given context, how the interested parties refer to them, and how the law and other normative systems, possibly reinterpreted in terms of the law, come into play. These issues will be addressed using material collected during fieldwork conducted in 2011 and 2012 in the steppe-like province (*wilāya*) of Naâma (West Algeria), in the district (*daïra*) of Aïn Sefra.

Agricultural Land In Steppe-Like Environments

The question of land in Algeria continues to remain an important issue in the wake of the policies of dispossession, nationalisation and socialisation implemented during the colonial period (1830-1962) and after Independence (1962). During the colonial period, we should bear in mind that, as from the decree (*senatus-consultum*) of 22 April 1863 on the constitution of property in Algeria,

---

3 See Ben Hounet *and al.* (2011), in particular the Appendix on property rights and issues. Also useful is von Benda-Beckmann, von Benda-Beckmann and Wiber (2006).

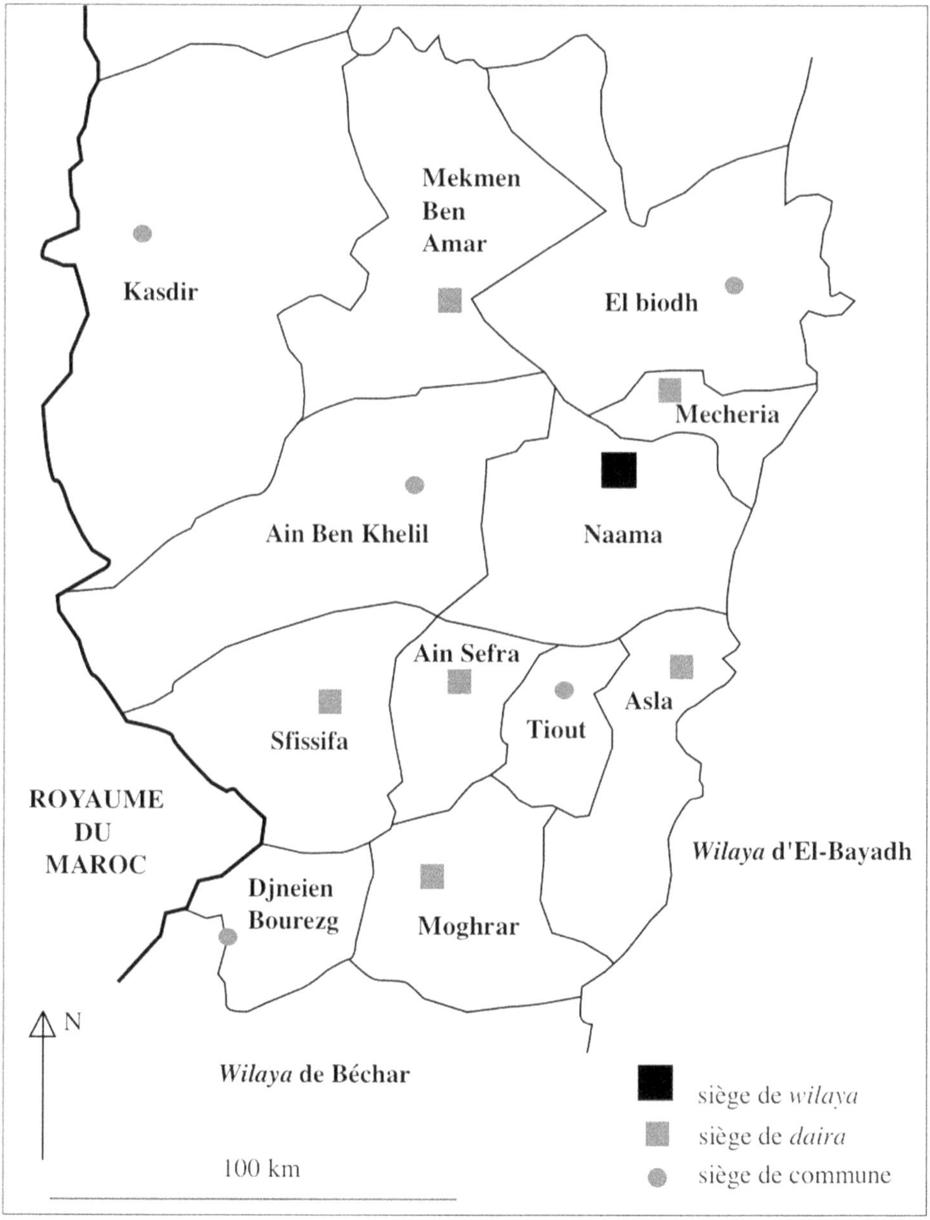

MAP 5.1 *Administrative division of Naama province*

in the areas occupied by the Indigenous (muslim arab and berber speaking groups) (Guignard, 2010), laws were passed to promote individual property, mainly on behalf of European settlers and companies. According to Jean-Claude Vatin (1983: 319) who refers to Charles Robert Ageron's work (1979), "100,000 hectares of land were owned by Europeans in 1850, 2,700,000 a century later"; "between 1871 and 1919 close to one million hectares (897,000) were handed to settlers. [...] The Muslims had lost, by 1919, seven and a half million hectares, which the state and individuals, and major capitalist companies, shared among themselves."

Around 1879, Karl Marx analysed land seizures in Algeria. The North African plateaus and steppes had, in his opinion, been the indivisible property of the nomadic tribes who roamed there. Passed down from generation to generation, this tribal property underwent only the following changes: "1) (gradual) division of the tribe into branches; 2) inclusion of members belonging to foreign tribes" (Marx 1970: 384). He then showed how, especially after the Warnier Act (1873), which was intended to put an end to joint tribal property rights, the spoliation of land took place, particularly through the confiscation and sale of land belonging to tribes suspected of rebellion.

Besides Marx's interpretation in terms of indivisible property, other analyses have been made of the status of the land over which nomadic tribes ranged. Some studies on tribal lands in Tunisia, before the French protectorate, state that "collective lands" very often belonged to tribes in the form of joint property, and that some tribes even had deeds attesting ownership (Daumas, 1912). Such land clearly had an acknowledged owner, and property rights were legally indivisible. Such joint holdings were wrongly considered to belong to the state (de Montety, 1927: 30). At the turn of the 19th century, Maurice Pouyanne maintained that a large proportion of tribal land in Algeria at the time was held in private ownership (*melk*). By contrast, collective tribal lands (*'arsh*) were inalienable: "Landholders cannot sell, pledge, or rent their land; it is the community of the believers [...] who has the enjoyment thereof" (Pouyanne, 1900: 97).

Let us add to this short summary of land tenure during the colonial period that dispossession mainly affected areas in the north, in the Tell Atlas farming area. In the southern territories (the Sahara and part of the steppe-like region), which were under military administration, the Arabic- or Berber-speaking tribes were relatively protected from this process. In his study of Aïn Sefra, Captain Mesnier (1914: 48), Head of the Accounts Department of the Saharan Oases (*Territoire des Oasis sahariennes*), wrote that the decree of 22 April 1863 "was only applied exceptionally in the military territory [...] Individual property did not develop in the military territory since pastures are only for collective enjoyment. Were they shared among the native population, disputes would always arise." The military policy of avoiding useless conflicts and the prevailing view of the steppes at the time as arid regions that were not suitable for colonisation (Lehuraux, 1931) may account for the difference in treatment between the south and north of the country.

In general, the principle result of the "dispossession of the fellahs" (Sari, 1978) under colonial rule was to make the nascent Algerian state into a colossal landowner. In order to have its land worked, the state then transferred rights, totally or partially, definitively or temporarily, to other parties, notably to private persons (Wilson, 2010; Belhimer, 2012). On the steppes, less affected by the process of dispossession, ownership of joint grazing lands (*ʿarsh*) was transferred by the Pastoral Code to the State in the mid-1970s at the context of agrarian reform.

The implementation of this reform's third phase, which had to do with pastoralism, started in 1975, the objective being to develop and modernise pastoral practices on the steppes by supporting small-scale herdsmen who lived off their work, and by restricting large-scale herders. This later policy was short-lived, and ended in the mid-1980s. Besides the direct assistance (in money and livestock) offered to small-scale herdsmen, the reform provided for setting up pastoral villages, such as Oulakak (40 km to the west of Aïn Sefra). Every pastoral village was to have a school for the nomads' children, a cultural centre and facilities for herdsmen: wells, collective farms to raise and look after livestock, etc. These villages were to help nomads settle and modernise their breeding practices, which were considered to be archaic. These objectives were not met, and the pastoral villages amounted to secondary residences for semi-nomads, and sheds for livestock. By favouring small-scale herdsmen who lived off their work, the agrarian reform did, however, somewhat hamper the development of a capitalistic pastoral economy in the hands of a few major landowners. In the words of M'Hamed Boukhobza (1989: 15): "Although the experiment was short-lived, it did lead to the state appropriating all pastoral land on the steppes."[4]

Once the agrarian reforms had been halted and the reforestation policy had failed, the government embarked on a development policy for small "farms" with the aim of settling nomads, combating desertification and promoting agriculture. In 1983, APFA was adopted; it mainly targeted the Sahara and the steppes. What characterised the 1980s was the gradual introduction of

4 Bedrani, Benadjila and Ghazi (1995: 14) state that, on the central Algerian steppe, "Legally, the rangelands belong to the state's private domain and, in all the zones studied, private property with a legal, written title of ownership is extremely rare, including farmlands". This observation can be extended to all steppe-like regions in the country. See also Boukhobza (1989) on the precise measures taken under agrarian reform and their success.

arrangements in favour of individual private property (not only in agriculture but also in urban contexts), in contrast to previous policies, which had focused on nationalisation/socialisation of the land and the creation of cooperatives, particularly agricultural ones. These new land management policies, especially the APFA, were not easy to implement and did not have the expected results. We shall demonstrate this through the case of Naâma Province, in the district of Aïn Sefra.

The district of Aïn Sefra lies in the traditional territory of the ʿAmūr tribal confederation. Before colonial rule, these nomads ranged at high altitude from east to west along the Ksour Mountains. The confederation has three main tribes: Swala, Awlād Salim and Awlād Būbkar, which in 1957 numbered 3,765, 1,500 and 3,908 persons, respectively (Bison, 1957: 16). Since (to the best of my knowledge) no census has been carried out since then, it is difficult to estimate how many people now belong to this confederation. Up to the end of the 1980s, there were statistics concerning the number of nomads per tribe but, since then, the authorities have refused to conduct a census of this sort. Taking into account the proportion of the ʿAmūr compared with other groups, we might estimate the confederation's population at approximately 45,000, the largest group in the southern part of Naâma Province. If we also include the return of families who fled to Morocco during the War of Independence, the Awlād Būbkar would now be the biggest tribe in the confederation. The Swala would be slightly less numerous; and the Awlād Salim would still be the smallest. Between 20% and 30% of the ʿAmūr still live in tents (*khayma*). The other members of the confederation mainly live in the localities of Tiout, Sfissifa, Moghrar and, above all, Aïn Sefra. This town, with its nearly 50,000 inhabitants (in 2010), is located at the foot of the Mekter and Aissa Mountains. Along the western edge of the town lies a large dune, and to the east runs the national road from Naâma to Bechar.

In addition to the tribes of the ʿAmūr confederation, the district has a population of varied origins, among them the *Ahl Qṣūr*, people of the *qṣūr* (fortified villages). There are five *qṣūr* in the south of Naâma Province: Sfissifa, Tiout, Moghrar Tahtani, Moghrar Fougani and Asla (and three others in El Bayadh Province). Until the early 1960s, these villages were inhabited by groups who lived off agriculture and spoke Chelha (a Berber dialect). In the aftermath of Independence, several groups moved to more "comfortable" dwellings on the outskirts of these villages or in towns (particularly, Aïn Sefra), while still others emigrated to France to look for work. Although a few families still live there, most of these fortified villages have been abandoned. Adults may still speak Chelha, but it is used less and less, mainly because children go to state-run schools where only Arabic and foreign languages are taught.

People from the Arabic-speaking *qṣūr* of Aïn Sefra are called Awlād Sidi Būtkhil, the name of the patron saint of this fortified village, which was built in the sixteenth century. Considered to be of Arab origin, the Awlād Sidi Būtkhil are not classified as *Ahl Qṣūr*. A few *shurfa* families, of Alawite origin (the same as the current Moroccan monarchy) live in the area, but they are few in number. There are also a few *hartani* families of slave origin, whose ancestors apparently came from the Sahara during the colonial period.[5] In Aïn Sefra and other towns of the district, there are inhabitants from other provinces, notably white-collar workers and civil servants from northern Algeria and merchants of Kabyle origin.[6]

Doing fieldwork in the district of Aïn Sefra (with its two municipalities: Aïn Sefra and Tiout) turned out to be a wise choice for observing changes in land appropriation and tenure. Not only was the town, historically, an important centre in the former French Southern Territories, but the district also lies in one of the largest steppe-like provinces in Algeria. Most importantly, the issues of the APFA, land development, pastoralism and urban expansion are all relevant locally.

Implementation of the APFA in Aïn Sefra (Naâma Province)

In 2002, almost 20 years after the promulgation of the APFA, 13,762.4 ha of the land in Naâma Province (less than 1% of the agro-pastoral land) had been attributed under the APFA to 4,920 beneficiaries in the province. The province's total surface area is 29,514 km^2 (100ha = 1 km^2), three-quarters of it (22,034.6 km^2) being set aside for farming (both agriculture and livestock). In 2002, the agricultural area used was only 20,495 ha, around 1% of the agricultural land; grass and rangeland covered the remaining 99% of the 22,034.6 km.^{2}

According to the report of the Agricultural Services subdivision in the Aïn Sefra district in 2008, when the APFA programme was suspended, 2,327 persons had benefitted from the programme: 1,648 in the municipality of Aïn Sefra and 679 in Tiout. In 2008, 490 applications (399 in Aïn Sefra, 91 in Tiout) for land grants with tenure were accepted, 105 (75 in Aïn Sefra, 30 in Tiout) were refused, and 81 (54 in Aïn Sefra, 27 in Tiout) were applications being renewed for a five-year period (from persons who had already received land for a five-year period

5 In Aïn Sefra, a locality now called Moulay Hachemi bore the name "Negro Village" during the colonial period. Only black people lived there. Since Independence, other groups have settled there.

6 On the social and anthropological composition of the population, see Ben Hounet (2009a).

but had not achieved the objectives agreed under the first application). In the same year, 2008, there were 711 (577 in Aïn Sefra, 134 in Tiout) beneficiaries whose agreements had run for less than five years (whose development had not yet been valued).

By 2008, there had been in the municipality of Aïn Sefra 1,648 beneficiaries, and 285 refusals (of persons who, having received land grants in 2003 or before, had not been able to develop the land by the end of the five-year period). In summary, approximately 83% of the applicants under the APFA had obtained the title deeds to the land at the end of the five-year period, and approximately 17% had failed.

On the suspension of the APFA programme (for reasons already pointed out), a few disputes were left unsettled, concerning the attribution of farming plots, and mainly related to the assessment of the land development achieved at the end of the five-year period. The transfer of property rights to agricultural land encountered practical difficulties in pastoral areas: bureaucratic procedures (often arbitrary) slowed down or even prevented the granting of deeds to certain applicants (while favouring others); and there were also conflicts about the use of rights on rangelands. Clearly, it was less difficult to acquire ownership of agricultural land when it was part of the applicant's clan's traditional territory (*'aqīla, farqa*) and when the applicant had the means (economic and social capital) to develop it. It was apparently more complicated when the applicant did not belong to the clan who traditionally used the territory – despite the law in force and the state's promotion of land development.

During 2011 and 2012 (at the time of my fieldwork), after the APFA's suspension, the various administrations involved in the development of agricultural land were the district offices of the Departments of State-held Lands, of Agriculture and of Water Resources, not forgetting the two municipalities and the district of Aïn Sefra. They were still following up on cases under the APFA that had not yet reached the end of the five-year period.

Officials in these Departments confirmed that the APFA had boosted agriculture in the district, which was a primary objective of the law. However, there were inadequacies. Some applicants, once they had been granted a deed, no longer developed the land, even though the government had assisted them (by drilling wells and providing rural housing and agricultural equipment). Some of them had even abandoned their land; others were letting their land to tenants or had sold it for various activities, or had simply kept the house there as a secondary residence. Once the deed of title to the land had been granted, the new proprietors were not legally compelled in any way to pursue the development of their land or to produce agricultural crops. Furthermore, land had been granted to persons who had neither the means nor the know-how to develop their land satisfactorily. Lastly, some of the land granted under the APFA was simply not suitable for agriculture (because of lack of water, poor soil, etc.).

Several persons working in the district offices of these Departments were dubious about the APFA's success. They pointed out that less than half of the land granted had been satisfactorily (and lastingly) developed. As for the new law on land, some of these officials said that the law was not the key. In the words of an employee of the Agriculture Department:

> We found it hard to make people work on the land that they were going to own. But the situation is not any better with the new law. We must put ourselves in their shoes: why work land that is not mine and that I'll never own? Property is not an empty word (*melk haja*).

According to an inspector from the district's Department of State-owned Lands (interviewed in March 2011), most of these cases involved herdsmen, who, according to him, did not have the necessary agricultural know-how, unlike people from traditional villages (*qṣūr*) in the district who were "used" to tending gardens and had acquired practical experience, on which they could build to meet the development requirements of the APFA programme. This dualistic vision, frequent in the region, of farming versus herding, sets people from the *qṣūr* at odds with nomads on the basis of a social division of labour. It is, however, simplistic, since it does not take into account the fact that some people have changed status, or that the division of labour as it now exists in the district is complex. I would add that the State-owned Lands inspector himself came from a *qṣūr*. I have met farmers from these villages who, for want of know-how and time, joined up with people who came from other environments and did have some agricultural know-how.

As for the beneficiaries interviewed, many of them mentioned the difficulty of producing agricultural crops in the long term and the lack of aid and advice on farming in a steppe-like environment. The land grants made in the context of the APFA thus provided interested parties with the opportunity to obtain individual deeds to land that, while long considered to be jointly-owned grazing lands (called *ʿarsh*), had later become state property. However, the objective of increasing agricultural production had not been achieved.

The implementation of the APFA on the outskirts of Aïn Sefra blocked the expansion of the municipality westwards, in particular along the Dzira oued (river). The implementation of the APFA was bound to spawn lawsuits and disputes over ownership of the land and owners' rights, for reasons we shall now examine. Analysing these disputes can help us detect the normative systems that come into play: how various parties invoke rules and norms, how and why legal proceedings are initiated, and how the authorities (judiciary or administrative) who apply the law intervene.

Conflicts and Forms of Dispute Settlement

The district services in charge of the APFA had to manage a few conflicts over the application of the law (particularly between proprietors and herdsmen), but very few cases were brought to court – to my knowledge, only four (including two brought by the same plaintiff) before the court (*maḥkama*) in Aïn Sefra. Most disputes were settled by the people involved, with or without the mediation of the Departments in charge of the APFA. I discuss below a dispute settlement of this sort, and two cases brought to court. These examples illustrate potential conflicts and ways of settling them.

The first dispute was settled in December 2011 by the district services in charge of the APFA (see the records in the Appendix). A semi-nomadic herdsman was in conflict with a beneficiary of APFA in the locality of El Hammar; the former complained that the boundary of the other's field prevented him from reaching watering holes. The district services decided to make a 60 m-wide trail to the watering hole to facilitate the herdsman. Besides being profitable to the parties concerned (since the dispute was settled out of court), this sort of amicable settlement reduces the number of legal problems and complications associated with the local implementation of a national programme. The district administrative services were responsible not only for applying the APFA locally but also for making it a success: for the Department heads, any lawsuit represented a failure for which they were partly responsible and which they must report. As a consequence, several cases were settled by the district-level services in charge of the APFA.

We should not forget that many staff in these services come from the district or nearby, and often know personally the people involved in disputes. Negotiations involve people with similar (local) origins but different concerns, owing to their positions. Staff from the State-owned Lands Department (which is under the Ministry of Finance) or the Agriculture Service will have different concerns again. Given this proximity to the parties involved, district officials cited their moral sense of duty, responsibility or empathy to justify their involvement and their tendency to seek amicable settlements of such disputes.[7]

7 Many conflicts concern poorly-marked boundaries. To deal with disputes of this sort, provincial authorities have, since 2010, advised using GPS for surveys and delimitating the properties.

The second (double) lawsuit from a (single) plaintiff concerned a field that receives rain, in the locality of El Euch. It had been granted to B.M., about 10 km to the north of the municipality of Aïn Sefra. Though not the legal owner of the field, B.M, a very old man, had had the plot as a concession since the 1940s. He had started working the land (approximately 60 ha in the 1940s) under an operating permit. The land was re-attributed to him in 1963 (immediately after Independence). He farmed 40 ha till 1970, while paying ground rent to the State-owned Lands Department. Under the agrarian reform measures the concession had to be used as rangeland, and B.M. was not allowed to plough from 1975 to 1980. He then resumed farming (various cereals) without authorisation. He cleared the land, 10-15 ha at a time, for almost ten years.

Two people, first (in 2003) his nephew and then (in 2005) someone else, filed applications under the APFA for the fields previously allocated to B.M. and thus acquired the land. B.M. pressed charges against them. His first complaint, against his nephew, was rejected in 2004. His request to have "his lands" returned to him was turned down after a legal inquiry. B.M. then filed a suit (in November 2003), again before the investigating magistrate (in March 2004), but in vain. The tribunal of Aïn Sefra was in the process of handling the second case in 2012. As in the first case, B.M's complaint will probably be turned down.

It should be pointed out that, during the colonial period, ploughing permits could be revoked. Since, by virtue of Act 90-25 of 18 November 1990, collective grazing lands (*ʿarsh*) became state property, B.M. was never able to acquire a deed of title to the land he was farming. As a consequence, his complaints were always rejected. During my interview with him, he was unable to understand the bureaucratic rationale, which was based on written title to the land. On several occasions, he brought up how he had used the land over the years, having farmed it since the 1940s. He thought he was in the right and that the land was his since he had ploughed it for so long. He often added that people in the area knew that this land "belonged to him", the right stemming from using the land for so long overriding any new legislation (the APFA). Why, then, did he decide to take legal action when he had been told that it was very unlikely that the court would decide in his favour? For him, it was "a matter of principle". Although his lawyer had warned him that his complaints would probably be rejected, he adamantly insisted on legal action to demonstrate his disagreement, regardless of the ruling.

The third case presents another way of seeking justice. The dispute set at odds a doctor, who lived in the municipality of Aïn Sefra, and pastoral families who have now pitched tent near the locality of El Euch, about 10 km north of the municipality. In 2008, the doctor obtained a grant of five hectares under the APFA; the APFA anticipated that the land, located on a trail used by herdsmen, was to be developed by 2013. It had been cordoned off in March 2011 so that it could be developed. The herdsmen then realised that their tents were one kilometre from the boundary, and that the latter cut off their herds' route to grasslands in the south. After a verbal exchange with the doctor, the herdsmen reported the situation to the police. The police checked the claims and, once the doctor had proved his claim under the APFA, they asked the herdsmen to leave the land. Approximately fifteen herdsmen later returned to see the grantee, and argued with him. The police intervened and, once more, asked the herdsmen to leave. The herdsmen took the dispute to the head of the district. Having checked the claims, he told the herdsmen that the beneficiary of the APFA land was indeed in possession of valid documents, and was within his rights. The party that brought the action to court for acts of aggression and vandalism was the doctor. He claimed that the herdsmen had uprooted some of what he had planted, specifically a tree, and had caused material damage. According to the herdsmen, there was nothing on the land; and the motive for the accusation was to establish mitigating circumstances for leaving the land abandoned. The case was brought to court in Aïn Sefra in April/May 2011. The plaintiff and nine herdsmen were summoned to court. The judge's decision was *barā'a* (a declaration of innocence and the release of both parties) and that the case should be closed.

During interviews, the herdsmen told me how discouraged they were by their appeals to the administration to defend their position. They emphasised the growing number of APFA-related disputes in the district, and stressed how hard it was to prove their case in court. Since judges, like the police and local officials, mainly consulted the administration's paperwork, and the customary practices of herdsmen (based on oral traditions) were not recognised by the administrative departments. These herdsmen considered the justice system to be biased against them in APFA-related cases.

As we can see from the disputes under consideration, an amicable settlement was preferred both by the parties involved and by the administrations in charge of the APFA. This is why few cases came to court. The administration had adopted a legal rationale, based on written documents (title deeds to the land, even before Independence); but this came into conflict with arguments based on "rights to the land" by virtue of use or of customary practices, and the needs related to pastoralism. The study of these disputes enables us to see how these different normative systems are invoked in cases of land tenure. Although there is a tendency to adapt the APFA to the local reality of pastoralism, and to settle conflicts out of court, when a dispute *is* brought to court, the grounds of a decision are the legally authenticated (administrative, judicial) documents. Herdsmen, like others who "use" the land, are aware of this and try various ways to defend their rights to use the land: amicable agreements, appeals to the authorities, and legal action.

Conclusion

Property, although of paramount importance for an economy, cannot be reduced to its economic aspect; it is multifunctional (von Benda-Beckmann, von Benda Beckmann and Wiber, 2006: 2-3). It is a factor in forging the identity of individuals and groups. As von Benda-Beckmann, von Benda-Beckmann and Wiber have pointed out, a variety of ideologies and legal arrangements, which refer to different sources of legitimacy, coexist in many modern states when it comes to property rights. This is certainly the case with land tenure under the APFA in the steppe-like and Saharan areas of Algeria. The implementation of the APFA has had an impact on the identities of individuals and groups, and on relations between them, especially between "new farmers" on granted land and herdsmen. Land tenure has long been associated with sedentary groups. New lines of tension have arisen on the steppelands, particularly those close to the municipality of Aïn Sefra, where most of the APFA applications were filed. People tended to ask for land there because of the proximity of the town, and the road networks. To implement the APFA and settle the conflicts arising, several institutions were involved, each with its own understanding of property rights. I have mentioned the services in charge of the APFA: the municipality, the district and administrative departments (Agriculture, State-owned Lands, Water Resources) as well as the police and the courts. But non-official institutions were also involved in settling disputes, particularly the elders (*kbār*) of lineages, especially among the herdsmen (Ben Hounet 2010a, 2010b).

As the example of the APFA shows, ideas about property rights changed not only at the level of the state, but also on the ground, particularly during the implementation of this national programme. As pointed out, the APFA already signalled a switch by the state in favour of private property, in contrast with previous policies of nationalisation. The recent programme of granting concessions is evidence of further changes in the underlying ideology, this time favouring a profit-seeking and managerial rationale in the development of agricultural land and resources. Locally, the implementation of the APFA transforms the ideologies and normative systems referred to. For example, what the inspector from the district's State-owned Lands Department said about the difference between people from the *qṣūr* and people of nomadic origin changed between the first interview in March 2011 and the last one in September 2012.

The increasing amount of granted land under the APFA and the difficulty that herdsmen have defending their cases and viewpoints before the administrations and the courts in Aïn Sefra, results in an increase in the state's legislative authority when compared with customary pastoral practices, which themselves are changing (Ben Hounet, 2009b). The herdsmen interviewed seemed to have understood this without challenging the decisions made by administrative officials. However, many herdsmen have also benefitted from grants under the APFA (Ben Hounet, 2009b). Those whose pastoral practices are somewhat restricted by the farmed plots granted under the APFA endeavour to find amicable settlements, as in the case cited, or to circumvent the plots and even, possibly, the law.

References

Ageron, Charles Robert. 1979. *Histoire de l'Algérie contemporaine: De l'insurrection de 1871 au déclenchement de la guerre d'Algérie (1954)*, vol. 2. Paris: Presses Universitaires de France.

Bedrani, Slimane, Sofiane Benadjila and Meriem Ghazi. 1995. "Contribution à la connaissance des zones steppiques algériennes: Les résultats du suivi triennal d'agropasteurs de la steppe centrale", *Cahiers du Centre de Recherche en Economie Appliquée et pour le Développement* (Algiers) 38: 11-46.

Belhimer, Ammar. 2012. "Le régime juridique de la propriété foncière en Algérie", *Les Programmes du Centre Jacques Berque* 1: 1-16. <http://www.cjb.ma/component/k2/item/2299-les-programmes-du-cjb-n-1.html> (accessed 17 August 2017).

Ben Hounet, Yazid. 2009a. *L'Algérie des tribus: Le fait tribal dans le Haut Sud-Ouest contemporain* (Connaissances des Homes). Paris: Editions L'Harmattan, Collection.

Ben Hounet, Yazid. 2009b. "Le poids du nomadisme dans les steppes algériennes", *Etudes Rurales* 184: 107122

Ben Hounet, Yazid. 2010a, "La tribu comme champ social semi autonome", *L'Homme* 194 (April-June): 57-74.

Ben Hounet, Yazid. 2010b. "La *diya* (prix du sang): Gestion sociale de la violence et logiques sacrificielles en Algérie (Sud-Oranais)", *Annales de la Fondation Fyssen* 24: 196-215.

Ben Hounet, Yazid, Barbara Casciarri, Baudouin Dupret, François Ireton and Alice Wilson. 2011. "Pratiques de l'appropriation foncière en contexte musulman", *Transcontinentales* 10-11. <http://transcontinentales.revues.org/1275> (accessed 15 August 2017).

Bison, L. (chef d'annexe). 1957. Monographie de l'Annexe d'Ain Sefra (mise à jour au 31 décembre 1957), Ministère de l'Algérie, Territoires du Sud. Document disponible au Service Historique des Armées de Terre (SHAT), Vincennes.

Boukhobza, M'hamed. 1989. "Société nomade et État en Algérie", *Politique Africaine* 34: 7-18.

Daumas, Paul. 1912. *Les populations indigènes et la terre collective de tribu en Tunisie.* Tunis: Borrel.

de Montety. Henri. 1927. *Une loi agraire en Tunisie.* Cahors: Imprimerie de Coueslant.

Denoix, Sylvie. 1996. "Introduction: Formes juridiques, enjeux sociaux et stratégies foncières", *Revue du Monde Musulman et de la Méditerranée* 79-80: 9-22.

Guignard, Didier. 2010. "Conservatoire ou révolutionnaire? Le sénatus-consulte de 1863 appliqué au régime foncier d'Algérie", *Revue d'Histoire du XIXe Siècle* 41: 81-95.

Lehuraux, Léon. 1931. *Le nomadisme et la colonisation dans les Hauts Plateaux de l'Algérie.* Paris: Éditions du Comité de l'Afrique Française.

Marx, Karl. 1970. "Le système foncier en Algérie (extraits du cahier de notes sur les sociétés pré capitalistes, datant de 1879 environ)", *Cahiers du CERM.* Paris: Éditions Sociales.

Mesnier (Capitaine). 1914. *Monographie du Territoire d'Aïn Sefra.* Oran: Imprimerie L. Fouque.

Pouyanne, Maurice. 1900. *La propriété foncière en Algérie.* Algiers: Adolphe Jourdan.

Sari, Djillali. 1978. *La dépossession des fellahs.* Algiers: SNED.

Vatin, Jean-Claude. 1983. *L'Algérie politique: Histoire et société.* Paris: Presse de la Fondation Nationale des Sciences Politiques.

von Benda-Beckmann Frantz, Keebet von Benda-Beckmann and Melanie Wiber. 2006. "The Properties of Property", in *Changing the Properties of Property*, ed. F. von Benda-Beckmann, K. von Benda-Beckmann and M. Wiber. New York: Berghahn, pp. 1-39.

Wilson, Alice. 2010. "Anthropological Studies of Land Tenure in Muslim Settings", *Les Programmes du Centre Jacques Berque* 2: 1-18. www.cjb.ma/images/stories/Programme_02_Wilson.pdf (accessed 17 August 2017).

Appendix (translated from Arabic)

People's Democratic Republic of Algeria. Visit report

On this day, corresponding to 13 December of the year 2011, the *ad hoc* commission went to the area called "El Hammar" further to a complaint filed by the herdsman Z.B. regarding a trail.
We
— B.M, representing the Subdivision of the Agricultural Services
— R.B., representing the Municipality of Aïn Sefra
— D.A, representing the Department of State-owned Lands
— K.A, representing the Forestry Services
have observed as follows:
Z.B. and his sons occupy the plot of agricultural land belonging to H.M. (decision No. 2096 of 16/02/2002). The herdsman Z.B. roams there with his sheep, searching for drinking water and pastures, namely along the trail reserved for herdsmen in direction of the *djebel* (mountain) called "Dir el Hairech".
T.A. began ploughing operations on the farmlands listed below:
1 – by decision No. 704 of 1994, *i.e.*, 3 hectares to the benefit of T.A.
2 – by decision No.3628 of 2004, *i.e.*, 5 hectares to the benefit of T.A.
3 – by decision No.3627 of 2004, *i.e.*, 5 hectares to the benefit of T.A.
4 – by decision No.3626 of 2004, *i.e.*, 5 hectares to the benefit of T.A.
Moreover, the interested party laid the boundaries (using a tractor) of certain plots which did not belong to him; this upset the herdsman Z.B.

After a hearing with the two parties, it appeared that the problem mostly had to do with the existence of the trail to the watering holes for sheep at the locality of Dir el Hairech.

In fine, the commission ruled to move the trail, 60 metres in width, leading to the watering holes.

Report executed on the same day, month and year.

CHAPTER 6

Anomie and the Post-Colonial State: Local Justice in the M'zab

Nejm Benessaiah

> We need religion to keep the moral order. Without it there would be chaos.
>
> FIELD NOTES, BANK MANAGER, 14 MARCH 2013, GHARDAIA.

∴

Introduction

The Mozabite Berbers (or Amazigh) of Algeria have historically managed their own affairs for over a millennium. They have resisted the overtures of the colonial and post-colonial states in their personal spheres of interest. Ibadi Islam and its interpretation through the *ittifāqāt* (agreements) and custom formed the basis of the regulation of everyday life, including land succession and the arbitration of conflicts. More recently, the Mozabite population has been integrated into the Algerian nation-state through a complex process, which I shall explore here. This integration has entailed a further complication of the ways in which (quasi-)formalised regulatory bodies interact within the hegemony of statutory law.

The Algerian judicial sphere is constituted by a plurality of systems including French law, *sharīʿa,* and customary law (Christelow, 2014: 6). How these systems interact, through individual actors, may be described in terms of a dynamic state of contested non-equilibria (Gramsci, 1977: 182), whereby the hegemony of statutory law and thus the status quo of the ruling elite is maintained in an unstable manner. Consent must therefore be continually manufactured and remade. In situations of political contestation, individual actors may be able to extend their agency by exploiting regulatory plurality to their own advantage. For example, many Mozabites tend to view Algerian civil law as illegitimate because of its French colonial origins. Others take a strategic view, and employ different laws for different purposes. This chapter investigates

 | DOI 10.1163/9789004362116_008

how the presence of multiple systems of law influences the decision-making process of disputants in Beni Isguen, central Algeria. It elucidates how this multiplicity destabilises the certainty and clear legitimacy of local authority and local ethics. Rather than becoming entangled in definitions of law, a focus on social regulatory practices may be more useful, by arguing for continuity between formal and informal ordering practices whereby norms inform rules and agreements, although new policies may also come from innovative reflection based on ethical multiplicity. In addition to such debates between actors, more powerful structures such as the French civil code, along with globalised media, ensure that structural elements play a powerful role in influencing local value systems. This play between explicit and implicit, agentive and structural processes of ethical engagement and influence contributes to recent debates regarding the encounters between ethical systems across borders, begun by Mair and Evans (2015).

People of the M'zab

The Mozabites originate primarily from the *Iznaten* (Zenete or Zenata) Berber ethnic group. The principal language of Mozabites is Tumzabt, a branch of the Berber (Tamazight) language, of the Afro-Asiatic family. I conducted research over 11 months in 2013-2014, primarily in the town of Beni Isguen, where approximately 7,000 Mozabites reside. Beni Isguen is part of a pentapolis, located in central Algeria, within the northern Saharan desert, 400 miles south of Algiers. Its inhabitants practise the faith of the Islamic Ibadi sect. The primary means of livelihood is trade, supplemented by oasis agriculture. Beni Isguen is known locally to be the most conservative of all the Mozabite *qṣūr* (Arab. plural of *qṣar*: fortified town), retaining many customs and practices such as traditional dress and religious observances. It is looked to by the other *qṣūr* of the M'zab as a source of heritage, through, for example, its reformulation of Ibadi legal codes. It is also a UNESCO World Heritage Site. The M'zab is interesting to legal anthropologists because of the doctrinal practice of spiritual *dissociation* (Arab. *barāʾa*) – from non-Ibadis and from the state – which has characterised the ideological and political position of Mozabites regarding the successive dominant political elites (including caliphs, Ottoman deys, French administrators, and so forth). The way the hegemony of the state has been resisted and utilised by various parties both as a political strategy and for ideological reasons is the object of the present discussion. Shifting views on inheritance will be presented within the context of local custom, atomisation of the family, globalisation and the media, and post-colonial encounters with French law.

"Abandoned" Oasis Lands

The present proliferation of inheritance disputes over land tenure in Beni Isguen offers a useful prism through which to view how individuals are affected by and utilise multiple legal systems at the everyday level. Despite being an abundantly productive oasis, and the Mozabite reputation for prodigious activity, many plots lie fallow.[1] In fact, Nejib, a local palm tree expert, estimates that perhaps 40% of the oasis lies in this state. These are not fallow lands in the traditional sense, however, as the land is completely barren, the soil is bare, trees (if any) are dying, and so on. These contrast with adjacent plots that remain verdant, bursting with a vibrant abundance of date palms, fruit trees and brightly coloured bougainvillea and other flowers. The local proverb that "the difference between a desert and an oasis is man" is strikingly clear here, showing how lack of maintenance rapidly results in the conversion of these human-made fruit forests into desert. In the course of my daily movements through the oasis, I observed a lot of this degraded land, sometimes with a note written in red spray paint on a door, declaring its status as "*abandonné*" (abandoned) (in French and Arabic).

How could these plots remain abandoned while farmers express their fears of urban encroachment upon arable land? I soon asked my companion, Nejib, whether the mosque or another local authority could intercede and redistribute the land to those who needed it. He replied that they could not, as the land was tied up in private lawsuits. "Before", Nejib remarked, "the surviving family head managed the land so that it remained undivided. Now everybody wants his or her share. Although they are Muslim, they deny Qur'anic law; people aren't God-fearing anymore." This statement reveals that the traditional authorities and the mosque in particular no longer retain the influence necessary to adjudicate in local disputes. Furthermore, the patriarchal institutions that previously prevented and mediated inheritance disputes and the fragmentation of family plots through succession (see also Rae, 2002: 11) are also in decline.[2] Below, I explore further the causes and ramifications of this shift in power, and ask whether it really entails a sense of anomie, or something

1 Unfortunately, many oases in Algeria, especially those not converted to modern-style monoculture and mechanistic techniques, are in a state of decline for a variety of reasons, outmigration playing a large part. This is not the primary reason for land abandonment in Beni Isguen, however, as I argue elsewhere (Benessaiah, 2015).

2 Family plots tend to shrink over time, for with any more than a single offspring per generation, property must be divided between them (three to five offspring per family was common in the M'zab). This problem was solved in the past through the management of the collective family property by the male family head through his authoritarian status.

different. Before exploring the reasons for these changes in the M'zab, I shall first describe how social institutions in the valley were organised historically.

Historical Forms of Social Control

A variety of formal and informal institutions regulated Mozabite life. They were largely based on religious ideas of piety, that is, how to be a good Muslim, but they also served practical functions, dictated by a dense population. Local Berber norms were implicitly mixed with idealised, openly debated scriptural moral forms. Historically, unsanctioned behaviour was formally punished through *tabrī'a* (excommunication) by the *ʿazzāba* (clerics), who effectively ruled as a theocracy. *Tabrī'a* simultaneously shamed the offending individual and reinforced the moral norms of society, as the culprit had to confess and ask for forgiveness at each Friday prayer in front of the entire community until he or she was pardoned. In a discussion on Mozabite *qanūn* (laws) in the late nineteenth century, Émile Masqueray described the powerful *ʿazzāba* clerics as "masters of conscience through confession, alone able to repress crimes through banishment, presidents of all meetings, custodians of all contracts, severe guardians of morality and old customs" (Masqueray, 1878: 215, my translation from the French). Yet the clerics were also seen as wise and fair judges, and even the local Arabs wished to be judged by them. Punishment given by the *ʿazzāba* could take the form of banishment, compensation, public penance, prison or baton blows (Masqueray, 1878: 225).

Judgements were made through a reading of the primary and secondary religious texts, as clarified by Pierre Bourdieu (1962: 42-43), in reference to:

> the law of the Koran and according to the *ittifāqāt,* the written compilation of Mozabite customs. These *ittifāqāt*, which can be modified at any time to settle current problems, but which are always interpreted by reference to religious jurisprudence, govern political life as well as private morals and provide for archaic but very formidable punishments.

Beyond the usual crimes of theft, adultery, violence and murder, the breaking of cultural taboos was also punishable; these included use of alcohol, tobacco and coffee, breaking marriage customs such as the amount of allowable dowry, playing music and dancing, and so on (Bourdieu, 1962: 47; for detailed categories of offences and punishments, see Amat, 1888: 47-50). The *ʿazzāba* had another powerful deterrent at their disposal: the withdrawal of religious services. This meant no prayers would be held, and bodies would not be washed upon death to prepare for burial.

Over time, the *ayyen* (a secular council, similar to the *djemʿaa*) gradually gained power and independence from the *ʿazzāba*'s supervision (Bourdieu

1962; Bennoune, 1986), and is now integrated into the regional bureaucratic framework of the national government, although the clerics retains considerable moral influence. Today the use of *tabrīʾa* as punishment is virtually non-existent, yet the moral weight of normative behaviour is strong, and so a sort of informal *tabrīʾa* exists, such that those perceived to be immoral are simply avoided. In this manner, formal cultural measures may be said to have morphed rather than declined; they are maintained through informal practices in Mozabite society.

Formalised codes and practices were conventionally reinforced by informal norms. Punishment was pre-empted, for example, through what I term *social visibility*, that is, the visibility of acts to others in intimately familiar settings, which obliges individuals to regulate themselves passively. Formalised monitoring was maintained throughout the outdoor spaces by *el-oumna* (officials who regulate irrigation, building work and so on, sanctioned through the mosque), and within the domestic sphere by mothers-in-law and networks of gossip (Farrag, 1971). Indeed, while the fear of punishment in the next life is perhaps greater than fear of punishment in this, the normative aspect of social life arguably provides an even stronger constraint: the fear of diminishing one's family honour and one's standing in society. In such a relatively small, face-to-face society, an individual's actions always require a broader consideration of their social consequences than in more complex, anonymous societies. The potential stigma of social shame due to anti-social or immoral behaviour by a family member is an extremely powerful prophylactic. Hence, prevention as well as punishment begins at home. While I do not contend that such practices should be included within a definition of law as such, they do constitute a legitimate focus of study for legal anthropologists within a broader framework of regulation.

Islamic Land Tenure Law

In solving issues related to property, local authorities are guided by a particular interpretation of Islamic law. However, Mozabites often challenge such rulings. Hamza, another palm tree specialist, describes how *sharīʾa* is contested in everyday situations:

> The entire Islamic world shares inheritance laws of all private belongings, *mulk*. For example, if you have a shop, it will be sold and divided into equal parts, or half for a woman. Alternatively, if it runs well and makes a good profit, one of them may run it, and give a share of the proceeds to the others. Nevertheless, often people contest the divisions, claiming that one is worth more than the other. This causes them to be stuck in litiga-

> tion, even on to the next generation. This is not good; they should be divided straight away. Alternatively, a father may leave a will, but should not give a favoured son more.

The application of jurisprudence then, must attempt to apply the *sharīʿa* to everyday realities, since the Qur'an determines proper usage and succession of land according to certain categories. However, Hamza is pointing to a general reason why inheritance may be contested, which I shall return to later. First, it would be helpful to give a definition of Islamic land tenure (from Forni, 2003):

> Land tenure can be defined as the group of rights of individuals, households or communities with respect to land. Water also can be accessed under different types of rights. Tenure includes not only property rights, but also use rights, of a permanent or seasonal nature. A tenure system may include rights sanctioned both by law and by custom. That is, alongside the formal legal systems, following defined administrative procedures, there also exist customary rules accepted by the majority of users.

Land ownership in the Islamic world is generally classified into four categories: 1) private land, *mulk*, in which one has full rights of ownership, alienation and usufruct; 2) state land, *mīrī*, where the state provides usufruct, codified during the Ottoman period (lan\d code of 1858) to counter the power of large landholders; 3) public land, *waqf* (or sometimes *hābūs* in North Africa) which is inalienable, usually for charitable use; and 4) so-called "dead' land, *mawāt*, often used for communal grazing, and a political "grey area" (Rae, 2002: 7-9). Land and water tenure are governed today through a legal plurality combining *sharīʿa*, customary "law" or *ʿurf*, and national statutory law. I describe below how these "laws" interact through litigants, prosecutors and judges.

In the Beni Isguen oasis, most of these land categories are in use, with the majority being in private ownership. The riverbeds are communally owned, and those who cannot afford land may plant date palms there, which then become privately owned. This is in accordance with the local Islamic interpretation, namely that water that is not held in artificially made constructions is communal property.

Finally, as indicated in Hamza's statement, there is the notion of joint land management and conversely – an important source of dispute – that one share may be (perceived to be) worth more than others. For instance, although a plot of land may be divided equally according to land surface, one of the divisions might contain a dwelling, making it more desirable. This clearly presents a difficult situation, and one solution is to sell the whole property and divide the proceeds. Such disputes have increased in number as a result of notions of shifting or multiple centres of authority. Before returning to this point, I describe below in more detail the local customary "laws", or *ʿurf*, upon which dispute settlement is based, and how these intersect with *sharīʿa*.

Customary Law, *ʿUrf*, and Dispute in the M'zab

Local disputes were historically resolved according to *ʿurf* (similar to *ʿāda* in Central Asia), or customary "law", consisting of encoded verbal rules or agreements.[3] Nejib explained *ʿurf* and its relation to *sharīʿa* by means of a story:

> One day the Prophet Mohammed saw a man pollinating a palm tree and said, "Why are you doing that? You should leave it alone to pollinate naturally by the wind." The man did as he was told, and at harvest season the production of dates was very poor. When the Prophet learned of this, he exclaimed, "Indeed, there are some things which I do not know, and different regions have their own specificities, with their own ways and laws not covered in the Holy Qur'an. For this there is *ʿurf*."

This example reveals the interaction between pre-Islamic local custom, and *sharīʿa*. Sartori and Shahar (2012: 648) describe the relationship of *ʿurf* to *sharīʿa* thus:

> The sharp distinction between Islamic law and *ʿurf* / *ʿāda*, taken for granted by Western students of Islamic law for decades, has been challenged in recent years by scholars who emphasised the fuzzy boundaries between *sharīʿa* and custom. In particular, anthropologists studying the socio-legal sphere in Muslim societies have contended that Muslim laymen hardly make a distinction between *sharīʿa* and custom in their everyday lives. It appears that jurists, too, have been tolerant towards custom and have viewed it as perfectly Islamic, as long as it does not violate Qur'anic prescriptions.

---

3 Some opponents of legal pluralism have argued that customary law is largely a colonial invention (e.g. Ranger et al., 1997). While in many ways this statement contains much truth, especially in the codification of custom in written form, it is also demonstrable that *ʿurf* has pre-colonial origins (Scheele, 2008).

This was indeed the case in Beni Isguen, where judges appeared to accommodate custom when it was fitting, and did not contradict *sharīʿa*. Sartori and Shahar (2012: 649) go on to note, however, that Islamic jurists:

> have perceived these as two distinct normative orders, and it is precisely this distinctiveness that enabled them to interrogate the relations between Islamic law and custom and discuss the circumstances under which law-abiding Muslims are allowed to act in accordance with local customs. Apparently, the fuzzy boundaries between *sharīʿa* and *ʿurf* in daily life made it all the more necessary for jurists to distinguish between them at the doctrinal and discursive levels.

In the past, people usually attempted to resolve disputes locally before they escalated through a variety of mediators and arbitrators. Indeed, these intermediaries were necessary, for access to limited resources, not to mention densely occupied living spaces and intense heat, can frequently give rise to quarrels.[4] I once witnessed a disagreement over building on a footpath. The responsible party claimed that it was public property and thus free to use, while his neighbour claimed that the path, adjacent to his land, was in fact his property. This dispute was probably resolved informally and quite simply by consultation with a Mozabite expert on property use, as private and public usage have clear precedents related to the *ittifāqāt* and *sharīʿa* as described above.

I was informed that, before taking disputes before the *ʿazzāba* for ruling, people usually tried to diffuse problems by appealing to family members. For example, if an individual felt wronged by someone, they might trust the moral authority of the offender's family to persuade him to act otherwise. If this first port of call failed, then an appeal would be made to the *ʿashīra*, the clan council, to compel the parties to resolve their problems equitably. If this also failed, then the clerics, whose elevated social standing usually gave them the necessary gravitas to compel a solution would judge the problem. Religious experts might also consult them if the problem contained ambiguities necessitating debate. The formal approach of the *ʿazzāba* was thus:

4 Historically, disputes took place between individuals, clans (or *ṣafs*) or even whole towns, often leading to violent conflict, which, according to Roberts (2002), inspired theorists such as Masqueray (1886) to conceive of ideas of segmentation that led to Durkheim's (1984) mechanical society and later formulations by Evans-Prichard (1940) and Gellner (1969).

1. Look for the rule in the Qur'an. If not then,
2. Look for it in the Hadith, the sayings of the Prophet. If not there, then,
3. Look for similar examples in the Qur'an and try to weigh up the pros and cons for the people. If not there, then,
4. Look to *'urf*, customary law. If not,
5. Look to civil law.

Today, the dispute resolution process is more complicated. While many Mozabites prefer to solve problems locally, some revert to civil law. This practice, Nejib exclaimed, inverted the correct order of things. Using the metaphor of a house, he claimed that "You can't build a house from the top. You have to start with the foundations, the local layers. The customary and civil law should be complementary, yet [here] they are inverted." Direct recourse to civil law, he suggested, inverted the right order of things, insinuating that state law unnecessarily overcomplicated issues that could be dealt with locally. Furthermore, Nejib argued that local institutions are better geared toward local problems, as they can find culturally sensitive, tailor-made solutions, whereas the state tends to offer one-size-fits-all policies. Nevertheless, certain local parties, tired of the limitations and laboriousness of local processes, have opted to circumvent these by appealing directly to the state, as we shall see.

'Urf in the Everyday

How does *'urf* guide the decision-making of specialists? The ethical underpinnings of *'urf* are such that they commonly protect the sanctity of the family over business interests. For example, if a bakery is opened next to a family residence and it makes a disturbance (as bakeries usually begin work early in the morning), then the family has the right to demand that the bakery move. I was curious as to how decisions were reached and how new applications of *'urf* were made, and it became clear that consultation was a key part. As Nejib expounded:

> The Qu'ran has allowed customary law to be applied to deal with particulars of a situation; it says "Apply the legality and the right custom." People try a new law for a decade or so, and consult people as to its efficacy and worth. Custom is the accumulation of experience over time. Another example is *shafa'a*: if you sell a house, you must ask your neighbours, otherwise they can cut in on the contract [right of pre-emption]. This is for conserving community. Yet another example of *'urf* is where in the past, all neighbours around a well would give up a piece of land around it including the space for the animal to pull the line. Now neighbours "steal"

> that land as they have electricity [for pumps]. However, it is collective land. The Algerian law does not know about these things, so there is conflict. There is a French hangover of rules from that time. They have updated their rules; however, here we have not. Such rules are adapted to French and European customs and geography, not ours. Another example is that custom stipulates that houses cannot be built higher than others, for access to sunlight, but now people go to *al-hukūma* [local government] and they say you can build as high as you like. People can say nothing. In addition, they may put windows, but this is *haram. L'oumna* [the water guards] in the past would have said, "Close it." If the perpetrators did not listen to these words, then the issue would be taken to the *ʿashīra*; at that time people were very afraid of this authority. People respected these institutions then; there was solidarity. France broke everything. People say, "A bad agreement is better than going to court."

Today, new voluntary associations appear to be taking up the mantle of local governance, with the recent opening-up of civil society in the Algerian political sphere. These associations take collective action based on mutual agreement around common interests. The problem of how to prevent or punish broken agreements without the force of locally recognised sanctions remains, however (Benessaiah and Shaffer, forthcoming).

From these examples, it is clear that the influence of local institutions has been waning for some time because, as some people put it, people are "not God fearing", or "because the French took the power away". In issues such as divorce, people still prefer to consult the customary authorities. Furthermore, my interlocutors often tried to keep women away from the courts, preferring to deal with such disputes locally (although I observed that this was not always the case).

Atomisation of the Extended Family

Today, social norms and rules dictating land succession and management are less clear-cut or have less weight than formerly, and are actively contested in national courts. The cultural institution of the family once protected inherited land from dwindling into ever-smaller plots by succession, through the management and redistribution of resources by the patriarch. His authority effectively prevented or lessened inheritance disputes. I have investigated how this institution has been socially reproduced and what caused its decline in Mozabite society today:

> On a cool winter's day, Bessem and Nejib visit us for dinner. Once again, I enquire into how the problem of inheritance has been managed so as not to continually diminish the date palm gardens. Bessem replies, "In the past, families operated like Christian families, with one son managing the garden, one professor, one doctor, two practising commerce in the north, and one imam or lawyer. The two tradesmen would invest some money in the palm grove, and everyone would get their share of dates or from the sale of dates. However, sometimes, and more regularly now, one would complain of not having an equal income and would demand their share. Then the family would either buy their part, or sell part of the palm grove, dividing it into a smaller size, or even sell the whole plot and divide it." (Field notes, 25 December 2012)

The conversation referred to above describes how, historically, resources such as land tended to be managed in common, presided over by the head of the household (see Crawford, 2008: 15, for a comparison with the Moroccan context). Bessem pointed out that families, as in medieval Europe, once operated as microcosms of society, in that sons would actively choose different careers, such as priests, lawyers, teachers, soldiers and farmers, so that each could draw on the benefits of the various social, economic and political fields for the overall prosperity of the family. The proceeds of each, such as the seasonal produce of the land, would be shared roughly equally among members.[5] This arrangement no longer seems to be prevalent.

Recently, a certain atomisation has been taking place in Mozabite society, dissolving these microcosms and the redistribution that took place through them. As noted by Amina Farrag (1971), this drive to small, atomised families is most probably related to the ability of wealthier individuals to break away and set up independent households, instead of being forced to wait for the patriarch to die in order to inherit and finally gain authority, as in poorer Berber communities, such as in Highland Morocco (Crawford, 2008: 15). As one individual maintained, this can be exacerbated further by individuals from outside the family, such as a spouse, wishing to make a claim. Certain factors, analysed below, have caused family members to cease to acquiesce to the ascendancy of the older male, especially after the death of the father, and to seek instead the monetary value of their share of the communal resources.

---

5 Bessem indicated that the local radical Mozabite thinker, Abderrahmane Hadj-Nacer (2011), influenced him in coming to this understanding regarding extended household management.

The desire for money rather than shares in family land is often motivated by the emerging value placed on privacy. In breaking off and starting their own households, young wealthy families avoid the "social gaze" and thus the normative modes of conduct imposed by "social visibility". Their new and independent houses are enclosed within walls that serve as an effective barrier to this mechanism of social control in the M'zab. Walls are more prevalent in Mozabite oases than in others I have encountered in North Africa, and they are erected and maintained according to local norms regarding the privacy of the family. Thus, new norms of privacy may be seen to be offsetting conventional, informal systems of control through visibility and the social gaze, for even Farrag's mothers-in-law cannot see inside independent households. It is the wealthy who are most able to afford such walls. Thus, class and access to social capital creates difference, with the wealthy being able to eschew traditional normative practices, while the working class remain more tightly bound within the social gaze.

Regarding the reallocation of property following a death, paradoxically, despite the Ibadi (and indeed wider Amazigh) doctrine of equality, newly held notions of *individual* equality may explain the downfall of family oasis plots. This paradox can be explained, however, if one understands that notional equality applies to household heads, but in practice a hierarchy of age and gender exists *within* households (Crawford, 2008: 12). While hierarchy between generations still exists, it appears that equality is sought between siblings. Thus, the eldest sibling is no longer the most important, and is no longer able to take on the mantle of "patriarch" of the family household. It appears likely that notions of individual rights have increased with the uptake of statutory law to resolve disputes, and with the emphasis on private property and the individual as values that may challenge those of communal ownership and the group. In this, we see a direct challenge to values that have helped maintain and reproduce the Mozabite hierarchical status quo. These new values have arguably been slipping into the Mozabite worldview through engagement with the state judicial system, for such ethical norms are embedded in the "Western" liberal values underpinning the French legal codes.

This is what Bourdieu (1961: 84) has argued in his claim that, in Algeria, atomisation was driven by the promotion of private property by French laws (see also Fowler, 1997: 15). Of course, family-managed farms were already privately owned, but Bourdieu seems to be arguing that with privatisation came a "modern", individualistic ethos, perhaps alongside this emphasis on individual rights. Following Fuller's (1994) assertion that it would be more fruitful to investigate the meeting of value systems than to counterpose "legal systems", I shall explore next how local values may have been affected by the rise of the global media in the M'zab.

Globalisation and Changing Values

Since the 1960s, anthropologists have paid more attention to the embeddedness of the societies they study within global scales of colonial disruption and the effects of world markets (whilst revealing the particularity of each case and the local meanings of these global processes), rather than studying them in isolation. The Mozabites, on the one hand, actively sought such separation from the wider world, not entirely unlike a monastic order, in order to practise their faith in solitude. The limited capacity of their desert environmental resources, however, along with an expanding population, forced the Mozabites to take up alternative means of livelihood such as trade. In this they became extremely successful, playing an influential role in financing the great Saharan trade routes that crossed the Ghardaia region. It was feared, however, that men travelling away from the valley would become polluted by contact with other lifeworlds. Bourdieu (1962: 40) claims that the men returning underwent a process of ritual purification on their return. As men were seen as being at risk through contact with the non-Ibadi Other, they were expected to practise spiritual *dissociation* from them, while maintaining the compact of *el-amena*, faithfulness, to the community, and to their families. This meant that in many ways, Mozabite women had more autonomy in the M'zab, because they had to take care of domestic business matters. The Mozabite women were and are still seen as central pillars of Mozabite culture, also because it was they who raised the young Mozabites.

Non-Mozabite custom was banned by the clerics, who would place an offending person who maintained such tabooed practices in *tabrīʾa*. Cafes and hotels are not allowed within the walls of the *qṣar*, and tourism remains highly regulated. Until recently, state education was also discouraged. Thus, when other cultural influences arrived in the form of radio, telephone, satellite and finally the Internet, these were all explicitly banned. However, the demand for these forms of communication was so great that the *ʿazzāba* was powerless to prevent this technological revolution.

The previously unquestioned normative order has been gradually challenged by confrontation with different cultural forms and expressions made visible by the global mass media. Omar Ben Enis, a young Mozabite friend, complained to me that many young people had been experimenting with (what he saw as) unacceptable, alternative forms of identity through the platform of social media.

> People may have seemed a bit harsh in the past, closed off to people, who are open-minded today, e.g. being open to foreigners, but maybe we

> are letting bad things in. This is my view. Like now, people on Facebook are calling themselves "emo" or crazy person. This did not happen three years ago, it is the detrimental effects of globalisation.

They were creating avatars, and through these avatars were expressing themselves, in the largely unregulated space of online social networks, in ways less acceptable to society. In these spaces, the highly normative constraint of the "social gaze" is mostly absent and, with hidden identities, the young people can find outlets for different forms of behaviour, perhaps influenced by the various cultural fads they encounter in the mediascape. The effects of such alternative narratives on viewers can be profound, for, as Appadurai (1996: 35) puts it:

> The lines between the realistic and the fictional landscapes they see are blurred, so that the farther away these audiences are from the direct experiences of metropolitan life, the more likely they are to construct imagined worlds that are chimerical, aesthetic, even fantastic objects, particularly if assessed by the criteria of some other perspective, some other imagined world.

In thus engaging with the wider world as never before, the previously sacrosanct inner sanctum within the fortified walls of the *qṣar*, symbolically defended through the practice of dissociation as expounded by the family and mosque, has been breached from within, by this "Trojan horse" of mass media. This hidden intruder, the personal computer or mobile phone connected to the worldwide web, enables young Mozabites inside the walls of the old town to engage with an unprecedented, unregulated flow of information, ideas and images. Individuals are now debating how conformity with social norms may limit processes of creativity, now referring, for example, to economically successful "Western" role models, such as Apple's (now deceased former CEO) Steve Jobs.

Discussing the negative effects of globalisation, I asked Omar Blidi, a petrochemical engineer, about what he meant when he claimed "the culture is getting lost". He replied:

> In the past, we were isolated. With the event of globalisation, the young people question their ways and culture, and perhaps see themselves as "retarded, ignorant". Plus, now there are many people around with different ways. Religion is being lost, and this is tied up very strongly with culture or identity. People don't listen to the *ʿazzāba* as much anymore. [I ask him for an example of culture or religion getting lost, he replies:] for

> example, neighbours wouldn't make problems over land, this wouldn't have happened in the past (by God fearing people), now they go to the courts.

Omar's comments bring us back to the land question, that through questioning their culture, people have become less awed by local religious authorities such as the *ʿashīra* and the family head. Indeed, all forms of authority seem to be threatened. One Mozabite elder claimed that loss of respect for religious tradition and authority would result in moral degeneration, indeed, in a total breakdown of everyday order, anomie. He exclaimed, "Then we would become just like the French, where anything goes, such as homosexuality, just like animals."

On the other hand, some Mozabites felt that such challenges refreshed their sense of religion rather than threatening it with extinction. Doubt has led many to a deepened sense of faith, by being exposed to alternative individual relationships to Islam. This means that enhanced contact with the Other not only weakens Mozabite identity, but through critical reflection can strengthen it. This flow of ideas has not been simply a one-way process either (Comaroff, 2001); certain features of French architecture such as Le Corbusier's "Modulor" and the Chapel of Ronchamp, and Gaudi's Guell Park are said to have been inspired by the buildings and motifs found in the M'zab, such as the ancient mausoleum of Sidi Brahim (Pavard, Bossu-Picat and Rollet, 1975; Cataldi, Abdelhamid and Selva, 1996). This questioning encourages reflection on the notion of "authenticity". Identity here is based on change and inner reflection rather than on "tradition" (see also Theodossopoulos, 2013). Such reflexivity may be said to entail a sort of indigenous anthropology (Sahlins, 2015), in which local order and praxis are compared with those of other societies around the world.

So far, I have described how alternative value systems interact both explicitly and more subtly. Clearly, these encounters do not take place on an equal playing field, as legitimacy is demanded by both religious and state authorities. Values may also be embedded implicitly within official discourses of science and law. Thus, while overt values may be debated and resisted, more subtle ones can slip in unnoticed through such authoritative and bureaucratic discourses. For example, Benmoussa (2013) describes how, through a legal loophole, certain individuals in southern Algerian tribes are starting to sell land that should be held for communal grazing, with an emphasis on privatisation slowly becoming the norm (see also Ben Hounet et al. 2011; Ben Hounet 2013[6]). Whereas Benmoussa inaccurately ascribes this to the forces of globali-

6 Especially regarding the implementation of the "Accession à la Propriété Foncière Agricole"

sation, it would be more accurate to attribute it to colonialism, for it was the French government that restructured land tenure laws in an overarching drive toward privatisation of land. It is to this momentous process that we now turn.

Civil Law and Colonialism in Algeria

> Before, the mosque protected the oasis, ensured that the law, *ʿurf*, dictated when certain things were done in the oasis, such as cutting the palm branches. In Morocco it is different; there they have the king, who protects their interests. Here, there is conflict with the state; they don't act in the peoples' interests. Now the mosque here is only for praying, and it is the population and the government together. It was the French who took away the power of *el-oumna* and the mosque. (Salah Ba Ali, farmer, 19 September 2013)

On the African continent, customary law was mainly created in reaction to or indeed by the colonial rulers (Ranger, 1997: 456).[7] However, in the Islamic world, *sharīʿa* existed prior to colonial civil or common law, and coexisted with pre-existing local custom. This resulted in a plurality of laws, since, although the colonial rulers needed to apply European codified law in criminal and commercial cases to facilitate market expansion, they had to leave certain elements intact, such as family law or personal-status law, in order to ensure social stability (Sartori and Shahar, 2012). Keeping control meant maintaining a delicate balance, especially allowing Muslim communities to continue to practise the Islamic faith, of which a central tenet is *sharīʿa*, undisturbed (Christelow, 2014: 4). Customary laws were of course subservient to colonial authority (Nasr, 2001: 43). Moreover, indigenous systems of law were not merely incorporated into statutory law, but were adjusted, with unsatisfactory ones being criminalised as dangerous or primitive (Sartori and Shahar, 2012). An important factor of legal pluralism under colonial rule is that colonial powers were able to apply legal codes from different pre-existing ethnic divisions, in order to maintain a divide-and-rule policy (ibid.).

(APFA) law in 1983, after the "Réforme Agraire" that was implemented under the Presidency of Houari Boumediene.

7 As Ranger et al. (1997: 456) unequivocally put it: "What were called customary law, customary land rights, customary political structure and so on, were in fact *all* invented by colonial codification."

Interestingly, pluralistic hegemonic regimes, rather than being solely sites of power and subordination, have been used for counter-hegemonic purposes by indigenous populations (Nader, 2002: 36), or have been manipulated opportunistically, as a way out of customary practices, such as with traditional inheritance rights (for example, civil law gave women equal property rights [Rae, 2002: 9]). Indeed, a multiplicity of legal regimes has afforded a kind of "forum shopping" by litigants based on opportunistic self-interest, as occurs in the M'zab (von Benda-Beckmann, 1981).

Colonial subjugation varied from direct to indirect rule. Algerians experienced a particularly brutal form of direct colonial rule (Fanon, 1959; 1963), where the French centralised and bureaucratised a formerly highly variable judicial order by introducing a court of appeal which oversaw the previously independent *qāḍī* law (Islamic jurisprudence) system[8] (Christelow, 2014: 9). The first phase of colonial rule entailed removing all vestiges of Ottoman political structures; the colonisers regarded the Algerians as never having had an indigenous state. The sultan or *bey* remained as a symbol of national sovereignty, as in Morocco and Tunisia. Then they eradicated all tribal structures, and reassigned their fragmented remains to territorial units or *communes* under direct French administration. Colonial rule differed significantly, however, between the Northern Department under civil administration, and the 'Territoires du Sud' (Southern Territories) which were under military administration (Ben Hounet, 2007). The *commune* leader or *qā'id* was selected by the French, often from outside the area, and thus was usually despised by the local population for subservience to the colonials and for their domineering habits (ibid.: 12).

The M'zab was left alone by the French colonial administration for the first 50 years; apparently, the new administration admired the Mozabites' disciplined capacities for self-organisation. Finally, in 1882, the French annexed the M'zab as punishment for aiding and sheltering members of a resistance movement led by Abd al-Qadir, and they also tripled their taxes (Amat, 1888: 238). Yet, following annexation, the Mozabites continued to resist, as Bennoune (1986: 110) puts it:

> ...[the *'azzāba*] organized the total boycott and avoidance of the French administration and the means of its presence: schools, hospitals, military service and even tax evasion. In a word, the Mozabites tried to minimize

8 In the 1880s, the French attempted to eliminate Islamic courts entirely. This led to the first popular protest movement in Algeria after 60 years of colonial rule, and eventually the French withdrew this policy (Christelow, 2014: 9).

> as much as possible their dealings and relations with the colonial power and the medium of its domination.

Thus, the Mozabites largely continued to attend to their own affairs, preferring to solve their problems and conflicts internally, according to their own methods of justice, resolution or punishment. However, a new precedent was set, and an alternative seat of justice was available for those who did not agree with the judgements of the Mozabite authorities, or who wished to subvert traditional arrangements regarding land tenure, inheritance, and authority (the household patriarch, the *ʿashīra*, the *ʿazzāba*).

Such a shift in the centres of authority and identity has been alluded to by Scheele (2009: 107-111) in her work on the Kabyles of Northern Algeria. I argue that, at a certain point, Mozabite individuals from the wealthier sections of society, who were already subverting the practice of *tabrīʾa* by forming their own bourgeois circles, turned to another centre of authority, that of the postcolonial Algerian nation-state. This was probably more attractive than accepting the authority of the previous colonial rulers, as the new state had a self-proclaimed Islamic identity. This view was supported by several individuals in the M'zab when discussing changes regarding local power. For example, Nejib informed me that:

> In the past before the French when a crisis happened, the community found solutions to problems and then put them into writing. The French removed power from the mosque to make decisions and placed an outsider *muqaddam* who didn't understand people or local history. He couldn't find a solution to the problems. The mosque used to be able to solve disputes by reference to Islamic law, solving disputes quickly so that the land doesn't lose value, unlike now. Now power is centralised as civil law.

Further, in discussing the matter with Bechir, a student of city planning:

> From our point of view, the French didn't really manage to interfere. Now power is given to central government, because they are an Islamic institution, but they respect local specificities. General regulations sometimes don't fit with local regulations. They often allow exceptions; however, e.g. we are free to deal with the mosque about 90%. In other mosques in Algeria, the imam is chosen by the Ministry of Religion; this is important, as religion is the most important thing in Mozabite society. In addition, there are no police officers. This change in power dynamics took place gradually since Independence.

Moreover, Salah Ba Ali (a Mozabite NGO director) added that judges played an important role in balancing the alternative avenues available for arriving at justice; indeed, they often favoured local processes when applicable, such as those incorporating *'urf*. Through the discretion of such judges, a certain harmony could be found between the various systems, showing that conflict was not always the norm.

The brutal French colonial rule was experienced more violently in Algeria than anywhere else, and the disruptive effects were far-reaching. We can see these effects into the post-colonial period, for as the fledging state attempted to oppose the dominant imperial powers in its formation, including attempts at socialism, the colonial structures, especially the legal system, resisted and endured. This took some time to reach the M'zab in its remote enclave in the desert, protected by the parochial *'azzāba*. Some Mozabites decided to strategically engage with the new Islamic Algerian state[9] because it was seen as morally and ideologically aligned with local interests. This arguably opened up the possibility of choosing an alternative pathway for litigating disputes. Colonialism was not therefore simply experienced as a loss of local agency; it provided alternatives for those who wished and were able to exploit them.

Conclusion: Anomie or New Horizons?

Among the bodies of "law" – from local customary and Islamic, to the colonial and post-colonial state laws – which could be said to be the most important in controlling, regulating, and motivating behaviour at the local level? Usually, with the creation of the nation-state, dispute settlement between parties is delegated from the local to the national level, in the form of law courts. This appears to follow a trend whereby the notion of individual *rights* ends up usurping the moral prerogative of *social care* for one's fellow household members and neighbours. This understanding redirects our gaze away from ineffectual critiques of legal pluralism, toward a more insightful wider analysis of different ideological systems, as Fuller (1994), drawing on Geertz (1983), would have us do.

Put another way, as I have documented above, the rise of the state and a new legal framework, with its corresponding "social contract" (i.e. taxation in return for supposed government protection of private property through the state's legal apparatus), have supplanted social allegiance to one's family and

9 I refer here to Algeria's proclaimed identity as an Islamic, Arab nation rather than in legal terms, as in Mauritania and Sudan. Algeria is a Democratic and Popular Republic.

neighbours. This situation is especially prevalent in large "faceless" societies, where social inequalities exacerbate fear, making it less likely that strangers will intervene in another's misfortune (Nader, 2002: 55). Indeed, in the M'zab, it is evident that the wealthy class, by drawing on the technologies of the state, take the lead in breaking away from traditional practices for imposing order, such as religion, *tabrīʾa*, the patriarch, gossip and suchlike. This accords with arguments I have made elsewhere (Benessaiah, 2015), in that they can afford to deal with problems through the use of money, rather than having to go through long drawn-out negotiations with peers, as dictated by reciprocal work. In such cases, rather than go through the customary channels (family, *ʿashīra*, *ʿazzāba*), many of those who can afford it employ lawyers. Although this has led to more, rather than less protracted disputes, receiving individual shares has become more important to many than joint management of land and resources. Perhaps in the creation of barriers to visibility by the wealthy, Mozabite society is moving away from a face-to-face society and thus formal litigation processes are becoming necessary. However, many people agree (as with Nejib's analogy of the house, above), that the national law courts have little understanding of local norms and practices, whereas local authorities may be able to give a more nuanced ruling. It is clear that local power dynamics influence people's decision-making in present-day disputes; some perceive the national law courts as being more neutral in their decision-making, as having less personal interest; yet others think quite the opposite, as state interests in the M'zab are also seen as less than neutral.

The move by certain individuals toward a state-centred social contract based on taxation – again, based on the idea of the individual consumer – thus replaces a local social contract comprising messy, complex obligations. The latter are not predicated on the exchange of money and the threat of force, but on the circulation of obligations, and a withdrawal of cooperation if obligations are not met (see Roberts, 1979: 30). This conceptualisation of contract theory goes beyond mere "forum shopping" as the search for strategic advantage (von Benda-Beckmann, 1982). In response to critics of legal pluralism, an analysis of multiple regulatory systems need not entail a dilution of the notion of law, but can offer a critical perspective on power relations between individuals and state actors.

Differences in the perceived quality of different land plots appeared to be a key factor in some of these inheritance conflicts. In the M'zab, formal laws, whether written or verbal, often contain an explicit moral dimension. Islamic interpretations are used to substantiate the representation of an ideal Muslim community, which is largely imagined and reconstructed by the *ʿazzāba* clerics during sermons, repeated in Qur'anic schools to pupils, and in the home or at work by mothers and fathers to their children. I have shown that oral customary law, scriptural Islamic law and state statutory law may be in conflict (and become the object of "forum shopping" by individuals), yet they also can interact "harmoniously" (when referred to by "enlightened" judges).

Is the M'zab, therefore, experiencing a state of anomie due to cultural contact with worldviews beyond it? Mozabite society is becoming more fractured, with increasing socio-economic inequality. This would not be a problem in a post-modern consumer-oriented neoliberal society, where any issue can (apparently) be resolved through money, if one has enough of it. However, when people truly need each other in order to survive, this is not enough. In the M'zab, the management of natural resources, which requires the participation of the whole community, requires a social consciousness beyond individual consumerism. Following a recent natural disaster, many have been questioning such notions as "individualism" and "community", and the competing visions of a locally desirable society they project.

Acknowledgements

This research was in part funded by the Royal Anthropological Institute, and the Kent Innovation awards. It was improved by feedback from Raj Puri, Matt Hodges and Irene Calis.

Bibliography

Amat, C. 1888. *Le M'zab et les M'zabites*. Paris: Challamel.

Appadurai, A. 1996. *Modernity at Large: Cultural Dimensions of Globalization*. Minneapolis: University of Minnesota Press.

Benessaiah, N.L. 2015. "Authority, Anarchy and Equity: Explaining Agrarian Change in the Algerian Sahara". PhD thesis. University of Kent.

Benessaiah, N.L. and J. Shaffer, forthcoming. "Relative Scales, Fluid Responses: A Polyphonic Approach to Participatory Water Governance", under review, *Ambio.*

Ben Hounet, Y. 2007. "Des tribus en Algérie?". *Cahiers de la Méditerranée* 75: 150-171. <http://cdlm.revues.org/4013> (accessed 16 August 2017).

Ben Hounet,Y. 2013. "Propriété, appropriation foncière et pratiques du droit en milieu steppique (Algérie)", *Etudes Rurales* 2 (192): 61-77. www.cairn.info/revue-etudes-rurales-2013-2-page-61.htm (accessed 16 August 2017).

Ben Hounet, Y., B. Casciarri, B. Dupret, F. Ireton and A. Wilson. 2011. "Pratiques de l'appropriation foncière en contexte musulman", *Transcontinentales* 10-11. <http://transcontinentales.revues.org/1275> (accessed 16 August 2017).

Benmoussa, B. 2013. "An Effect of Globalisation? The Individual Appropriation of *'arch* Lands in Algeria", *The Journal of North African Studies* 18 (5): 668-677.
Bennoune, M. 1986. "Cultural Ecological Theory and the Formation of the Ibadite Desert Confederacy", *Dialectical Anthropology* 11 (1): 93-117.
Bourdieu, P. 1962. *The Algerians*. Translated by A.C.M. Ross. Boston, MA: Beacon Press.
Cataldi, G., R. Abdelhamid and F. Selva, F. 1996. "The Town of Ghardaïa in M'zab, Algeria: Between Tradition and Modernity", *Traditional Dwellings and Settlements Review* 7 (2): 63-74.
Christelow, A. 2014. *Muslim Law Courts and the French Colonial State in Algeria*. Princeton, NJ: Princeton University Press.
Comaroff, J.L. 2001. "Colonialism, Culture, and the Law: A Foreword", *Law & Social Inquiry* 26 (2): 305-314.
Crawford, D. 2008. *Moroccan Households in the World Economy: Labor and Inequality in a Berber Village*. Baton Rouge: Louisiana State University Press.
Durkheim, É. 1984. *The Division of Labour in Society*. London: Macmillan.
Evans-Pritchard, E.E. 1940. *The Nuer*. Oxford: Oxford University Press.
Fanon, F. 1959. *Black Skin, White Masks*. New York: Grove Press.
Fanon, F. 1963. *The Wretched of the Earth*. New York: Grove Press.
Farrag, A. 1971. "Social Control amongst the Mzabite Women of Beni-Isguen", *Middle Eastern Studies* 7 (3): 317-327.
Forni, N. 2003. "Land Tenure Policies in the Near East", *Land Reform, FAO* 1. <ftp://193.43.36.93/docrep/fao/005/Y8999T/Y8999T03.pdf> (accessed 16 August 2017).
Fowler, B. 1997. *Pierre Bourdieu and Cultural Theory: Critical Investigations*. London: SAGE.
Fuller, C. 1994. "Legal Anthropology: Legal Pluralism and Legal Thought", *Anthropology Today* 10 (3): 9-12.
Geertz, C. 1983. "Local Knowledge: Fact and Law in Comparative Perspective", in ed. *Local Knowledge: Further Essays in Interpretive Anthropology*, ed. C. Geertz. New York: Basic Books, 167-234.
Gellner, E. 1969. *Saints of the Atlas*. London: Weidenfeld and Nicolson.
Gramsci, A. 1977. *Selections from Political Writings (1910-1920)*. Selected and edited by Q. Hoare & translated by J. Mathews. London: Lawrence and Wishart.
Hadj-Nacer, A. 2011. *La Martingale Algérienne: Réflexions sur une crise*. Algiers: Éditions Barzakh.
Mair, J., and N.H. Evans. 2015. "Ethics across Borders: Incommensurability and Affinity", *HAU: Journal of Ethnographic Theory* 5 (2): 201-225.
Masqueray, E. 1878. *Chronique d'Abou Zakaria*. Paris: Aillaud.
Masqueray, E. 1886. "Formation des cités chez les populations sédentaires de l'Algérie: (Kabyles du Djurdjura, Chaouïa de l'Aourâs, Beni Mezâb)". Thesis. L'Université impériale de France, Paris.

Nader, L. 2002. *The Life of the Law: Anthropological Projects*. Berkley: University of California Press.

Nasr, S.V.R. 2001. *Islamic Leviathan : Islam and the Making of State Power*. Oxford: Oxford University Press.

Pavard, C., C. Bossu-Picat and P. Rollet. 1975. *Lumières du M'Zab*. Paris: Delroisse.

Rae, J. 2002. "An Overview of Land Tenure in the Near East Region", Part 1. <http://www.fao.org/wairdocs/aq202e/aq202e.pdf> (accessed 8 June 2015).

Ranger, T. 1997. "The Invention of Tradition in Colonial Africa", in *Perspectives on Africa: A Reader in Culture, History, and Representation*, ed. R.R. Grinker, S.C. Lubkemann and C. Steiner. New York: John Wiley & Sons, 450-461. Also in *The Invention of Tradition*, ed. T. Ranger and E. Hobsbawm, Cambridge: Cambridge University Press, 2012, 211-262.

Roberts, H. 2002. "Perspectives on Berber Politics: On Gellner and Masqueray, or Durkheim's Mistake", *Journal of the Royal Anthropological Institute* 8 (1): 107-126.

Roberts, S. 1979. *Order and Dispute*. London: Penguin.

Sahlins, M. 2015. "An Anthropological Manifesto: Or the Origin of the State", *Anthropology Today* 31 (2): 8-11.

Sartori, P., and I. Shahar. 2012. "Legal Pluralism in Muslim-Majority Colonies: Mapping the Terrain", *Journal of the Economic and Social History of the Orient* 55 (4-5): 637-663.

Scheele, J., 2008. A taste for law: rule-making in Kabylia (Algeria). *Comparative studies in society and history*, *50*(4), pp.895-919.

Scheele, J. 2009. *Village Matters: Knowledge, Politics and Community in Kabylia, Algeria*. Woodbridge: James Currey.

Theodossopoulos, D. 2013. "Laying Claim to Authenticity: Five Anthropological Dilemmas", *Anthropological Quarterly* 86 (2): 337-360.

von Benda-Beckmann, K. 1981. "Forum Shopping and Shopping Forums: Dispute Processing in a Minangkabau Village in West Sumatra", *The Journal of Legal Pluralism and Unofficial Law* 13 (19): 117-159.

CHAPTER 7

To Compensate or Not to Compensate? Law, Property and Sahrawi Refugees in Algeria

Alice Wilson

Law, Property and Refugees

Property is often the subject of disputes. Yet property given as compensation can also constitute a means of helping resolve a dispute. This chapter considers the (re)emergence of turning to property as compensation to resolve disputes in a somewhat unusual setting: the case is that of Sahrawi refugees, whose presence in refugee camps in south-west Algeria dates back to 1976.

Sahrawi refugees' turn to property to offer compensation in internal disputes offers an interesting perspective on the relationship between law and property. Refugees are often associated both with dispossession, and with a legal framework that suggests the potential rights of refugees to reparations (which can take the form of compensation) for property lost upon becoming refugees. The rights of refugees to such reparations and potential compensation are increasingly recognised by scholars (Leckie, 2003) and in policy (UN Sub-Commission on the Promotion and Protection of Human Rights, 2005).[1] An emphasis on refugees' potential rights as refugees can, however, affect long-term refugees' attitudes to property in internal disputes between refugees. In a study of the autonomously-run Palestinian refugee camps in Lebanon in the 1970s, Julie Peteet (2005: 141) reports one interlocutor's view that, although the PLO set about organising reconciliation (*sulha* [sic]) – a process that can entail discussions about compensation for the injured party – in order to resolve internal disputes amongst refugees, in practice refugees were under pressure to let grievances go "in the name of the revolution" (*bism thawra* [sic]). National identity and potential rights as refugees were meant to take priority over potential rights to compensation in internal disputes. A relationship between law and property that might have held outside exile was, in exile, meant to be overridden.

1 For a contrasting view that there is not consensus on the right of refugees to reparations for property lost, see de Greiff (2006: 7).

 | DOI 10.1163/9789004362116_009

Initially, the experience of Sahrawi refugees in Algeria, like that of Palestinian refugees living under the PLO in refugee camps in Lebanon in the 1970s, saw a suspension of potential claims to material compensation in internal disputes. Fieldwork undertaken with Sahrawi refugees from 2006 to 2012 nevertheless suggests that in the 2000s grounds were emerging for Sahrawi refugees to turn to property to make compensation payments in order to resolve internal disputes. Such claims or payments were not uniformly made, however, which points to the ongoing complexity of the relationship between law and property for long-term refugees. There were not only material barriers (arising from the aftermath of material dispossession) to making compensation claims and payments. There were also political and moral barriers concerning whether such claims were appropriate in exile.

In the following sections, I first introduce the Sahrawi refugees and their refugee camps in south-west Algeria. I then consider the kinds of disputes over property, and the recourse to property for compensation payments, that are likely to have been prominent in the pre-exile lives of those who became refugees. To do so, I review property disputes and compensation as observed in the north-west Sahara by a colonial officer who worked in the 1950s in southern Algeria, at times with some of those who later would go on to identity as Sahrawis. I go on to describe the contrasting situation that arose in exile, where the initial material dispossession of the refugees meant that there were fewer opportunities either for disputes over property, or for the offering of compensation. Nevertheless, by the 2000s, when material conditions had improved in the camps, in some circumstances compensation payments began to re-emerge. I conclude by reflecting on refugees' ambiguous relationship to potential rights to compensation in intra-refugee disputes.

Sahrawi Refugees in Algeria

Since early 1976, the area around the Algerian town and military base of Tindouf, in the south-west Algerian Sahara, has hosted a population of Sahrawi refugees from the neighbouring disputed territory, Western Sahara. Sahrawis speak the Hassaniya dialect of Arabic, and many of them identify with a Bedouin heritage. Sedentarisation became common in present-day Western Sahara only from the 1950s.[2] Refugees fled Western Sahara (or, in some cases,

2 For a discussion of the extent to which Sahrawi refugees may identity with a mobile pastoralist background, even if not all refugees were practising mobile pastoralism in the period immediately prior to becoming refugees, see Wilson (2014a).

northern Mauritania and southern Morocco) in the wake of Morocco's partial annexation of Western Sahara in 1975. This partial annexation paralysed the territory's decolonisation.[3] Various UN resolutions from the 1960s to the present, and the advisory finding of the International Court of Justice (1975), have recognised the right of the people of Western Sahara to self-determination. Nevertheless, Morocco claims the territory as historically part of its kingdom. It has annexed some three-quarters of the territory, which it rules as part of Morocco.[4]

The territory of Western Sahara is also claimed, however, by Morocco's rival, the national liberation movement of Western Sahara, known as the Polisario Front (henceforth Polisario).[5] The movement was founded in 1973 to resist the then Spanish colonial rulers of Spanish Sahara. From 1975, Polisario opposed Morocco (and, from 1975 to 1979, Mauritania) in claiming the territory. From 1975 to 1991, Morocco and Polisario fought a war that neither was able to win outright. In 1991, the UN brokered a ceasefire, and then set up a mission, Minurso, focused on organising a referendum (on self-determination) in Western Sahara. All efforts to hold the referendum have, however, thus far ended in political stalemate (see Jensen, 2005). At the collapse of the last plan put forward by the former UN envoy to Western Sahara, James Baker, Morocco refused the inclusion of independence as an option in a referendum, and Polisario insisted on its inclusion.

The protracted stalemate during the ceasefire period has seen the conflict assume alternative battlefronts over reputation, legitimacy and the eligibility of voters for a potential referendum on self-determination (see Zunes and Mundy, 2010). For its part, Polisario enjoys a strong legal position (at least on paper), thanks to the consistent international recognition of the right of the people of Western Sahara to self-determination. But Morocco benefits from strong support from France and the US, and thus enjoys a strong political position. Morocco has so far been able to prevent the implementation of decolonisation, despite increasing concerns about the human rights situation in annexed Western Sahara (Human Rights Watch, 2008; 2012).

As the conflict has dragged on, a population of Sahrawi refugees – who may have numbered some 160,000 by the late 2000s – have found themselves

3 On the Western Sahara conflict, see Hodges (1983); Zunes and Mundy (2010).

4 With the exception of Mauritania 1975-1979, when Mauritania was a co-annexing power with Morocco prior to Mauritania's withdrawal and subsequent recognition of Morocco's rival, to date Morocco's claims to Western Sahara have not been officially recognised by a third state.

5 As of 1979, Polisario has been recognised by the UN as the sole representative of the people of Western Sahara.

growing old, becoming adults and growing up in exile in refugee camps in Algeria, near Tindouf.[6] At the time of writing, the refugee camps are forty years old. Whilst the camps are located in Algeria, the refugees are governed by Polisario. Authority over the refugee camps and the territory between them has been delegated by Algeria to Polisario. In practice, the liberation movement governs the civilian refugee population, in a close fusion with the state authority that it founded in 1976 for Western Sahara, the Sahrawi Arab Democratic Republic (SADR). The governing authority in which Polisario and SADR are intertwined has state-like qualities. SADR has achieved degrees of international and multi-lateral recognition.[7] The refugee camps have their own ministries, a parliament, police, prisons and law-courts administering SADR laws. Perhaps to an even greater degree than other long-term exiled communities (Peteet, 2005; Frésia, 2009; McConnell, 2016), Sahrawi refugees have become citizens-in-exile of a state-like administration of their own (see Wilson, 2016).

Locked in an overarching conflict for the sovereignty of Western Sahara, over the course of nearly forty years of exile, the refugees have inevitably faced their own internal conflicts. Before considering some examples that indicate the changing nature of these disputes, and the evolving manner of dealing with them, I consider an account from the colonial period that suggests some insights into disputes and their resolution amongst some of those who came to see themselves as Sahrawis.

Disputes in the North-West Sahara: Colonial Perspectives

Until the 1950s, mobile pastoralism was an important source of livelihood for the inhabitants of the north-west Sahara (see Caro Baroja, 1955; Caratini, 1989). Since pasturelands were not formally owned by particular tribes, but rather dominant tribes exerted priority claims to pasturelands and their water resources, the main source of material wealth was movable. It took the form of

6 For a discussion of population figures for the camps, see Chatty, Fiddian-Qasmiyeh and Crivello (2010: 41). The Sahrawi population in annexed Western Sahara may be slightly larger than the population in exile. The UN figures for 2000 for provisional approved adult Sahrawi voters are 41,150 for Moroccan-controlled Western Sahara and 33,998 for the refugee camps (Zunes and Mundy, 2010: 214). The annexed and exiled Sahrawi populations are increasingly in touch through migration movements (see Wilson, 2014b) and thanks to mobile phones (see Deubel, 2012).

7 For a list of 80 recognitions by states as at 2006, including 22 cancellations or suspensions, see Pazzanita (2006: 376-378). SADR has been a full member of the African Union since 1984.

animals (camels, sheep and goats), as well as people (slaves). According to one colonial officer's account of the disputes he was asked to resolve in the early 1950s between mobile pastoralists in the area (Denis, 2001), many everyday disputes took place over property in the form of animals.

Pierre Denis was a French colonial administrator who presided over courts for settling disputes between mobile pastoralists in southern Algeria in the early 1950s. Denis worked in various locations, and with persons from a variety of backgrounds, including Touareg and people whom he calls "Arab nomads". He also worked with Rgaybāt, one of the large tribes now identified and identifying as Sahrawi. Denis's work with them included hearing cases in the vicinity of Tindouf, the town near which the Sahrawi refugee camps are now located. Founded in 1852 by members of the Tajakant tribe, Tindouf had been sacked by members of the Rbaybāt tribe in 1895. In refugees' oral histories of some families' movements in the early decades of the twentieth century, Rgaybāt families had remained present in the vicinity of Tindouf, and others travelled there periodically from pasturelands in Western Sahara and further afield.

Denis heard 150 cases, on which he reflects in an account published some fifty years later (Denis, 2001). He combines personal memoirs with an analysis from the point of view of a colonial officer. The cases took place over three years, from 1950 to 1952. Denis does not specify how many cases were from each of the three groups he identifies ("Arab nomads", Touareg and Rgaybāt). The cases with which he dealt were brought to him on local initiative. In his view, cases were brought to the French in order for a decision to be imposed when it had not been possible to reach a solution through internal mediation. Such internal mediation varied between "Arabs", Touareg and Rgaybāt, as Denis discusses. Amongst the Rgaybāt and other tribes present in what became Western Sahara, a tribal council, known as a *jamāʿa*,[8] is reported to have had authority in taking decisions in disputes (see Caro Baroja, 1955).

Echoing many a colonial administrator, Denis reflects on perceived difficulties that he experienced in dealing with local disputes. Animals could be owned by several individuals as a result of shared inheritance, which could exacerbate disputes. Animals could also be bought without being seen, and sometimes left with the original owner for years before being claimed. Not only were animals themselves mobile, but so were their owners. If the Touareg with whom Denis worked tended to move around distances of some 100 km, Denis recalls that the Rgaybāt moved across distances of hundreds of

8 Unless otherwise stated, my transliterations favour, where different, the pronunciation by speakers of the Hassaniya dialect of Arabic over the pronunciation in classical Arabic.

kilometres. This could make it difficult to call up witnesses for a case. Furthermore, there was no established common calendar of dates in use amongst mobile pastoralists of different trajectories and tribes. Rather, people referred to years through significant events that had occurred in their own experience. These references therefore varied according to people's experiences. In Denis's view, the need for the French presence to impose justice was clear.

The degree to which the cases that reached Denis – those that had resisted resolution through alternative means – were representative of the wider cases arising remains an open question. Yet the broad trend that Denis identifies seems plausible as a pattern for disputes in the north-west Sahara: the majority of the cases that were brought to him concerned animals. Of the corpus of 150 cases, Denis classifies 72 as concerned with "animals" (such as, for instance, someone selling on an animal, only for their ownership of the whole animal to be contested by another party). A further fourteen cases concern theft, and some of these deal with the theft of animals. For example, Denis (2001: 36) reflects, what should be done in a case where an animal that has been stolen is then sold on to someone who buys it?

Nine further cases concern the animal loaning system known as *mnīḥa*. According to this loaning system, male and female camels could be lent by their owner to another person or persons, who would have the right to the usufruct of the animals (Caro Baroja, 1955: 103-104; Caratini, 1989: 56-57; Denis, 2001: 38). The milk of female camels could be drunk, and male camels could be used to carry goods. This loaning system has been analysed as a means of circulating property that reinforced hierarchical power relations. Typically, those who borrowed animals were – or thereby became – dependent on those who lent them the animals (Caratini, 1989: 57; Denis, 2001: 38). Such loans could last for years. Borrowers should not in principle sell or kill an animal under their care, and the offspring of any loaned animals should be returned, with the original animals, to the owners at the end of the loan. Denis notes a distinction between the loaning practices of Rgaybāt, and their "Arab" and Touareg counterparts. If an animal died during a *mnīḥa* loan as a result of mistreatment by the animal's custodians, it was customary amongst the Rgaybāt to leave punishment to "divine justice". In contrast, Touareg or "Arab" owners might seek out a more immediate dispensation of justice (Denis, 2001: 38).

Ten further cases reviewed by Denis concerned lost animals. Disputes in such cases arose from the etiquette of care for animals lost in the desert. Someone finding a lost animal should water it, if otherwise the animal would die. But to water an animal so much that it is able to move on further away from its owner, and thus become more difficult to find, would be wrong. Another question was whether, if someone found a lost animal and then looked after it, but it died or was mistreated, this led to liability to the owner. If a lost animal was restored to its owner, then disputes could arise about whether the owner was responsible to pay for the upkeep of the animal during that period, or only for the distance covered to return the animal (Denis, 2001: 40-42).

Not only animals were owned and came to be disputed. Slavery was still practised, and six cases with which Denis dealt concerned slaves. In four cases, owners of slaves who had escaped demanded their return; these cases were dismissed. In another case, two parties each claimed to own the same slave; the case was resolved by allowing the slave to choose the party with which he wished to remain (Denis, 2001: 50).

It emerges, then, that many of the disputes Denis handled were over property, and the majority of these cases concerned animals. Alongside these cases, Denis lists twenty-nine cases concerning debt, eight concerning servants, nine cases of divorce disputes, and three cases of murder and injuries. One potential point in common between disputes over property and disputes of other kinds (such as relations between people, of marriage, debt, labour and injury), is that property could be an important means of achieving reconciliation between disputing parties. For example, in cases of theft, according to Denis, the Rgaybāt required the stolen property to be returned four-fold or two-fold to the original owner (Denis, 2001: 36). According to Caro Baroja (1955: 440-441), however, for the Rgaybāt (as well as for the Izargiyen tribe), four times the stolen property should be returned.[9] In other words, if one camel was stolen, then four should be given by the thief to the original owner. In a context where, although money certainly circulated amongst mobile pastoralists, there might nevertheless be a preference to make payments in commodities, there could be fixed forms of property recognised as potentially due to parties. For example, amongst the Ait Ousa tribe and the Rgaybāt, for each lost camel restored to its owner, the owner should hand over 15 m of cloth (Denis, 2001: 42).

A form of the recourse to property to resolve a dispute that has become (in) famous in the Middle East and North Africa is the payment of compensation in the case of homicide, *diya*, often translated as blood money. Compensation payments following murder are by no means particular to Muslims or the Middle East region;[10] within the Middle East, blood money also has pre-Islamic

9 The punishment for theft varied between tribes. For example, amongst the Ait Lahsen, the penalty for theft was the return of the stolen item and, in addition, a sheep or goat suitable for slaughtering (Caro Baroja, 1955: 439).

10 Evans-Pritchard (1940) famously analysed blood money amongst the Nuer of southern Sudan in the early twentieth century. Blood money was also formerly practised in

precedents. But *diya*, a compensation payment that can obviate the need to avenge murder with the death of someone from amongst the perpetrator's agnates, is praised in the Qur'an as a form of God's mercy (Q 2: 178-179). In the case of involuntary homicide, *diya* is enjoined upon Muslims (Q 4: 92). There are many discussions of the practice of *diya* in the Muslim Middle East and North Africa in pre-colonial, colonial and post-colonial times. Analyses have examined the political nuances of the liability to contribute to *diya* payments, and the social importance of such debts as a form of social lubrication that avoids a breakdown of relationships.[11] In contemporary Iran, Saudi Arabia and Sudan, *diya* has been incorporated into state law as part of the attempt to implement Islamic law (*sharīʿa*).

In the area that would become Western Sahara (as in many other parts of the Middle East and North Africa), the close male agnates of the murderer would be responsible for raising the amount of *diya* to be paid to the close male agnates of the victim. In theory, the amount for the *diya* was set at 100 camels. Denis (2001: 61) suggests that this should include 25 two-year-old female camels (*bentelboun*), 25 three-year-old female camels (*jeddaa*), and 25 two-and-a-half-year-old male camels (*amsakhser*).[12] Nevertheless, in practice the two parties to the dispute would negotiate the number of camels to be handed over. Once decided, each family amongst the close agnates of the culprit would be instructed as to the age and sex of the camel(s) to be handed over (Denis, 2001: 61).

The animals handed over in *diya* can be understood both as a form of compensation to the injured party, and as a means, through the exchange of things, of mediating the relationship between parties to a dispute. Both principles run through other instances of the exchange of property in the resolution of disputes, such as in compensation for injury and for divorce settlements. In a divorce case discussed by Denis, the woman's family claimed that the husband was impotent. The groom himself claimed that the bride's family had kept the bride under such close watch so as to prevent him from finding an opportunity to consummate the marriage. The groom alleged that the bride's family wished her to be able to emerge from the marriage as a virgin, and to go on to marry a

medieval and early modern times in parts of northern Europe. For example, see Brown (1986) on blood money in Scotland in the early modern period.

11 See, for example Dresch (1989); Peters (1990); Weir (2007). For a review of anthropological discussions of *diya* in the Middle East and North Africa region, see Ben Hounet (2012).

12 For an alternative breakdown of the distribution of camels in the Maliki school of Islamic jurisprudence, followed in the north-west Sahara, see Malik ibn Anas (1989: 358-370), discussed in Ben Hounet (2012).

richer husband. (The groom-to-bride prestation, *mahr*, was higher for a virgin.) The divorce was eventually agreed with the bride's party giving two four-year-old camels to the groom, which Denis (2001: 58) interprets as both a return of (part of) the groom's wedding gifts, and a form of compensation.

The insights offered by Denis's account into disputes in the north-west Sahara in the colonial period demonstrate that property was not only a common object of dispute. It was also a crucial element in the pursuit of justice for claimants, and in the means of renewing, restoring or appeasing relations between disputing parties. The conditions of widespread material dispossession that befell those Sahrawis who became refugees near Tindouf affected both potential roles for property in disputes occurring in exile.

Disputes in Exile

Echoing the experiences of other refugee populations who have experienced intense dispossession (Sa'di and Abu-Lughod, 2007; Chatty 2010), Sahrawi refugees remembered the early period in exile as a time of intense material dispossession resulting from the exile itself. Indeed, many refugees arrived in exile without significant possessions. Those from urban backgrounds had fled their homes, and those hailing from the pasturelands had, in many cases, arrived in exile with neither livestock nor the tents in which they had lived (Hodges, 1983: 233). Such a context of material dispossession meant that, in practice, there were fewer opportunities for the previously common category of disputes about property, namely disputes over animals.[13] There being fewer possessions in circulation in general, there was also less opportunity for theft in the early years. In addition, some of the broader contextual problems, at least as perceived by Denis, such as the mobility of both animals (the main object of disputes) and persons (both litigants and witnesses) and the lack of a common overall calendar between litigants, changed in exile. The refugees were, especially in the early years, geographically focused in the space of the refugee camps. They were also encouraged to identify with a common chronology, reinforced upon them by the creation of new national dates to commemorate. These included dates such as 27 February (the founding of

13 In the 1970s and 1980s, Polisario developed animal herds of its own (and it indeed still owned such "public" herds in the 2000s). In refugees' memories of this period, for those refugees in the refugee camps who acquired animals in exile, typically sheep or goats, these were kept at that time in communal pens, overseen by the camp authorities (see Wilson, 2016).

SADR), and 9 June (the date of the death of the first Secretary General of Polisario and President of SADR, El Ouali Mustafa Sayed). Such dates were not only commemorated, but became inscribed on the geography of the refugee camps when public buildings, such as schools, were named after them.

In the early context of widespread material dispossession, although common potential sources of disputes (animals) had been minimalised, the potential for disputes between persons nevertheless remained. The most common kind of dispute that refugees recalled from this early period concerned marital relations. With fathers and husbands usually serving on the front during the period of active warfare between Polisario and Morocco, men were usually away from their wives and families for long periods. Prolonged absences were remembered as a potential cause of marital tension, possibly leading to requests for divorce.

Amongst Hassanophones, as amongst other Saharans (but in contrast to many Arab settings), a divorced women does not suffer from a stigma that is likely to obstruct her remarriage. So, there was already a potential openness towards divorce amongst Sahrawis, and an expectation that women could go on to remarry. Nevertheless, Polisario was – and remains – a pro-natalist liberation movement, keen to oversee the reproduction of future generations of Sahrawis who could continue to pursue self-determination. In this context, requests for divorce were channelled, in the early years of exile, to a forum for dispute resolution set up in exile by Polisario, through which it sought to pursue some of its own agendas as a governing authority.

Following in the steps of the colonial authorities whom Denis had served, Polisario set up a forum, endorsed by the state-like authorities of the refugee camps, for resolving disputes. In the late 1970s and 1980s, this forum took the form of a Popular Committee for Social Affairs and Justice (see Wilson, 2016). This was one of a range of Popular Committees that ran public services in the refugee camps. These Committees were modelled on the popular committees of Qaddafi's popular revolution in Libya. The committee responsible for resolving disputes has commonly come to be known as the Justice Committee. It was composed of women refugees (at this time, most adult men were away serving on the front), assisted by a legal specialist, known as a *mukhtaṣṣ*. It was the responsibility of the *mukhtaṣṣ* to ensure that the decisions of the Committee were compliant with Islamic law.

The Justice Committee can be seen as a forum through which Polisario attempted to pursue some of its own goals as a governing authority. For example, I explore elsewhere (Wilson, 2016) the extent to which the staging of dispute resolution in an almost all-female setting was a means of achieving a detribalisation of the administration of justice. Such detribalisation was in line with Polisario's wider early policies to undermine tribalism in the name of building a state authority for all Sahrawis. Prior to Polisario's embarking on what it saw as its revolution (*thawra*), discussion surrounding the resolution of disputes, *ṣulḥ*, or reconciliation, would have taken place between gatherings of male tribal elders. In the Justice Committee, these activities were displaced onto a group of women drawn from diverse tribal and social backgrounds – effectively "detribalising" *ṣulḥ* or the negotiation of resolutions for disputes.

The Justice Committee was also perceived by Polisario as a potential means of pursuing a particular kind of marriage agenda. Sophie Caratini (2000: 446) describes how one of the Justice Committee's jobs was to persuade parents of potential brides to consent to give their daughters in marriage to men hailing from different tribes. Historically, marriage patterns amongst Hassanophones favoured both "close marriage" with a relative, or women marrying into other tribes for the purpose of making suitable political alliances or relationships – to the exclusion of women marrying "down" the social scale (Caratini, 1989; Bonte, 2008). Part of the revolutionary agenda was to seek to promote marriages that contravened the former restrictions on women marrying men of a lower ranking tribe (see Wilson, 2016). The Justice Committee played a role in furthering the agenda for "revolutionary" marriage.

In addition, it appears that the Justice Committee was envisaged as a means of pursuing a pro-marriage, and by implication, pro-natalist agenda. Some of the women I interviewed who had taken part in a Justice Committee recalled that the Committee had, in the first instance, sought ways of resolving a marital dispute between couples in order to preserve the marriage (and the potential birth of more children, it was implied), but it is unclear whether such attempts prevailed in practice. According to Caratini (2000: 445), the number of divorces in exile increased.[14] A former *mukhtaṣṣ* whom I interviewed also recalled, laughingly, that his job had often been difficult, because, as the only man there, "every time a problem came up about marriage, the women would turn to me and blame 'you men'. I would tell them, 'You can't blame it all on me personally!'"

14 A rise in the number of divorces has been noted for refugee communities elsewhere. For example, Jonathan Bascom (1998: 138) found that the incidence of divorce has increased amongst Ethiopian refugees in Sudan. He suggests that this may have arisen from changes within households, and men helping less with domestic work. In the Sahrawi case, as well as there being a pre-exile precedent for tolerance for women's re-marriage after divorce, the initial fall in exile of the bridewealth required of a groom further decreased the barriers for re-marriage.

The early years in exile were represented by refugees – and their observers (Zunes, 1988; Caratini 2000) – as a time of few disputes between refugees. In a context of dispossession, property was far less commonly a cause of disputes, and it was also far less common for property to be taken up as a source of compensation between disputing parties. Yet by the 2000s, property was re-emerging both as a potential source of disputes, and as a potential resource for resolving disputes.

New Kinds of Disputes

The ceasefire of 1991 led to many changes in the Sahrawi refugee camps. Significant protests in the camps in 1988 had been violently put down by Polisario (see Zunes, 1999). But this led to a political crisis and, in the early 1990s, a political opening or "Sahrawi perestroika" (Shelley, 2004: 179). Important political reforms were undertaken, aimed at curbing unaccountable powers amongst the leadership of Polisario (see Wilson, 2016). The end of active warfare also led to new economic opportunities for the refugees. They now found more opportunities to migrate to Spain (see Gómez Martín, 2011), often as workers who sent remittances to family members in the camps. Thanks to various income sources – such as remittances, pensions from Spain for former Spanish colonial employees, local wages from NGOs or international aid organisations, and philanthropic gifts from host families in Europe who had hosted Sahrawi refugee children in summer programmes – from the late 1990s refugee entrepreneurs set up thriving markets in the refugee camps. For refugees who could access surplus income (and the opportunity to do so varied widely between refugee families), there were many new kinds of commodities to buy in the refugee camps.

In a sense, then, private property had re-emerged on a significant scale in the refugee camps. This development caused consternation amongst those refugees who felt that the accompanying rise of socio-economic differentiation between refugee families was a betrayal of revolutionary principles (see San Martín, 2010; Wilson, 2016). The resurgence of private property in turn created new trends in the kinds of disputes that emerged. There was also a transformation in the manner of seeking to deal with disputes. The Justice Committee, along with other Popular Committees, was disbanded in 1995. Whereas new Councils were formed to take over areas of former Committee work, such as health care, education and rations distributions, the Justice Committee was not replaced by a Council. Instead, Polisario set about professionalising the administration of justice in the refugee camps. New kinds of courts were established: a Court of First Instance, a Criminal Court and a Court of Appeal. These courts were staffed and serviced by legal professionals (judges and lawyers). The women of a neighbourhood were no longer charged with resolving disputes, as they had been in the days of the Justice Committee. In at least one case that I came across, a former *mukhtaṣṣ* became one of the new-style judges.[15]

What reconfigurations of the relationship between law and property did these changes bring? When the system of courts was introduced in the refugee camps, court archives were also established. The archive in the Court of First Instance in Ausserd refugee camp dated back, I was told, to 1997.[16] Although I requested access to the court archives, the request was not granted. It is possible that Polisario authorities, concerned with presenting a united image of the refugee community, were unwilling to facilitate a researcher's access to evidence of internal disputes between the refugees. I draw on interviews with judges and lawyers, and conversations with refugee interlocutors, to suggest some of the new patterns that emerged concerning law and property in the refugee camps.

According to some judges and interlocutors, a common kind of dispute concerned the re-sale of cars. In a sense, then, the "new" camel (see Chatty, 1986) had become a common object of dispute. There was a lively turnover of sales of cars in the refugee camps. Vehicles could reach the refugee camps via different routes. A common pattern was that refugees who had migrated to Europe (especially Spain) would save money to buy a car there. Popular models included a second-hand Mercedes saloon, or a Toyota Land Cruiser. Refugees wishing to bring these vehicles to the camps could then choose between one of two options. The car could be driven to an Algerian port, and then driven through Algeria to the refugee camps, or it could be shipped to a Moroccan port and driven down through Morocco and Moroccan-controlled Western Sahara, to Nouadhibou in Mauritania, across to Zouérate, and then to reach the camps via the Polisario-controlled areas of Western Sahara. The latter route was a considerably longer distance. In refugees' perception, though, the bureaucratic challenges of the Algerian route were greater. This might lead to the longer route being preferred. (Nevertheless, I came across cars that had been brought in through both routes.)

15 For a discussion of the professionalisation of justice in the Sahrawi refugee camps, see Wilson (2016). For a discussion of the effects of this professionalisation of justice on custom, see Wilson (2015).

16 The four biggest refugee camps are named after towns in Moroccan-controlled Western Sahara: El Ayoune, Smara, Dakhla and Ausserd.

Once the car had been brought to the camps, it could be sold locally to one of the refugee families who, through a route such as commerce or migration remittances, had become one of the wealthier families who could afford such cars. For instance, in 2012, my host family in Ausserd refugee camp welcomed back an uncle who had been working in Spain for a few years. He arrived back in the camp driving a Toyota SR5 that sported a Madrid licence plate. It still looked spruce, despite its long journey across the desert. He had travelled via Morocco, Moroccan-controlled Western Sahara, Mauritania and Polisario-controlled Western Sahara. His plan was to sell the car locally – and he was already in touch with potential buyers. Such a car might sell for 3,000-4,000 euros. His plan was to use the money to pay for his wedding, and then in the coming weeks to return to Spain (without his wife) to work again, perhaps to bring another car back on his return.

Disputes about the sale of cars would be taken to the Court of First Instance. As judges explained to me, all contracts for buying and selling were dealt with in the refugee camps through Maliki jurisprudence. At least in the late 2000s, there were as yet no SADR codified laws for sales or contracts.[17]

If disputes over sales were amongst the affairs that kept judges in the Court of First Instance busy, a common kind of case that came before the Criminal Court concerned theft. According to an interlocutor who worked as a teacher in the male prison in the refugee camps, this was the most common crime for which prisoners were serving sentences. Whilst I did not have the opportunity to find out the kinds of theft for which prisoners had been detained, refugees talked about, and took precautions against, the kinds of theft they perceived to be likely. Mud-brick rooms that contained valuable items, such as a television, stereo system or satellite dish, were locked up when these rooms were left unoccupied. A cautious refugee who had money, I learned, would protect it by burying it in the sand. (A concerned host remonstrated with me that I should do the same with my own money.)

It might seem at first surprising that the kinds of disputes over property that Sahrawi refugees most readily discussed, both amongst themselves and when questioned on this directly, concerned cars and theft. What of disputes over housing, and productive resources such as land and animals? In a sense, the Sahrawi refugee community was not subject to some of the pressures in these areas that have marked other refugee communities. Where refugee camps for Palestinians are constrained for space to accommodate new refugee homes (Peteet, 2005; Feldman, 2015), the Sahrawi refugee camps are located in a vast

17 There were SADR codified laws for other areas, such as the penal code and the penal procedural code. See Wilson (2016).

stretch of inhospitable desert. At each stage when population pressure has called for spaces for new homes, either a new camp or new districts in existing camps have been founded. I heard of one rumoured dispute between families about one home being built too close to another, which occurred in the 27th February camp (later renamed Boudjour) in the late 2000s. As the only camp at the time with access to mains electricity, space to build there within access to electricity was highly coveted. My interlocutors in 27th February were unable to share more than vague rumours of the dispute with me, and this kind of dispute seemed to be rare in a wider context of space being available for families prepared to relocate, if necessary, to the edge of a refugee camp.

Small scale animal husbandry of sheep and goats was common in the refugee camps, with families often having an individual pen for a few privately owned animals. I heard of disagreement as to the appropriate location of these animal pens, but not of disputes over ownership of these animals. It is possible that, in the pasturelands of Polisario-controlled Western Sahara, which were several hours drive away from the camps and where camel-raising was a common activity, there may have been the kinds of disputes over animals that would have struck Denis as familiar.

Productive land resources can be the subject of intra-refugee disputes and tensions, and can cause disputes between refugees and host communities (Frésia, 2009; James, 2009). In the Sahrawi refugee case, the (scant) horticultural activity that took place in some camps was organised collectively by Polisario, and the produce distributed amongst refugees. Local Algerians from Tindouf were also not allowed to enter the refugee camps without a permit, so possibilities for conflicts between Algerian host and Sahrawi refugee populations were scarce. By no means was the Sahrawi refugee community lacking in internal disputes – but the circumstances of exile concentrated tension in particular areas rather than others.

If property had re-emerged as a potential source of disputes, there was also a trend in the 2000s towards, in some cases, refugees making demands on other refugees for compensation for wrongs suffered, and this compensation could take the form of property. For example, the family of my host mother in Ausserd, Māghalāha, told me that, in the mid 2000s, one of her relatives came to receive compensation for an injury.[18] The young man in question had been hit in a car accident. A car without mirrors hit the car in which he was travelling, and the young man was injured. At first he was sent to the hospital in Tindouf, and from there he was sent on to the hospital in Algiers – a sign of the gravity of the injury. The young man was left, Māghalāha's daughter Khanātha

18 All names of interlocutors are pseudonyms.

explained, unable to move. The driver of the mirror-less car had come from a different tribe, and elders from his tribe now approached elders from the tribe of the injured young man, asking what compensation they would like.[19] The family of the injured young man asked for a car, and for some money, which they received in due course. Khanātha went on to explain that her relative later got better, and was able to drive the car that he had been given. He worked as a taxi driver, taking fares from Ausserd to neighbouring camps.

Māghalāha's family members took an approving view of the handing over of compensation in this case. At the time the car was given, they explained, the injured young man was unable to move and might face a lifetime of not only being dependent, but also being unable to provide for others in his own family. It was right in the circumstances, they felt, for the tribe of the driver who had been at fault to provide the family of the victim with a source of income. Whilst the injured young man recovered enough to be able to drive the car himself, he retained some injury to his leg which affected the way he walked. Since he would therefore be restricted in the kind of work he could do, Māghalāha's family felt that it was right that he should continue to benefit from the opportunity to earn an income with which the compensation had provided him.

Not all cases of compensation payment were spoken of with such approval, however. Another relative of Māghalāha's family had found himself obliged to make a compensation payment of a different kind. There is a tradition amongst Hassanophones whereby a wife who has been offended by her husband can become angry or "*mughṭāḍa*" with him. This requires him to make her significant gifts in order to appease her and to be able to assume marital relations. Whilst the use of the term "*mughṭāḍa*" for this state of affairs seems to be particular to Hassanophones, comparable practices have been observed elsewhere in the arabophone world – where a wife may become *zalane* [sic] (angry) (Peters, 1978) or *hardane* [sic] (angry) (Ginat, 1982) – as well as in the non-arabophone Sahara (Lhote, 1944: 294). One of Māghalāha's male relatives had been married to his wife for many years, but had gone to work in Spain, from where he sent remittances to support his wife and children in the refugee camps. Nevertheless, in the 2000s the man took a second wife in Spain. When the first wife heard about this, she became *mughṭāḍa*. The husband found himself obliged to make compensation payments in order to appease her. Khanātha explained that he gave his first wife the following: new mud-brick rooms in the refugee camps, a car, a camel for slaughtering, a sheep for

19 The interlocutors named the relevant tribes to me when they discussed the cases presented here. Nevertheless, because it was sensitive to name tribes in the refugee camps, I choose not to name the implicated tribes.

slaughtering, jewellery and "a lot of money". "Was she satisfied?" I asked. "Yes," Khanātha replied. But at this point, Māghalāha's sister, with whom we were talking – a woman whose own marital history had entailed four marriages and four divorces, and who still received offers of marriage – interjected with her view of whether her relative had been able adequately to make up for his offending action. She called out: "Utfū!" (a Hassaniya expletive expressing strong disapproval). Where the first compensation case had been discussed as an appropriate resolution, in this second case, even the generous gifts offered to the first wife were not deemed by all observers to be a satisfactory recompense.

Whilst in these two cases some compensation was offered and accepted by injured parties, in practice compensation that could be claimed was not always requested, or, when offered, was not always accepted. One case of accidental death and one case of murder illustrate that compensation could be offered or owed, but foregone.

Mbārak, a young bureaucrat in his late twenties, recounted this story of how a young relative of his was killed in a car accident in the mid 2000s. His female relative on his father's side had been walking along, holding the hand of her young son, who was about two years old. A car came along with faulty breaks. (This was a common condition of the old cars in circulation in the refugee camps, as I experienced myself on a number of occasions.) The car hit the young boy, who died. The boy who died and the driver of the car came from different tribes. Elders from the driver's tribe approached elders from the dead boy's tribe. Over tea, Mbārak explained, the first group asked the second what they wanted in compensation for the death. The elders of the little boy's tribe, however, said that it was an accident, and that they did not want to ask for any compensation.

Accidental deaths – very often as a result of car accidents – were not unusual in the refugee camps. Murder cases, however, were much rarer. In interview in 2008, several judges who were familiar with the history of the Criminal Court in the refugee camps believed that, at that time, there had been five cases of murder since the refugee camps had been formed. Māghalāha's family were familiar with one of the cases, which had occurred in the mid 2000s. A member of Māghalāha's tribe had been murdered. In the account of 'Abdi, Māghalāha's son, the murdered man had a large amount of money – between three and four thousand euros. "A friend" came to him one evening, took him to the marketplace for dinner, and then, with another man, took him out to the desert, to the south of Smara camp, where they strangled him with his turban. ('Abdi thought that they might possibly have knifed him too.) But the victim had hidden his money (allegedly in his shop). His killers left him in the desert.

The next day, neighbours noticed that he had not opened his shop. A search began and his body was eventually found. The corpse was taken to Tindouf for examination, and inquiries were made as to who had been seen with the dead man before his death. People at the restaurant were able to say who had been with him, and the two men who had killed him were found. ʿAbdi named the two tribes from which the perpetrators hailed, both different from the tribe of the victim. He went on to describe how the victim's father was approached – in ʿAbdi's account by the police – and asked what he wanted to do next. According to SADR penal law, the family of the victim was entitled to compensation. Article 220 of the SADR penal code states that indemnity must be paid in accordance with *diya* in cases of homicide and injury. Nevertheless, the victim's father allegedly replied that he did not want compensation. The two men went to prison. As in the case of the little boy who died in the car accident, the family of the victim gave up their right to compensation.

Exile and the Ambiguities of Compensation

Sahrawi refugees have experienced a changing relationship to law and property. Initially, the material dispossession of exile impeded the likelihood of property being the object of a dispute – in contrast to what seems to have been commonly the case before exile, at least according to Denis's (2001) experiences as a colonial officer. There was also little opportunity in the early days of exile for refugees facing disputes to resort to property as a means of offering compensation to resolve a dispute. Over time, however, as the economy changed in the refugee camps and private property re-emerged on a more significant scale, property became once again a potential object of dispute and opportunity for theft, and a potential resource for making compensation payments in disputes. By the mid 2000s, in at least some cases, there were refugees who were offering, and accepting, compensation in order to resolve disputes. Nevertheless, the opportunity to claim compensation – formally supported in the SADR penal code for cases of injury and homicide – was not always taken up, as we saw from the last two cases discussed. Why might the families of the victims have declined an offer of compensation, or the right to claim compensation?

Whilst I was not able to interview the families directly affected by these cases, I discussed this question with a number of interlocutors, who shared their views on the subject. Legal professionals were aware that the SADR penal code upheld the rights of families to compensation. Refugees might not be so readily familiar with the SADR management of compensation, but were very familiar with the principles of *diya* and other forms of compensation. In practice, though, refugees and legal professionals often expressed the view that it was controversial in exile to ask for compensation. Just as the right to freedom of association was "on hold" in the SADR constitution until the question of self-determination could be resolved, so refugees spoke of how it was "not right" (*mā hī zayna*) to demand compensation in exile. In some cases, judges suggested that the right to compensation existed in theory, but in practice should actually be taken up after exile.

The barriers to taking up compensation in exile were thus not only material – as had very much been the case in the early years of exile. When the improved material conditions of the later exile period lowered the material barriers, Sahrawi refugees – like their Palestinian counterparts observed by Julie Peteet – met political and moral barriers to taking up compensation claims. Encouraged to focus on the rights for the claiming of which they found themselves in exile, principally their right to self-determination, refugees could find themselves discouraged from claiming other rights, such as the right to compensation in intra-refugee disputes.

The relationship between law and property for long-term refugees is therefore complex. The image of a dispossessed refugee, who has been deprived of property because of a violation of legality, is powerful (Sa'di and Abu-Lughod, 2007; Chatty, 2010). There is also increasing scholarly and policy recognition of the rights of refugees to reparations for property lost, which may take the form of compensation for property lost on going into exile (Leckie, 2003). Sahrawi refugees in Algeria certainly suffered the loss of property upon becoming refugees. Nevertheless, the discussion here has suggested further nuances to explore in the relationship between refugees, law and property. Long-term refugees are likely to face intra-refugee disputes that emerge in exile. Property may be both a potential object of dispute, or, in the form of compensation, a potential means of resolving disputes. Yet in practice, moral and political pressures arising from the wider context of exile may see refugees forego their potential rights to compensation in intra-refugee disputes. For long-term Sahrawi refugees, it remains to be seen how the ambiguities of the right to compensation in exile may affect dispute resolution in a potential post-exile future.

References

Bascom, J. 1998. *Losing Place: Refugee Populations and Rural Transformations in East Africa*. New York: Berghahn.

Ben Hounet, Y. 2012. "'Cent dromadaires et quelques arrangements': Notes sur la diya (prix du sang) et son application actuelle au Soudan et en Algérie", *Revue des Mondes Musulmans et de la Méditerranée* 131: 203-221.

Bonte, P. 2008. *L'émirat de l'Adar mauritanien: Harim, compétition et protection dans une société tribale saharienne*. Paris: Karthala.

Brown, K.M. 1986. *Bloodfeud in Scotland 1573-1625: Violence, Justice and Politics in an Early Modern Society*. Edinburgh: Donald.

Caratini, S. 1989. *Les Rgaybāt (1610-1934): Territoire et société*, vol. 2. Paris: Harmattan.

Caratini, S. 2000. "Système de parenté sahraoui: L'impact de la révolution", *L'Homme* 154-155: 431-456.

Caro Baroja, J. 1955. *Estudios Saharianos*. Madrid: Consejo Superior de Investigaciones Científicas, Instituto de Estudios Africanos.

Chatty, D. 1986. *From Camel to Truck: The Bedouin in the Modern World*. New York: Vantage Press.

Chatty, D. 2010. *Displacement and Dispossession in the Modern Middle East*. Cambridge: Cambridge University Press.

Chatty, D., E. Fiddian-Qasmiyeh and G. Crivello. 2010. "Identity with/out Territory: Sahrawi Refugee Youth in Transnational Space", in: Chatty, D. (Ed.), *Deterritorialized Youth: Sahrawi and Afghan Refugees at the Margins of the Middle East*, ed. D. Chatty. Oxford: Berghahn, 37-84.

de Greiff, P. 2006. "Repairing the Past: Compensation for Victims of Human Rights Violations", in *The Handbook of Reparations*, ed. P. de Greiff. Oxford: Oxford University Press, 1-16.

Denis, P. 2001. *La justice chez les nomades algériens avant 1960*. Paris: Harmattan.

Deubel, T. 2012. "Poetics of Diaspora: Sahrawi Poets and Postcolonial Transformations of a Trans-Saharan Genre in Northwest Africa", *Journal of North African Studies* 16 (4): 295-314.

Dresch, P. 1989. *Tribes, Government and History in Yemen*. Oxford: Clarendon Press.

Evans-Pritchard, E.S. 1940. *The Nuer: A Description of the Modes of Livelihood and Political Institutions of a Nilotic People*. Oxford: Clarendon Press.

Feldman, I. 2015. "What is a Camp? Legitimacy and Experience in Spaces of Long-term Displacement", *Geoforum* 66: 244-252.

Frésia, M. 2009. *Les Mauritaniens réfugiés au Sénégal: Une anthropologie critique de l'asile et de l'aide humanitaire*. Paris: Harmattan.

Ginat, J. 1982. *Women in Muslim Rural Society*. New Brunswick, NJ: Transaction.

Gómez Martín, C. 2011. *La migración saharaui en España: Estrategias de visibilidad en el tercer tiempo del exilio*. Saarbrücken: Editorial Académica Española.

Hodges, T. 1983. *Western Sahara: Roots of a Desert War*. Beckenham: Croom Helm.

Human Rights Watch. 2008. *Human Rights in Western Sahara and in the Tindouf Refugee Camps*. New York: Human Rights Watch.

Human Rights Watch. 2012. *Morocco and Western Sahara*. New York: Human Rights Watch.

International Court of Justice. 1975. "Western Sahara" (International Court of Justice Western Sahara, General List No. 61 [1974-1975]). The Hague: ICJ.

James, W. 2009. *War and Survival in Sudan's Frontierlands: Voices from the Blue Nile*. Oxford: Oxford University Press.

Jensen, E. 2005. *Western Sahara: Anatomy of a Stalemate*. Boulder, CO: Lynne Rienner.

Leckie, S. 2003. *Returning Home: Housing and Property Restitution Rights of Refugees and Displaced Persons*. Ardsley, NY: Transnational.

Lhote, J. 1944. *Les Touaregs du Hoggar (Ahaggar)*. Paris: Payot.

Malik ibn Anas. 1989. *Al-Muwatta of Imam Malik ibn Anas: The First Formulation of Islamic Law*. New York: Kegan Paul International.

McConnell, F. 2009. *Rehearsing the State: The Governance Practices of the Exile Tibetan Government*. Oxford: John Wiley.

Pazzanita, A. 2006. *The Historical Dictionary of Western Sahara*. Lanham, MD: Scarecrow.

Peteet, J.M. 2005. *Landscape of Hope and Despair: Palestinian Refugee Camps*. Philadelphia: University of Pennsylvania Press.

Peters, E.L. 1978. "The Status of Women in Four Middle East Communities", in *Women in the Muslim World*, ed. N.R. Keddie and L. Beck. Cambridge, MA: Harvard University Press, 311-350.

Peters, E.L. 1990. *Bedouin of Cyrenaica: Studies in Personal and Corporate Power*. Cambridge: Cambridge University Press.

Sa'di, A.H. and L. Abu-Lughod. 2007. *Nakba: Palestine, 1948, and the Claims of Memory*. New York: Columbia University Press.

San Martín, P. 2010. *Western Sahara: The Refugee Nation*. Cardiff: University of Wales Press.

Shelley, T. 2004. *Endgame in the Western Sahara. What Future for Africa's Last Colony?* London: Zed.

UN Sub-Commission on the Promotion and Protection of Human Rights. 2005. "UN Principles of Housing and Property Restitution for Refugees and Displaced Persons". E/CN.4/Sub.2/2005/2017. <http://www.unhcr.org/uk/protection/idps/50f94d849/principles-housing-property-restitution-refugees-displaced-persons-pinheiro.html> (accessed 16 August 2017).

Weir, S. 2007. *A Tribal Order: Politics and Law in the Mountains of Yemen*. Austin: University of Texas Press.

Wilson, A. 2014a. "Ambiguities of Space and Control: When Refugee Camp and Nomadic Encampment Meet", *Nomadic Peoples* 18: 38-60.

Wilson, A. 2014b. "Cycles of Crisis: Migration and the Formation of New Political Identities in Western Sahara", in *Crises et migrations dans les pays du sud*, ed. M. Pérouse de Montclos, V. Petit, and N. Robin. Paris: Harmattan, 79-105.

Wilson, A. 2015. "Refracting Custom in Western Sahara's Quest for Statehood", *Political and Legal Anthropology Review* 38: 72-90.

Wilson, A. 2016. *Sovereignty in Exile: A Saharan Liberation Movement Governs*. Philadelphia: University of Pennsylvania Press.

Zunes, S. 1988. "Participatory Democracy in the Sahara: A Study of Polisario Self-Governance", *Scandinavian Journal of Development Alternatives* 7 (2-3): 141-157.

Zunes, S. 1999. "Unarmed Resistance in the Middle East and North Africa", in *Nonviolent Social Movements: A Geographical Perspective*, ed. S. Zunes, L.R. Kurts and S.B. Asher. Malden, MA: Blackwell, 41-51.

Zunes, S., and J. Mundy. 2010. *Western Sahara: War, Nationalism and Conflict Irresolution*. New York: Syracuse University Press.

CHAPTER 8

Kafāla and Succession: The Practices of Transfer of the "Parent's" Name and Goods to an Adopted Child

Emilie Barraud

It is commonly held that adoption does not exist in the Maghreb, in particular in Morocco and in Algeria, since "Islam forbids it" (Q 33:4, 5, 37). However, the ethnology of adoption, invites us to qualify this assertion. Adoption as defined in French law, that is, as an institution that has an impact on filiation, has no equivalent in Moroccan or Algerian law.[1] Yet this does not exclude the existence of forms of social, informal, sometimes illegal parenthood, and also the institutionalised form, *kafāla*. In this field, there is another common belief that a child "adopted" or fostered via the legal *kafāla* mechanism is not considered a legitimate child: he or she would not take the name his or her *kafīl* father (assignee of the right to foster), or inherit property from him, since "Islam forbids it" (adoptive filiation is prohibited). The norm would then be the absence of adoption and, if we accept that the *kafāla* is a form of adoption, the norm would be the absence of practices that transfer the name or goods outside of legitimate filiation (founded on the coincidence of consanguinity and of alliance), due to the authority of Islamic law. However, the ethnography of adoptive practices and of legal transfer practices in the framework of *kafāla* testifies to a more complex reality governed by other references than that of Islam. The purpose of this article is to shed light on this social reality in Algeria.

Prohibition of Adoption, and Legal Fostering (*Kafāla*)

Since 1984, Algerian law, with explicit reference to the *sharīʿa*, prohibits adoption as a legal act that establishes between the adopted child and the adoptive parent legal relationships analogous to those resulting from filiation. Article 46 (Chapter V) of the Family Code formally sets out that "adoption (*tabannī*) is prohibited by the *sharīʿa* and the law". The Algerian legislation uses a doubly imperative tone and refers to the authority of Islamic law. The *sharīʿa* is indeed

1 It was nevertheless set out in the Tunisian Personal Status Code in 1958.

 | DOI 10.1163/9789004362116_010

a material legal source invoked by the judge[2] when the law is silent. As regards adoption, the Family Code is not silent, but the legislation is intended to mark an official, firm position, so that the norm cannot be disputed.

My research has helped show that, in this regard, the rules of law do not always match the observed reality (Barraud, 2009; 2013). Here, as elsewhere, couples confronted by the crisis of sterility have always been able to bypass or even to infringe the laws, opting for forms of total or partial adoption of a child from their own, or a different, family. The still current phenomenon of illegal adoptions testifies to a discrepancy between the law and social aspirations, and demonstrates how the stigma attached to being a sterile couple, or the absolute necessity of toeing the line, leads to transgressing the law, the better to comply with the dominant model.

The Family Code prohibits adoption, but has replaced it since 1984 with another mode of family integration – the legal fostering of a minor, or *kafāla*. The legalisation of *kafāla* results from an awareness that it is vital to have a policy concerning abandoned children, a phenomenon traditionally kept secret, but which worsened drastically during the 1980s (Barraud, 2010). This form of fostering has gradually taken precedence as the privileged mode of managing and protecting abandoned children, a social category hitherto invisible and violently ostracised.

Legal fostering, *kafāla*, consists of the promise to undertake without payment the upkeep and protection of a minor, "as a father would do for his own son" (Art. 116). It makes the child eligible for "the same family and school services as the legitimate child" (Art.121). In the text, the bond derived from *kafāla* is twice compared to legitimate filiation, acting as a reference, but in no circumstances does legal fostering result in any filial bond between the adult and the child. The child does not take the name of or inherit from his or her *kafīl* (guardian or assignee of the legal fostering scheme); the rules of succession, determined by the Qur'an and incorporated into positive law, only acknowledge consanguinity and alliance. The *makfūl* (fostered child or beneficiary of the legal fostering scheme) is not considered a son or daughter and is therefore not registered in the family record book. By not recognising the filiation between the parents and the child, *kafāla* avoids any transgression of legitimate situations. This institution is socially reassuring since, as he or she is only partially affiliated, the fostered child does not pose a threat to the rights of the legitimate heirs.

2 Art. 1 of the Civil Law.

The prohibition of adoption finds its source in the Qur'an.[3] Etymologically, the word *kafāla* means security and guarantee, as well as taking care of and looking after somebody. On two occasions, the word appears in the Qur'an in the sense of "giving custody, appointing or designating someone as a guardian". Q 20:39 refers to the story of Moses when, entrusted to the waters of the river, he is discovered by Pharaoh's wife and returned to his mother (who pretends to be a wet-nurse): "Put him in the casket, and cast it into the river. Then the river will cast it on the bank, and he shall be picked up by an enemy of Mine and an enemy of his. And I cast upon you a love from Me, and that you might be reared under My eyes."

Q 3:37 refers to one of the episodes in the life of Mary, when she is entrusted to Zakariah after the child (Jesus) has been placed in the temple: "*wa-kaffalahā Zakariyyā*". This sentence may be interpreted in two ways (Aït Zaï, 1996: 97). In the first, "*Zakariyyā*" is the second direct object, subjected to the action of God, and in charge of a mission of protection and of supervision with respect to Mary: "Thereupon her Lord accepted her with a gracious acceptance, and made her grow up in a worthy fashion, and He charged *Zakariyyā* with her care" or "welcomed her in the best possible way and let her grow beautifully, and then entrusted her to *Zakariyyā*" or again "turned *Zakariyyā* into her guardian" (Aït Zaï 1996: 97). The other interpretation makes *Zakariyyā* the subject of the sentence: "And *Zakariyyā* is vouching for Mary." The latter reading is the one chosen by the later Algerian and Moroccan legislators. The individual is free to vouch voluntarily for someone. Although the term is employed in the Qur'anic text, Maliki *fiqh* did not formalise *kafāla*. The concept of *kafāla* takes its root in the function of the *kafīl* and should be understood as "a pure fact attached to the notions of guardianship and upkeep" (Aït Zaï, interview, Algiers 2006). In other words, *kafāla* has not been the object of a legal construction by jurists.

The minor who is fostered by *kafāla* may be of known or unknown filiation. If his parents can be traced, he keeps his original filiation. If not, the Civil Registry Code of 1970 (Art. 64)[4] and a law of 1976[5] are applicable to him, pursuant to which a patronym is compulsory for any person deprived thereof. Maliki *fiqh* classifies children into three categories: legitimate (born in wed-

3 Q 33:4, 5 and 37 are concerned with elective parenthood (Barraud, 2008).

4 "The registrar himself ascribes the first names to children born from unknown parents. The child is designated by a sequence of first names of which the last serves as a family name" (Ordinance 70-20 of 19 February 1970 governing civil status, *Official Journal* 1970, p. 233.

5 Ordinance 76-7 of 20 February 1976 requiring the choice of a family name for people deprived thereof (Art. 1), *Official Journal* 1976, p. 214.

lock), illegitimate (born out of wedlock) and of unknown origin (found). In today's Algeria, children born outside of a matrimonial framework (illegitimate children, from *zinā*[6]) are assimilable to children of unknown filiation, not recognised by their father (Barraud, 2010).

In 2001, the Ministry concerned announced 5,000 officially recorded births out of wedlock in Algeria (CNEAP, 2001). In 2007, the figure reached 7,000, not taking into account the reality of illegitimate sexual relations (especially preconjugal sexual relations, in the context of the prolonged celibacy of the younger generation), abandoned children, infanticide and illegal adoption practices. The Ministry of National Solidarity kept statistics for about 15 years on the number of abandoned children, showing an astonishingly stable 3,000 per annum, including 600 children born in the bush. However, these are official figures and there is every indication that the real figure is considerably higher.

Algerian law does not officially recognise the existence of illegitimate children, and the Family Code does not refer to them. The fate of these "non-standard" newborns, whose handicap is strictly social, is associated with the decision of the birth mother, commonly called a "single mother". If she has the support of her family and relational as well as material resources, she may keep the child and, since 2005, the law has authorised her to be recognised as the child's mother (Art. 44). The child is thus deprived of *nasab* (genealogical name, legitimate filiation) but bears the family name (*laqab*) of his mother, with the consent of the male heirs. Otherwise, the mother is forced to abandon her child as soon as he or she is born, and in great secrecy. Single mothers are the primary source of children for Algerian orphanages, abandoning their children, whose sole handicap is illegitimate birth, the absence of a name and of legitimate filiation (*nasab*).

The Transfer of the Name Outside Legitimate Filiation

During the first years of its being covered by legalisation, legal fostering was blatantly unsuccessful. There are many infertile couples who wish to adopt a child without a family, but most of them give up in order to avoid being singled out by society on account of a double shame: being sterile and fostering a child perceived as the "fruit of sin". Because the patronym of the parent and the child does not coincide, the *kafāla* is visible. It exposes the sterility of the *kafīl* and

6 *Zinā* occurs when the rules of marriage have not been respected and the matrimonial prohibitions have been infringed.

the shameful origins of the *makfūl*, who is no longer without status, but who remains set apart, stigmatised by his/her two first names and his/her unknown filiation. This is especially serious in a society that defines individuals by their kinship.

The Algerian parliament endeavoured to solve the problem of nominal stigmatisation by promulgating a surprising decree in 1992. The amendment on name matching is the result of joint work between the president of the AAEFAB (Algerian Association for Children and Voluntary Foster Families), the Ministry of Social Affairs and the High Islamic Council: the objective being to enable the better social and family integration of the *makfūl*, while respecting Islamic law. The prohibition on transmitting the father's name to the adopted child refers to a certain interpretation of Q 33:5: "Call them after their fathers. That is more just with Allah. And if you do not know their fathers, then they are your brethren in the faith and your kinsmen."

But can we compare the name as it was conceived in seventh-century Arabia to the modern patronym? At the time of the Prophet and before marital status was introduced by the French in Algeria (1865), a person was designated by a first name (*ism*), followed by the *nasab* (genealogical name: a list of the father's and male antecedants' first names, each preceded by *ibn* – "son of"). A third element, the *laqab* (honorific name) was institutionalised by law as the "family name". The opponents of the project defended an interpretation whereby the name was transmitted through filiation alone, and they feared the possible ambiguity arising from the *kafīl* and *makfūl* bearing the same patronym. The child ran the risk of being mistaken for the son of the *kafīl* in the eyes of the community. In other words, they feared "a shift towards adoption" (Pruvost, 1996: 174). The proponents of the project focused the debate on the notion of *ijtihād*,[7] arguing that Islam cannot accomplish its mission – to ground a right capable of organising the needs of society and developing solutions adapted to modern social problems – without making this effort to reflect.

Calling for attempts to reconcile Qur'anic precepts with new social requirements, they developed a process of reasoning concerning the modern family name which, now compulsory for any Algerian citizen, enables a transition from "a traditional definition of the person by the *nasab* [...] to a personal identity" (Borrmans, 1977: 349). They succeeded in convincing their opponents that a shared name in the framework of *kafāla* would have no impact on filiation. In August 1991, the Ministry of Religious Affairs informed the president of the AAEFAB, Mr Tifadi, after a long interview with the President of the

---

7 *Ijtihād* – independent judgement (within Islam law), whereby the prescriptions of the sacred texts may be adapted to the needs and development of society.

Association of Ulemas, that: "If the purpose of this kinship is not to make the child benefit from inheritance nor to proscribe what is not proscribed, such as the marriage of the daughter with the foster father, then it is possible to give the name."

The authorisation of the same name was legalised in January 1992.[8] Let us note that this date coincides with that of the signature by Algeria of the United Nations Convention on the Rights of the Child (UNCRC), which saw the emergence of an important new term of reference: "the best interests of the child". This was one of the four guiding principles of this Convention, which makes the child a "subject of rights". Since then, the *makfūl* may bear the patronym of his/her *kafīl*, but always the *laqab*, never the *nasab*. The fostered child bears the family name of his/her adoptive parents but has no place among the possible heirs. Since 1992, the number of legal fostering cases involving a change of name has soared in Algeria. All the actors and observers of *kafāla* consider this decree to be a measure well-adapted to social aspirations. However, there is a blatant gap between the rules of Islamic law and the resulting governmental reforms on the one hand, and social practices and aspirations on the other.

Most of the time, Algerian *kafīl*s think in terms of adoption. They wish to be seen as the exclusive parents of the youngest child, who ideally resembles them physically as closely as possible, who has been definitively abandoned and whose filiation is unknown, and to whom they will pass on their name and much more. Everything possible is done to disguise the adoptive situation, to emerge from marginalisation (caused by sterility) and to return to the norm by copying the family model. The provisions of *kafāla* therefore thwart the aspirations of those who experience child fostering as a full adoption.[9]

Consequently, over the last few decades, in view of contemporary social developments, changes in the representation of the abandoned child, and the battle led by the AAEFAB and adoptive parents, the *kafāla* model has been revised to adapt it to new social necessities and aspirations. However, these changes transgress certain rules, to the extent that the *kafāla* model increasingly tends towards the prohibited adoption model, especially in its simple

8 Executive Decree 92-24 of 13 January 1992, complement of Decree 71-157 of 3 June 1971 regarding the change of name, *Official Journal* 1992, p. 113.

9 Legal fostering is temporary and revocable. The child can be returned to his biological parents, even if he has lived in his adoptive family for many years. The *makfūl* does not become an heir. *Kafāla* is still often performed in the name of the husband alone. In case of divorce or death, the *makfūl* is inherited just as an owned object would be. These factors explain the success, even today, of illegal adoptions, in spite of the arrangements and compromises granted by parliament.

form.[10] Focusing on majority practice concerning the elaboration of the legislation on *kafāla*, its adjustments, its application and especially the experience people have of it, we may venture the hypothesis that the law, in this specific domain, seems less and less subordinate to Islamic authority. The sole difference that may be observed between simple adoption and *kafāla* is that the child is integrated into the family of the *kafīl* but does not figure among the possible heirs.[11]

From the Object Child Whom We Bequeath to the Loved Child to Whom We Bequeath

> From the perspective of the rules of inheritance, the makfūl is as if she were an only daughter, or as if there were no children at all. The makfūl does not exist. As if that were not enough, the makfūl is transferred with the goods. (official of the Direction des affaires sociales [DAS] in Algiers, 2012)

Bearing the same name as the father is not essential to filiation, but this does not deal with the issue of inheritance. The problem arises in very specific terms inasmuch as the *makfūl*, far from ranking among the heirs, is considered to be part of the inheritance. At the death of his *kafīl*, on a par with any other possession, he becomes, as it were part of the assets: "In case of death, the legal right of fostering is transferred to the heirs if they commit themselves to fulfil it. If not, the judge assigns the custody of the child to the competent institution for assistance" (Art. 125). The heirs are the legitimate children of the *kafīl* and the *makfūl*'s adoptive brothers, but not of his adoptive mother. Thus, the *makfūl*, unlike any legitimate child, is covered neither by the rules relating to succession nor by the right of custody (*ḥaḍāna*), which is devolved to the mother when the father passes away (Art. 64).[12]

10 In France, simple adoption is an adoption whereby legal bonds remain between the child and his family of origin (Articles 360 ff of the French Civil Code). Its conditions are much less demanding and its effects less radical than full adoption.

11 In addition, in simple adoption, the adopted child takes the status of "son of" his adoptive parents; in other words, a bond of filiation is created.

12 In case of the divorce of the *kafīl* couple, judges generally refuse to rule on the right of custody. As illustrated by judgement n°1288/07 of 15 May 2007, Tribunal of Cheraga, for example, in this abstract of a discriminatory argument by a family judge: "Whereas the defendant has asked for custody of the young girl taken in *kafāla* and the refusal of the applicant to pay alimony, and to place at her disposal a domicile so as to exert a right of

These laws, which enclose the *makfūl* in an irreducible situation of alterity so as to protect the interests of the legitimate heirs, only partially reflect the observable social reality. Indeed, reading the legal norms does not enable us to conclude that all the children fostered under *kafāla* are systematically returned to the DAS at the death of their *kafīl* father, or that they are never the beneficiaries of bequeathed goods within their adoptive family. The ethnographic approach combined with the study of legal cases and the solutions found in case law reveal other concepts and norms of reference such as "filial love", "equality for children and citizens" and "the best interests of the child", which support these bequest practices. When a *kafīl* father dies, the judge must rule in the interests of the child, which most often results in the *makfūl* remaining with the wife of the *kafīl*, i.e. in the custody of his adoptive mother. Similarly, we have seen that the rule of legitimacy acts against fostered children, to block their share of the inheritance from their adoptive parents. Should it be deduced, then, that this rule is systematically applied every time a child is fostered under *kafāla* in an Algerian family? We cannot make this assumption. In many cases, "conservatory" provisions are taken by the adoptive parents to protect the fostered child, which are governed by strategies that circumvent the Islamic prohibition of adoptive filiation.

"Gift" as a Remedy for the Inequalities of the Rules on Succession

In a book on "gift" (*hiba*), Yvon Linant de Bellefonds (1935: 16) gives a general definition of the term, valid for all Muslim sects: "The immediate transfer from the donor to the donee of the ownership of goods, for free and for worldly ends."[13] The Algerian Family Code defines it in equivalent terms and goes on to say: "It may relate to the donor's goods in all or in part" (Chap. II, Art. 205). Thus, in terms of gift (*hiba*), any person is legally entitled to deprive himself/herself, while he/she is alive, of the totality of his/her movable and immovable

custody therein, this request is inadmissible since the applicable legal provisions in this case only concern the legitimate children, this request is therefore rejected for lack of foundation." On appeal, the judges of the court of Blida confirmed on 3 December 2007 the decision of the court of Cheraga, on the grounds that the "provisions concerning *kafāla* are different from the provisions concerning custody", and consequently they rejected the request for custody lodged by the *kafīla* mother (*CIDDEF* [*Centre d'Information et de Documentation sur les Droits de l'Enfant et de la Femme*], *Kafala* case, June 2008, Algiers, p. 19).

13 In this respect, *hiba* differs from *ṣadaqa* (alms), which is given to please God and to merit his reward (Liant de Bellefonds, 1935: 18).

goods to the benefit of the person of his/her choice. And no restriction or reservation attaches to the donor, who may be a parent or an outsider, a man or a woman, major or minor, Muslim or not. Islamic *fiqh* does not place any restriction on the right to use this measure to make a gift *inter vivos* without a fee. Only the rules relating to the donor's capacity restrict this act of "giving".[14]

"Giving" is deemed morally reprehensible inasmuch as a man enjoying full capacity may dispossess his family totally to the benefit of an outsider. He is not compelled to give a share to his heirs. Making a "gift" can be a legal means to disinherit them. Nowadays, many heirs thus wronged, seeing a father or an uncle transferring assets, take legal action to contest the gift, but such actions have only been upheld where donors and notaries did not take prior precautions. Some members of the family, although legitimate heirs, are perceived as "outsiders" when daily bonds are loosened and when a conflict has affected the relationship. This is confirmed by an Algerian female notary in the case of an elderly woman living with her sister, her niece and her adopted daughter, who donated a third of her villa to each of them:

> She came to see us and said that she did not want her cousins to inherit her goods, that all her life, they had lived on their own, they had managed by themselves, without a father or a mother, and neither the cousins nor the uncles had come to visit them, and had never helped them. For her, these men were not entitled to inherit the villa. (Notary, Algiers 2012)

The consideration of members of the extended family as "outsiders", regarded with resentment and hostility, testifies to a major change in the representation of the Muslim family, a change that the lawyers of the time may not have anticipated. In the light of the conservatory provisions they elaborated, they clearly did not anticipate potential attitudes of the donor, who is encouraged to give, providing that his "detachment from worldly affairs" enables him to relieve the needy and to remedy social inequality. But this provision also required "that the spirit of family, so powerful in Islam, should not fuel the fear that the donation would be used for ends harmful to the family and, consequently, to society" (Linant de Bellefonds, 1935: 39). Nowadays, the use of a "gift" is intended to "modify the legal order of succession, by privileging certain heirs over others", such as a single daughter for example, and thus to "limit the effects of the rules of succession" (Rycx, 1987, 32).

---

14 The act of giving is not permitted for persons who are minors (*quṣār*), mentally unbalanced (*majnūn*), mentally deficient (*ma'tūh*), prodigal (*mubadhdhir* or *sāfiḥ*), neglectful (*mughaffal*), insolvant (*muflis*).

Contradictions, and the *Kafāla* Mechanism's Legal Discrimination Against the Child

In the Algerian Family Code, the *makfūl* child is not referred to in the chapter on succession. However, in the chapter relating to *kafāla*, Article 123 is devoted to the question of inheritance. If the *makfūl* does not inherit from his *kafīl*, the assignee of the right of fostering may conversely, "if he so desires, bequeath or donate, in the limit of the third of his assets, to the benefit of the child. Beyond this third, the testamentary provision is null and void, unless there is consent of the heirs" (Art. 123). Although deficient, this point of law raises certain issues. First of all, the *kafīl* may leave a testamentary bequest, which is limited to one-third of his assets. This provision is in compliance with the rules of succession that apply to any Algerian. But, according to Article 123, the *kafīl* does not seem to be able to "give" the child more than one-third of his assets, while the rules governing "gift" (*hiba*) are unequivocal: it is possible to give the totality of one's assets (Art. 205), and anybody can be the beneficiary of this beneficent act, in particular "the distressed" that the succession regime tends to prejudice. Such is the case of the *makfūl* child. Nevertheless, the latter is blatantly less well treated than in common law. Is it a mistake in the text? Is it the deliberate purpose of the legislation to limit the intention of the *kafīl* as a donor, and to reduce the share of the *makfūl* as a beneficiary? If this is the case, we must consider the social representations of the adopted child: as an intruder limiting the rights of the legal heirs.

A contradiction, along with a discrimination, is clearly apparent at the heart of the Code. Article 123 introduces the notion of donation (*tabarruʿ*), and as such is a commendable exception since this term appears only once in the Code. This mention is interesting because there is no legal device relating to donations, unlike gifts (*hiba*), which, in order to be valid must meet particular criteria (registration before a notary, transfer of property). In most legal documents, however, lawyers define the gift as a donation (*tabarruʿ*). In short, the confusion is absolute and paves the way for all kinds of interpretations, the more so since this problem has not been settled in legal doctrine. It has not yet been commented on by researchers, or taken into consideration by the judiciary: "It was foreign researchers who have pinpointed contradictions like this one (…) Algerian lawyers are not interested in family affairs; the subject is traditionally neglected in the justice system" (A barrister before the Supreme Court and the State Tribunal, Senior Lecturer, Oran 2012); or again: "I acknowledge that there is a problem; jurisprudence needs to take a different turn" (Magistrate, Law School, Algiers, 2012).

The Obstacles to Donation in the Case of *Kafāla*

Given these legal inconsistencies, practices are governed by the individual attitudes of the institutional actors (notaries, Land Registry, judges, etc.). This starts with the first interview with the notary, who may refuse the *kafīl*'s request, invoking the inescapable religious argument and instilling in his client an embarrassing sense of guilt:

> There are various trends among us as notaries, and some of us even disagree. Their line of thinking is that Islam prohibits depriving an heir. Mainly those with a religious tendency do everything they can to avoid donation. They say: "What? You are depriving the heirs? It is a sin in the eyes of the *sharīʿa*!" Let us consider the example of a young lady who adopts a child and is not married. The heirs are her parents, and if they are deceased, the brothers and sisters, otherwise the nephews and nieces. The notaries will tell her that she is depriving the heirs and it should not be done. So they try all possible means not to proceed to a donation. But nothing in the law prohibits it. (Notary, Algiers 2012)

With the notaries' participation, the rumour that the *kafīl* does not have the right to make a donation in favour of the adopted child is slowly gaining ground to block the intentions and initiatives of the more hesitant and most vulnerable people. Thus, many *kafīl* parents explain to me in a contrite tone that religion prohibits making a donation to the child fostered under *kafāla*.

When the *kafīl* is resolute, and signs the deed before a notary, a new obstacle may crop up: the Land Registry may weigh in. Under the aegis of the Ministry of Finance, this administration keeps a national record of the proprietors in each *dāʾira*. It controls the deeds and implements the transfer of goods. It can also formulate refusals, which must be founded: "Some members are lenient while others are quite rigid. They will say, in the case of a *kafīl*, that they are applying Article 123 and that they cannot perform the transfer of property" (Notary, Algiers 2012). The testimony of a *kafīl* who consulted lawyer Nadia Aït Zaï at the Information and Documentation Centre on the Rights of the Child and of Women (CIDDEF), after receiving a decision of rejection, was read out by her during an interview:

> In this document, the administration says that it cannot perform the transfer of property since it is a *makfûl* child and that according to Article 123, the donation is limited to a third. This decision is not widespread, but the issue has been raised. I advised this gentleman to sell. (Nadia Aït Zaï, CIDDEF, Algiers 2012)

Another example: "Conservation is no motivation. It rejects, sometimes for fanciful reasons, but you must persevere, you must go there, ask for explanations, show that you are not fooled. You must brawl rather than snivel and stand idly by" (A family law barrister, Oran 2012).

Rather than fighting to "eradicate the problem at the root", many *kafīl*s choose to transfer their property by disguised sales; they either they sell their property to the child,[15] or buy a property on behalf of the child:

> They are not advised not to give, but to buy. If you buy on behalf of the child, then when you pass away, the property is no longer part of the inheritance; it is excluded from the *fredah* [sharing the inheritance]. At the end of the day, it is a pitfall for the next of kin. (DAS official, Algiers 2012).

Although it has a cost (one-fifth of the amount is declared to the Treasury), the sale and purchase on behalf of a child are solutions to protect the *makfūl* while guarding against a legal conflict with the heirs. For even if the *kafīl* insists, and transfers to his *makfūl* a large part, or possibly all, of his assets, before a notary, and even if the transfer of property is ratified by the Land Registry, a sword of Damocles hangs over the donor: the risk of the donation being contested by the heirs. A judgement of 12 May 2011 illustrates a case of contestation confirmed by the Supreme Court (n°620402). When he was alive, a man gave (*hiba*) one-third of his assets to his wife and two-thirds to his *makfūl* child. When the donor passed away, the heirs, his brothers, commenced an action for annulment of the donation on two grounds: the donation was made when the donor was terminally ill (Art. 204)[16] and, in addition, in the framework of a *kafāla* (Art. 123). A judge commented on this judgement orally:

> The last illness, to the best of our knowledge, showed that he was bedridden and dying, and his mental faculties were therefore not complete. The

15 "Certain people declare a ridiculously low price and attention is drawn to the fact that the tax administration may effect a readjustment. They are advised to declare a reasonable price, since some people announce 500,000 dinars for a valuable villa. (…) Others may sell their property at a good price and buy another in the name of their child" (Notary, Algiers 2012).

16 A donation made by a person when suffering from a terminal disease or by a person afflicted with a serious disease or finding himself/herself in a dangerous situation, is considered as a bequest and is therefore limited to a third: "In the eyes of the Muslim jurisconsults, this is a true incapacity serving to protect the heirs who, due to the mortal disease, have already an acquired a right over the assets of the patient" (Linant de Bellefonds, 1935: 62).

> notaries asked for a medical certificate, but in spite of this the heirs still managed to cancel the donation. In this case, they invoked this last disease and they went even further. They explained that Article 205 enables one to give all one's goods, but since the recipient is a *makfūl*, Article 123 must be applied. There is a contradiction between *hiba* and *tabarruʿ* [voluntary donation], they discuss it, they give a far-fetched explanation in which they distinguish between gift and donation, and they eventually decide that in this case, it is a gift. They specify that the donation made to a *makfūl* complies with the provisions relating to gifts, which are limited to a third. (Judge, Law School, Algiers 2012)

The judge of the Supreme Court decided in favour of the heirs, cancelling the donation on the grounds that Article 123 had been infringed. The lawyers and members of the judiciary encountered during our ethnographic work all agree on the confused, "poorly written" and especially unusual character of this judgement. Judgements of this sort are indeed rare. This is partly because we only have access to the judgements pronounced and we cannot see all the applications that were refused. Also, the donation of the totality of one's assets to a *makfūl* child is rare in Algerian society, for all the reasons cited above. Rumour is very effective: "People are talking about it", "I was told", "Religion does not allow this", "It is not usual", "People are afraid of what will be said", "The heirs are going to contest it", "It should not be done." There are many *kafīl*s who, already undermined by being an "illegitimate parent" with respect to a child who is just as illegitimate, prefer to pursue other possibilities rather than persisting in a "donation at all costs". In fact, there are very few deeds of donation in favour of *makfūl* children. An example of such a document can be found in the Appendix. The use of rather general and abstract categories (donors and donees), specific to the language of law, and to what Fernanda Pirie (2013) defines as "legalism", enables the signatory to circumvent the possible problems raised by the relation between *kafīl* and *makfūl*.

To Wish or Not to Wish to Bequeath to the Fostered Child

Article 123 specifies that the *kafīl* may "if he so wishes" make a gift or bequest to the *makfūl*. Obviously, many *kafīl*s consider the fostered child as "a son", a subject of right, a loved one: "Even if there is no bond of filiation, there is filial love" (*kafīl* mother, Algiers, 2012). This love goes hand in hand with a desire to protect the child, which motivates them to transfer, or intend to transfer, their goods. Does this protect the adopted child? Yes, indeed, if he enjoys full family integration while his *kafīl* parents are alive. However, since they have often imposed on the extended family their individual choice of *kafāla*, the child runs a serious risk of violent rejection in the case of the premature death of his protectors: "The principle is that the *kafīl* and the *makfūl* solve their problems when they are alive. Once the *kafīl* has been buried, the child is entitled to nothing" (Nadia Aït Zaï, Algiers, 2012). Or again: "Generally speaking, the *makfūl* represents a danger for the extended family, who do not accept him. The slightest lapse on his part is enough for the heirs to come down on him" (Notary, Algiers, 2012). The following example illustrates the rejection the may affect the *makfūl*:

> When I worked in a "nursery" [orphanage] in the east, I met a handsome 23-year-old man who came there to eat and sleep. I wondered about him. I came to know his story. He had been "adopted" into a family of educated people, nice people. He had three sisters, legitimate daughters, and he was the only boy and the youngest. Their parents died in a road accident, and his sisters turned against him. His sisters made him pay everything he had because as a young boy, he had been mollycoddled. Consequently, they kicked him out of the house. The only links he had in Algeria were with the "nursery". (*kafīl* mother, researcher, Algiers, 2012)

The following testimony again reflects the *kafīl*'s desire to protect:

> I don't have any children [of my own]. I adopted. I have always considered this baby daughter as my own child, from her birth until now. She has come of age and if I die, they will throw her out. I want to protect her and any means are admissible. (*kafīl* mother, Oran, 2012)[17]

Some *kafīl*s give everything they possess (by *hiba*, gift), especially if the *makfūl* is an only child; others prefer the less controversial solution of the will (bequest limited to one-third). Some of them couple the conservatory provisions of the rules of succession with a donation, with the result that the *makfūl* may be seen as greatly favoured as compared with other heirs:

---

17 « I decided that I was going to sell a good for my daughter. It is a good which I financed but there is a problem with the family. If the good does not go to her, it will go to my nephews and nieces and I felt a pressure from them fifteen days ago. I was discussing with my sister my daughter's school problems and I was explaining to her that I had not solved the issues of inheritance because my daughter was quite upset. And she told me not to worry, that she pledged herself to give her the equivalent of a flat. I was flabbergasted, because it means that she is going to buy her a flat but she wants to keep MY flat and my daughter will go to live somewhere else. For me, it is inadmissible » (kafîl mother, Algiers 2012).

> Sometimes the *makfūl* receives more money and goods than the heir since he can benefit from a donation, as well as from a will later on. We can do both. I know cases where the *kafīl* gave the home and then made a will in addition at a later stage. Except that the adopted child can waive his right of inheritance if the *kafīl* is in debt, whereas in French law debts are inherited. (Notary, Algiers, 2012)

The case of mixed families, composed of legitimate children and of children fostered under *kafāla*, has further particularities. The *kafīl* defending the idea of the equality of all the children (adopted/legitimate, daughter/son) practises "fair" sharing while he is alive:

> I have four children, two biological, two adopted, two daughters, two sons. All my children are listed in the deed of donation I made seven years ago. My brother has three adopted children, he created a real-estate company and included them in it. (*kafīl* father, Algiers, 2012).

The law relating to legal fostering leaves the free choice of transfer to the *kafīl* and does not impose any duty of protection of the *makfūl* through inheritance. In this sense, from a legal viewpoint and in terms of inheritance, the interest of the legitimate family, a structural element of society, outweighs the interest of the fostered child. Thus, in practice, we can observe that not every *kafīl* wishes to transfer goods to the *makfūl*. First, some of them have no goods: "They have nothing and they are the happiest. From the start, the child knows that there will be nothing to scrounge and this will remain a close-knit family" (Notary, Algiers, 2012). As mentioned above, there are also those who do not feel strong enough to fight against the heirs and the administration – in short, society as whole. Lastly, there are reservations based on fear:

> A woman came to see me, explaining that she wanted to sell [her house to her adopted daughter] but was afraid that her [adopted] daughter might kick her out of the house one day – that once she gets married, her husband would force her to sell, to buy something else, in order to be integrated into the assets. (Notary, Algiers, 2012)

There is the fear of changed behaviour and of the possible ingratitudeof the *makfūl*:

> My wife told me to remove him from the house [i.e. cancel the donation to the *makfūl*], and it's true that he was given his share. But these children are very selfish, even if each of them is a particular case. (…) It is not

> simple to draw up a deed while one is alive; the child is 10 or 15 years old, and tomorrow, with the donation, he may become mean, violent. And when he starts to drink and to take drugs… (*kafīl* father, Algiers, 2012)

Or again:

> One of my nieces has been adopted by my sister-in-law. The grandparents of this little girl have many assets and they had shared them out before the adoption. The goods were to go to two daughters, one of them being my sister-in-law, and two sons. But the grandmother, before she passed away, decided to remove her daughter – of course, the one who adopted – from the inheritance. She said: "If ever there are problems with your [adopted] daughter, she might take the whole house and kick you out of the house." (*kafîl* mother, Algiers, 2012)

This fear of being "thrown out by one's adopted child" is not associated here with the legal measure of donation, since sale also raises reservations: "If I made a sale, it should mean that I would receive money but, in reality, I would not receive anything, and overnight I could find myself on the streets" (*kafîl* mother, 2012, Algiers).

All these testimonies reflect the socio-cultural representations of the abandoned and adopted child (Barraud, 2013). The society forcefully conveys the idea that all the affection, attention and protection given to the adopted child will be rewarded with ingratitude, especially in the case of a boy. There are many stories, real or fancied, recounting how the adopted son turned violently against his parents, as if the absence of a biological link motivated the betrayal of the adopted child. These stories are instrumentalised to support preconceptions according to which a child born illegitimate and adopted is essentially bad and ungrateful, so that "violence is par for the course" (*kafīl* father, Algiers, 2012). This fear of malevolent behaviour on the part of the adopted child is especially prevalent because a donation is irrevocable once it is made in favour of a child who is not the donor's biological son or daughter. Conversely, there is the possibility of including in the notarised deed a clause stipulating that the donor keeps the usufruct of the goods until his death.

Conclusion

It would seem that the problem of transfer of property remains unresolved for the *kafīl*. Adoptive parents delay making a decision as long as possible, with fear in their hearts, before precautions are taken. Too hesitant, ill-informed about the rules and the legal provisions, these parents, whenever they can, open savings accounts in the name of the child, in Algeria and sometimes abroad, and thus opt neither for sale nor for a bequest. They finance quality education (private schooling) for him so as to provide him with qualifications that will better enable him to live without relying on any family inheritance. Let us note that many still favour the illegal adoption of a boy at birth in order to "close the door on the heirs", whereas legal fostering, *kafāla*, concerns girls in most cases (Barraud, 2013: 119).

In conclusion, addressing the issue of succession in cases of *kafāla* sheds light on the conflictual encounter of two major principles: that of the equality of rights of all the children of a family (natural, legitimate, illegitimate, adopted), with reference to the UNCRC (1992), and that of legitimacy, under Islamic law. Ultimately, this conflict prompts us to reflect on a new definition of filiation in Algeria. Elective filial love, and all that it generates in terms of practice, is expressed in the majority of adoptive families. Gradually it becomes the norm to be integrated into the family system:

> What has happened, then, since times have changed, but laws have not, is that this new irrepressible need to give a name, to bequeath one's goods, to leave, before leaving this world, one's own signature is not any longer in terms of one's flesh and blood, but in the name of the love given, of all the attention lavished on a child, a life, with whom bonds, non-uterine but no less strong for all that, have been established, making of these bonds the backbone of a new law ....[18]

References

Aït Zaï, Nadia, 1996, La *kafâla* en droit algérien, *Les institutions traditionnelles du monde arabe,* Paris : Khartala,

Barraud, Emilie. 2008. "Adoption et kafâla dans l'espace migratoire franco-maghrébin", *L'Année du Maghreb* 4: 459-468

Barraud, Emilie. 2009. "Kafâla et migrations: L'adoption entre la France et le Maghreb." Thesis. Université de Provence Aix-Marseille.

Barraud, Emilie. 2010. "La filiation légitime à l'épreuve des mutations sociales au Maghreb", *Droit et Cultures* 59 (1): 91-118.

18 D. Jaydan, "*Kafala: Où en est-on dix ans après?*", Luxe Radio, 4 March 2014. <https://www.luxeradio.ma/les-matins-luxe-7h30-10h/kafala-ou-en-est-on-10-ans-apres.html> (accessed 4 March 2014).

Barraud, Emilie. 2013. *De terre et de sang: L'adoption entre France et Maghreb*. Paris: Non Lieu.

Borrmans, M. 1977. *Statut personnel et famille au Maghreb de 1940 à nos jours*. Paris: Mouton.

CNEAP (Centre national d'études et d'analyses pour la population et le développement). 2001. "Les enfants abandonnés pour cause de célibat maternel". Rapport final. Alger.

Linant de Bellefonds, Yvon. 1935. *Des donations en droit musulman*. Paris: Recueil de Sirey.

Pirie, Fernanda. 2013. *The Anthropology of Law*. Oxford: Oxford University Press.

Pruvost, Lucie. 1996. "Intégration familiale de l'enfant sans généalogie en Algérie et en Tunisie: Kafala ou adoption", *Studi Arabo-Islamici del PISAI* 8: 155-180.

Rycx, Jean-François. 1987. "Règles islamiques et droit positif en matière de succession: Présentation générale", in *Hériter en pays musulman: Habus, "lait vivant", manyahuli*, ed. M. Gast. Paris: CNRS, 19-42.

Appendix: Example of a Deed of Gift (*hiba*)

DEED of GIFT

Before Mr **** , Notary undersigned , undersigned :

came

Mr : ****, son of ***, merchant, residing at N° ** Street, *****, born in *** on ***, as can be seen from a copy of his birth certificate N° *** , bearer of the C.N.I N°*** issued by the Dā'ra of *** on *** .... of Algerian citizenship

Who has declared pursuant to article 202 and following the Family Code, having made a donation *inter vivos*, irrevocably with immediate transfer of the real estate designated below, committing himself to all the usual and regulatory guarantees in force in this matter ...

To

Mr : ***************

Present at the contractual session, and who accepts the building, designated below:

Designation

The undivided real estate rights, assessed at ** in premises, intended for the common exploitation of a ***, residing **, street *** and Dā'ra of ***, Wilāya of ** , the bulk of the plots on which are built the premises and the associated plot has a surface area of *** , plot N°02 , section ** of the Land Registry **. ....

So that this building exists, extends and continues with all its facilities and dependences and including advantages and dependences, without any exception or reservation, known by the trustee, who declares he has visited them and that he knows them. ....

Origin of property

The said building, object of this donation, is the property of the donors, since they have acquired it in the manner stipulated thus:

By virtue of the preliminary numbering process, complying with the executive decree N° ** of ** , relating to the constitution of the real estate book , modified and completed by Executive Decree 93-123 of 29/05/1993.
Then, the definitive numbering of said process was established for preserving the mortgages of **, on **, Volume **, Case **.

Origin of previous property

The parties expressly declare that they exempt the undersigned notary from verifying the origin of the property analysed above, and that they refer to the property deed analysed previously

Terms and conditions

The donation was consented to and accepted under order and lawful conditions in this context that the parties shall execute.
The donee will take the building in its current state, without recourse to the donors for any reason whatsoever and specifically without guarantee of the stated content, unless the difference between the gift as described and the actual property amount to more than one-twentieth (1/20) in profit or loss to the donee

....

He will benefit from the active utilities and will support the apparent or hidden passive, continuous or discontinued utilities, of public law or of private law, encumbering said building, at his own risks and perils, without recourse to the donor. This being so, the donor states that the said building is to the best of his knowledge not encumbered with any other utility than those which may result from the natural situation of the premises, in accordance with the law.
The donor will bear as of the day of coming into force the taxes, contributions and other charges to which the said building object of the donation is subject ...
The donor will also pay the duties and fees of the notary pertaining to the present act as well as its legal developments ....

Property and enjoyment

The donor will be proprietor as of this day of the given, undivided real estate properties and immediately enjoying their actual and effective possession

....

Evaluation

In order to pay all the necessary expenses pertaining to the present deed, both parties have assessed the portion given up to an amount of ** of Algerian Dinars (***,00 DA).

Land records

A copy of the present deed will be published in the Land Registry of the department of Remchi by the care of the undersigned notary at the donor's expense.

……………………………………

Civil status

The donors have stated, under penalty of regulatory sanctions, that they are of Algerian citizenship, that they are capacitated and are not initiating any measure or procedure, especially relating to incapacitated adults, so as to restrict their civil capacities or to block the free availability of their .goods. They are not and they have never been in a situation of personal bankruptcy, liquidation of assets, judicial remedies, receivership or cessation of payment. That no judgement was required, providing resolution, rescission or nullity of the deed by virtue of which they were proprietors: That the goods designated above are free of any debts and charges

………………………………………………………………

INSURANCE AGAINST DISASTER SITUATIONS

The building designated above is insured against disaster situations by virtue of the insurance policy taken with ** Assurance, Agency of **, under the N° /***, of 30/07/2013 for one year, of which a summary remains appended to the present documents after the usual mention ……………………………………………………

Place of abode

For the execution of the present contract and its consequences, both parties have chosen to elect as domicile their place of abode mentioned above.

In witness thereof

The present deed is enacted in Remchi in the notarial firm of the undersigned notary.
In the year ** ……………………………………………………………………
On ** (*-*)……………………………………………………………………

Deed enacted in the presence of both witnesses:

1°) Mr ** ....

2°) Mr **

After reading, both parties and the witnesses have signed with the notary.
Once the signatures have been made, there is the following statement:

Recorded at the registration office in TLEMCEN on *** ------------------------------------

Right ** Da --- Receipt N°**
Signed by the central inspector:

Rectangular stamp with the wording:
Stamp duty levied on the transaction
Round seal bearing in Arabic characters:
Notarial firm located at ** - Mr **

Index

Tamazight Terms

Organizations/Institutions

Authors

Concepts/Objects

www.ingramcontent.com/pod-product-compliance
Ingram Content Group UK Ltd.
Pitfield, Milton Keynes, MK11 3LW, UK
UKHW022209051026
15624UKWH00001B/79

9 789004 357624